IDEOLOGY AND THE IRISH QUESTION

Ideology and the Irish Question

ULSTER UNIONISM
AND IRISH NATIONALISM
1912–1916

PAUL BEW

CLARENDON PRESS · OXFORD

Oxford University Press, Great Clarendon Street, Oxford OX2 6DP

Oxford New York

Athens Auckland Bangkok Bogota Bombay Buenos Aires
Calcutta Cape Town Dar es Salaam Delhi Florence Hong Kong Istanbul
Karachi Kuala Lumpur Madras Madrid Melbourne Mexico City
Nairobi Paris Singapore Taipei Tokyo Toronto Warsaw

and associated companies in
Berlin Ibadan

Oxford is a registered trade mark of Oxford University Press

Published in the United States
by Oxford University Press Inc., New York

British Library Cataloguing in Publication Data

Data available

Library of Congress Cataloging in Publication Data
Bew, Paul.
Ideology and the Irish question: Ulster unionism and Irish
nationalism, 1912–1916/Paul A. Bew.
p. cm.
Includes index.
1. Ireland—Politics and government—1910–1921. 2. Ulster
(Northern Ireland and Ireland)—Politics and government.
3. Nationalism—Ireland—History—20th century. 4. Irish question.
I. Title.
DA690.B49 1995
941.5082'1—dc20 94–9295

ISBN 0–19–820202–4
ISBN 0–19–820708–5 (pbk)

1 3 5 7 9 10 8 6 4 2

Printed in Great Britain
on acid-free paper by
Biddles Ltd., Guildford and King's Lynn

Acknowledgements

THIS material first saw hesitant light of day in November 1990; at Professor John Vincent's Acton Society seminar in Bristol University and Dr Brendan Bradshaw's Irish Studies seminar in Cambridge. I am indebted to the encouragement of both men. My greatest debt though is to the new generation of modern Irish scholars—friends like George Boyce, Roy Foster, and Henry Patterson have sustained the project. My close colleagues Richard English, Alvin Jackson, Margaret O'Callaghan, and Graham Walker were marvellous supports. The graduate students in this department were a frequent source of insight. I am particularly grateful to Peter Semple; Enda Staunton; Keith Sweeney and Stephen Day; it is a pleasure here to salute Dr Patrick Maume, an outstanding emergent talent. Fergus Campbell, Noel Dorr, Michael Foy, Tom Garvin, Keith Haines, Tom Hennessy, Desmond Keenan, Peter Leppard, Garret FitzGerald, Alan O'Day, David Trimble, and George Woodman were most helpful at key points. Arthur Green read an early manuscript version and commented perceptively. Johathan Parry helped me to understand the British Liberal context. Adrian Guelke inspired both by his scholarship and personal courage. The text has been more fun to write because of the increasing interest of my wife, Greta Jones, in Irish history. The book is dedicated to the memory of two eminent scholars in the field of Irish Studies, Professor Frank Wright and Dr Denis J. Clarke who both died in 1993. Frank Wright was an outstanding student of ethnic conflict while Denis Clarke was one of the great historians of Irish America. They will be sorely missed.

Belfast, April 1994   PAUL BEW

Contents

Introduction

Against 'Partitionist' History

'The Irish parliamentary party so degraded the political process that no man or woman of sensitivity or idealism could have any part of it. . . . Did the utmost conciliation of John Redmond, for instance, make any difference to the Ulster Unionists?'

C. J. Haughey, *The Spirit of the Nation*, 310, 529

MR JOHN CUSACK. Sir Edward Carson persecuted many leaders of the nationalist movement—amongst them were Parnell and Davitt—whose names will never be forgotten by the Irish people (cheer).

Today the soul of this Apostle of Law and Order (Laughter) is bursting at the mention of the Imperial forces being brought to Ulster to preserve law and order. He has now constituted himself the High Priest of the Army in Ireland and elsewhere; he tried to bully the Crown, to corrupt the Army, to blackmail the Cabinet and to raise a general hell in these islands

MR JAMES GILSENAN. He will repent.

MR JOHN FLYNN. He will have to repent.

Trim Board of Guardians and UDC, *Leinster Leader*,
13 June 1914

The attempt to rescue one neglected and despised historic ideology—Ulster unionism during the home rule crisis—from oblivion may be regarded as brave. To attempt to rescue a second and contemporary ideology—'Redmondism', or constitutional Irish nationalism—considered foolhardy, especially when that second ideology was locked throughout its life in an apparent death struggle with the first. Such a project may also appear to be self-contradictory and futile. For some, the futility of the exercise would be confirmed by the fact that any positive re-evaluation of Redmondism—the claim for example that the Irish party leadership actually possessed a relatively viable political strategy—implies a certain criticism of the key founding event of the Irish state, the Easter Rising of 1916.

After all, in so far as there is anything new and positive to be said about Ulster unionism it must be to the detriment of the critiques made by its opponents on the Redmondite side and adopted—without any genuine acknowledgement—by nationalist critics ever since. On the other hand, any positive evaluation of Redmondism may well imply that unionist attacks during the home rule crisis were splenetic and exaggerated. Furthermore, the Easter Rising did receive a retrospective democratic endorsement of a sort in the general election of 1918, which annihilated Redmond's party, though a large proportion still opposed the party linked to the insurrection (Sinn Fein). Why examine too closely the origins of states, which can rarely stand too much scrutiny? Nevertheless, there are powerful reasons for attempting to reconstruct the assumptions of Sir Edward Carson's unionist movement and John Redmond's nationalist movement in the 1912–16 epoch. We ought at least to have a full picture of what Ulster unionists and Irish nationalists said about each other in this period. There is a sense in which the dialogue, tempestuous though it was, was a real and sustained one; after partition, exchanges on an all-Ireland basis became rather perfunctory and, if possible, even more hackneyed than before. Let us not forget that the Ireland of 1912–16 was still a unified administrative entity. The *Intelligence Notes* series of county reports, prepared annually for the judicial division of the Chief Secretary's office in Dublin Castle, represented a serious attempt by the county inspectors of the Royal Irish Constabulary to convey the diversity of conditions to be found in the thirty-two Irish counties. The *Notes* convey a picture of a country which was mostly peaceful, but still vulnerable both to sectarian Catholic–Protestant tension in the north-east and to agrarian conflicts, particularly in the west. Within a decade, the effort to hold together these diverse realities had collapsed and the country was formally partitioned.

The partition of Ireland in 1921 has inevitably had a major effect on subsequent interpretations. Historians have concentrated with great skill on either the development of southern nationalism, with its agrarian and cultural dimensions, or on the internal dynamics of unionist resistance to home rule. Much has been achieved by the best recent scholarly work, though the understanding of Ulster unionism, in particular, has been hindered by its treatment as merely a negative appendage to nationalism. But what has been lost is not just the sense of a thirty-two-county perspective which the police reports attempt to give; not just, in other words, the sense of an administrative order's ability (albeit a fading one) to hold the country together, but also—and this is a rather more profound problem—the full scope of the actual interaction of Ulster unionism and Irish nationalism. Knowledge of the internal dynamics of the 'two traditions' has increased, but there has been less progress made in understanding their interplay: certainly there has been no attempt to combine them in a scholarly analysis based on primary sources for both the north and south.

If we wish to begin to put this right there is no better place to start than the home rule crisis of 1912–14. The conflict of Ulster unionism and Irish nationalism was much more sustained then than in its earlier phases (1886 and 1893). Yet it remained predominantly peaceful and constitutional, which is not to deny that occasional outbreaks of violence and, more frequently, the orchestrated threat of force by both sides, played an important role. There was nothing like the violence of the epoch of 1920–3, a period so marked by bloody events and intercommunal atrocity as to render almost impossible any attempt at a relatively dispassionate focus on political and ideological discourse.

The home rule crisis has naturally been subject to competing interpretative reprises. For many mainstream nationalists it demonstrates that, having patiently played by the Westminster rules of the game—imposed after all by Britain—parliamentary Irish nationalists were deprived of the fruits of victory by illegal and anti-constitutional manœuvre. The descent of Ireland into violence after 1916 must therefore, at least partly, be the responsibility of the obdurate Ulster unionist and British Tory leadership in 1912. The nature of the unionist opposition to home rule is widely perceived to be the weak point in the project of a new revisionist 'anti-national' Irish historiography. As Martin Mansergh, the special adviser to Albert Reynolds, has observed: 'Even for the most revisionist historian, resistance to home rule is difficult to transform into a stand for liberal democratic ideals and enlightened values.'[1] In fact, the most important historians of modern Ireland have made no such effort to rehabilitate the anti-home rule cause.

F. S. L. Lyons has noted icily that 'the obstinate and in the end successful resistance of Ulster and English Unionists to the extremely moderate self-government which Parnell, Redmond and Dillon were

---

[1] 'A Rising Curve from Subversion to Statecraft', *Fortnight*, 292 (Feb. 1991), 28.

originally prepared to accept will always remain one of the great mysteries of politics';[2] in a massively influential book, Roy Foster has described the unionist opposition to home rule as being 'ludicrously extreme in retrospect';[3] and, in another recent and prize-winning work, Joseph Lee has insisted that Ulster unionist resistance to home rule is based above all on a sense of racial superiority: a 'master race' syndrome. Lest the overtones of South Africa and Nazi Germany be missed by an unusually obtuse reader, Professor Lee frequently employs the term *'Herrenvolk'* to describe the unionist community.[4] Most recently, Michael Laffan was merely summarizing a widespread view when he insisted that 'the Rising could not have taken place without the example of Edward Carson and . . . it was the Ulster Volunteer's defiance of parliamentary government which initiated Ireland's modern phase of violence'.[5]

These arguments remain in an important sense part of the contemporary Irish debate. In a paper submitted by the Irish government to the interparty talks on the future of Northern Ireland it is roundly declared—not without exaggeration:

Unionist recourse to paramilitary force, including the first illegal shipment of arms into Ireland of modern times in order to negate the will of the British Parliament on the issue was a major influence in turning the nationalist population to similar methods, with results which reverberate to the present day. It was, however, successful insofar as serious British negotiation with the nationalist tradition took place only after the creation of Northern Ireland as a special entity, dedicated to the rule of the Unionist community.[6]

This is a view which had been formally codified in the *New Ireland Forum Report*—the statement of faith of mainstream Irish nationalism—in May 1984:

During the Home Rule for Ireland debates in the British Parliament in 1912, many arguments were advanced by British political leaders in favour of

---

[2] *John Dillon* (London, 1968), 483.
[3] *Modern Ireland 1600–1972* (London, 1988), 470. For a challenge on this point, see Maurna Crozier (ed.), *Cultural Traditions in Northern Ireland* (Belfast, 1989), 48–9.
[4] *Ireland 1912–85: Politics and Society* (Cambridge, 1990), 4, 21, 59, 79, 596. But see K. T. Hoppen, 'Ireland, Britain and Europe', *Historical Journal*, 14/4 (1991), 512–13; G. Walker, 'Old History: Protestant Ulster in Lee's "Ireland" ', *Irish Review*, 12, (spring/summer 1992), 65.
[5] 'Insular Attitudes: The Revisionists and Their Critics', in Mairin Ni Dhonnchadha and Theo Dorgan (eds.), *Revising the Rising* (Derry, 1991), 111.
[6] 'Identity, Allegiance and Underlying Realities', 28 Aug. 1992.

maintaining the unity of Ireland. The British government had introduced a bill that proposed to give Ireland a separate Parliament with jurisdiction over her internal affairs while reserving power over key issues. However, faced with the unionist threat to resist this bill by unlawful force, the British government backed down, and when the Government of Ireland Act of 1914 was placed on the statute book in Westminster, there was a provision that it would not come into operation until after Parliament had an opportunity of making provision for Ulster by special amending legislation. The message—which was not lost on unionists—was that a threat by them to use violence would succeed. To the nationalists, the conclusion was that the democratic constitutional process was not to be allowed to be effective.[7]

Brian P. Murphy, a writer who has considerable sympathy for the 'lost republican ideal' is critical of the diluted nationalism of this report, but acknowledges that here, at least, is 'criticism of the unionist and English position'.[8] In particular, it has been stressed that the home rulers were prepared to accept a modest measure of self-government which fell far short of complete Irish independence. The Home Rule Bill of 1912 proposed to create a bicameral Irish parliament with an executive responsible to it. This parliament was to be allowed to make its own laws for peace, order, and good government, but the Royal Irish Constabulary was to remain under British control for at least six years. Extensive powers were reserved to the imperial parliament, including foreign affairs, war and peace, the position of the Crown, and the general control of taxation, the powers of the local parliament in this area being restricted to little more than the right to levy 10 per cent on or off existing duties.[9] In the areas of law and education, as well as finance, there were checks and safeguards limiting the autonomy of the Irish parliament. With a high degree of symbolism, Ireland retained a representation of forty-two members in the imperial parliament. The bill also included a clause which prohibited any law interfering with the free exercise of religion, and forbad endowing or giving any preference or privilege to any religious belief or religious ceremony as a condition of the validity of any marriage in Ireland.

There were many impressive critiques of the bill: in particular, it

---

[7] *New Ireland Forum Report* (Dublin, 1984), 9.

[8] *Patrick Pearse and the Lost Republican Ideal* (Dublin, 1991), 61.

[9] Lyons, *Dillon*, 237; A. T. Q. Stewart, *The Ulster Crisis* (London, 1967), 59. For the text of the Home Rule Bill, see John Redmond, *The Home Rule Bill* (London, 1912), 101–54. For an excellent review of home rule legislation, see Alan O'Day and John Stevenson (eds.), *Irish Historical Documents* (Dublin, 1991), 153–5.

was claimed that the provisions for future financial relations had much capacity for generating friction between London and Dublin. The classic unionist analysis came from the *Quarterly Review*, which argued that the control of Irish taxation constituted a 'nominal' supremacy which was likely to be a fertile source of 'collision' and 'acrimonious' conflict. On the other hand, the bill possessed features which were 'intolerable' to Great Britain. It made Ireland a pensioner on the British taxpayer—largely because of the recently increased government expenditure on old-age pensions—and a non-contributor to imperial defence and the national debt. More dramatically, the *Quarterly Review* insisted that the remaining forty-two Irish MPs at Westminster might be a source of trouble, giving Ireland 'such a grasp upon the finance of England, such a ready means of embarrassing British trade, domestic and foreign, such power throughout the executive of paralysing imperial control, such opportunity at Westminster of arresting British legislation and preventing British party policy that it would enable Ireland to compel concession after concession and thus would, eventually, lead to absolute independence'.[10] The fear here was that home rule would inevitably lead to the triumph of the hidden separatist agenda of Irish nationalism. As W. F. Monypenny pointed out: 'The fact is the bill leaves the ambiguity in the meaning of the supremacy of the UK Parliament to be determined by the play of forces.'[11] Or, as Sir Edward Carson forcefully put it in one of his major parliamentary speeches on home rule: 'What a farce it is to tell us that you are going to establish a Parliament, and all the paraphernalia of an independent Executive, answerable alone to that Parliament, and the moment any thing arises you will send men over from Downing Street here and say "Stop the parliament you set up".'[12]

Redmond, in fact, explicitly acknowledged the technical force of some of the unionist criticisms of the legislation.[13] But he felt that these arguments missed the point. Home rule, in his view, would open up an era of good feelings in Ireland. The atmosphere would be one of

---

[10] For this critique see 'The Home Rule Bill', *Quarterly Review*, 217/432 (July 1912).

[11] *The Two Irish Nations: An Essay on Home Rule* (London, 1913), 103.

[12] *Hansard*, 5th ser. xxxiv. 1436, 11 Apr. 1912.

[13] Redmond, *Home Rule Bill* 64. On the thorny issue of finance, see Patricia Jalland, 'Irish Home Rule Finance 1910–14', in Alan O'Day (ed.), *Reactions to Irish Nationalism* (Dublin, 1987), 307. Redmond referred to the quality of argument advanced by George Cave, KC, MP. See his essay 'The Constitutional Question', in S. Rosenbaum (ed.), *Against Home Rule: The Case for the Union* (first pub. 1912; reissued Port Washington, NY, and London, 1970), 82–106.

harmony and co-operation and not one of conflict. In his speech on the second reading on 9 May 1912 Redmond expressed the positive view with great force and eloquence:

I desire to point out that, underlying all these arguments and all these objections, there has been the supposition that the worst will happen and not the best when Home Rule is granted; that all parties to this new Treaty will be animated by bad faith and by malice and instead of there being a desire shown to make the best of things, on the contrary, it will be the set purpose of everyone concerned to utilise any defect that may appear in the machinery of the Bill, or any provision which on paper may seem illogical and unworkable in order to wreck the settlement.[14]

Redmond liked to quote an early speech by Parnell—'when he was engaged in a violent movement in Ireland'—on this point:

Home Rule would be the introduction of a system which would remove the rankling sting of suppressed but not extinct enmity. Give back to Ireland her nationality, her individual existence, and soothe thereby the wounded pride that goes for so much in history and that often turns the scale in the destinies of nations as well as of individuals. Such a system as that would teach Ireland to regard Imperial affairs with interest, as being the concern no longer of a master and oppressor, but of a dear colleague and sister, whose honour and dishonour would be alike hers and whose downfall could never be her profit, and to whom she would be bound by ties sacred because voluntarily assumed.[15]

    This formulation provokes a number of questions. Would home rule have worked in this way? What do we really know about the home rule movement of 1912? What type of government for Ireland might it have provided? In the midst of the crisis J. J. Horgan, an ardent home rule theorist and politician, protested about the difficulty of initiating a serious debate on that issue: 'The agitation for home rule so engrossed our thoughts and energies that we had not time to consider or discuss the vital elements of Home Rule itself.'[16] Today we are accustomed to relatively sophisticated analysis of unionist ideology;[17] for example, how important is a negative sectarian emotion as opposed to a more positive patriotic identification with the United Kingdom? But, apart

---

[14] Redmond, *Home Rule Bill*, 63.   [15] Ibid. 46.

[16] *Cork Examiner*, 15 Feb. 1912.

[17] See esp. Jennifer Todd, 'Two Traditions in Unionist Political Culture', *Irish Political Studies*, 2 (1987), 1–26. For a comprehensive survey of this literature see John Whyte, *Interpreting Northern Ireland* (Oxford, 1990), 122–30.

from some shrewd but brief comments, we have comparatively little to work with for the earlier period of the home rule crisis. The purpose of this work is to remedy this deficiency. The intention is to reconstruct the home rule debate of 1912–16 and illuminate the clash of the 'two traditions' in Ireland in a way that will make it more comprehensible. As the *doyen* of anti-revisionist historiography, Brendan Bradshaw has observed, in this case uncontroversially:

the history of the northern community seems as much in need of imaginative and empathetic elucidation as that of its southern neighbours. The plea, therefore, is for an account of Irish history capable of comprehending sympathetically the historical experience of both communities, and, by comprehending them, of mediating between the island's past and its present.[18]

The present work does, however, have another, related, project: that is, to add a new dimension to our understanding of the meaning of the 1916 rising. The rising led to the eclipse of constitutional 'Redmondite' nationalism. It was to be replaced by a more radical, uncompromising revolutionary nationalist tradition. Nicholas Mansergh has recently commented that, on the outbreak of the First World War, 'a majority, possibly, the great majority'[19] in Ireland supported the appeals of Redmondite nationalists, in favour of co-operation with Britain. He adds:

The subsequent and progressive alienation of Irish opinion from the party is not in doubt, but the timing and causes of it at grass roots level have not received systematic or satisfying explanation, maybe because historians with others have been blinded by the light of the sequel. Between Irish men whose thoughts were moulded in the pre-war years and the generations who came after there was the interposition of 1916, effecting a psychological transforma- tion so considerable as to constitute a near unbridgeable gulf in outlook and understanding between the generations.[20]

In similar fashion, Garret FitzGerald, a former Irish prime minister and son of one of the leading revolutionary nationalist leaders, has noted that 'it is of course very difficult for us to make the imaginative leap back to the mood of the 1912–16 period in Ireland'. He has further claimed: 'To generations born after independence the existence of an Irish State based on a powerful tradition of separatism

---

[18] 'Nationalism and Historical Scholarship in Modern Ireland', *Irish Historical Studies*, 26/104 (Nov. 1989), 351.
[19] *The Unresolved Question: The Anglo-Irish Settlement and its Undoing* (New Haven, Conn., and London, 1991), 80.   [20] Ibid. 81.

vis-à-vis Britain is so much a fact of life that it is almost impossible for these generations to conceive of an Ireland in which the existence of a sovereign, independent Irish State was to the vast majority of people a remote and uncertain objective to which very few were in fact totally committed.'[21] In support of this thesis, he quotes his own father's analysis of the 1912–14 period: according to Desmond FitzGerald:

Home rule was in the air. The overwhelming majority of the people supported Redmond. In so far as that support had waned it was due to a growing cynicism among the people. Home Rule had been promised so long and had not materialised. If it failed again there was no evidence to lead one to expect that the people would do more than shrug their shoulders and say they expected as much. On the other hand it did really look as though some Bill would become law. Those of us who thought of Home Rule as something utterly inadequate were a very small minority, without influence, impotent. ... In the circumstances of the time, in the cold light of reason, one could really have foreseen only the success of the Home Rule movement with a subordinate Government established, whose restricted powers would be acclaimed as fulfilling all aspirations, or the failure of Home Rule, which would have been acceptable to the majority of the people as a proof that it was too much to hope for. On the very declaration of war Mr Redmond made a statement assuring the English people that the Irish volunteers would protect Ireland. ... But more disturbing than that mere statement was the fact that immediately it became apparent that it really represented the views of the majority of the Irish people. ... There were reports of the success of recruiting, of Volunteer bands marching to the station to see off their comrades who had volunteered for service in the British Army. The Movement on which all our dreams had centred seemed merely to have channelled the martial spirit of the Irish people for the defence of England. Our dream castles toppled about us with a crash. It was brought home to us that the very fever that had possessed us was due to a subconscious awareness that the final end of the Irish Nation was at hand. For centuries England had held Ireland materially. But now it seemed she held her in a new and utterly complete way. Our national identity was obliterated not only politically but also in our minds. The Irish people had recognised themselves as part of England.[22]

Garrett FitzGerald's comment on his father's memoir is suggestive: 'The subsequent attempt, successful for two generations, to portray the Rising as part of an unbroken tradition of armed resistance to British rule, which involved effectively writing the Irish parliamentary

---

[21] *Irish Times*, 13–18 July 1991. A series of five articles by Dr FitzGerald on the meaning of the rising.   [22] Ibid.

party and its leader, John Redmond, out of history, totally obscured—
by negating—the actual rationale of the Rising.'[23] In short it is not
possible fully to assess the implications of the Easter Rising until we
know more about what was—in Irish domestic political terms—
destroyed by it. This will entail a full discussion of the elected political
leadership of the Irish people on the eve of the rising: the Irish
parliamentary party led by John Redmond. This party represented the
accumulated political capital of an increasingly self-confident, middle-
class, Catholic Ireland. They became the forgotten men of independent
Ireland. Three-quarters of a century after their destruction, they
deserve to be rescued from oblivion: not simply out of pious respect for
the lost aspirations of a dominant political class, but also because the
implications of the party's collapse for the evolution of the 'northern
question' have never fully been analysed. The many articles which
were published on the 75th anniversary of the Easter Rising of 1916
were notable precisely for their failure to engage with this topic.

Did the Redmondites clearly cease to speak for the Irish people after
1914?[24] In a famous article published some twenty years ago, Father
Francis Shaw challenged one particular canon of Irish history: 'The
canon of history of which I speak, stamps the generation of 1916 as
nationally degenerate, a generation in need of redemption by the
shedding of blood.'[25] Shaw clearly doubted that such a redemption
was required; an angry critic soon reminded him that his family
tradition placed him firmly on the Redmondite side.[26] The same point
was to be made against another modern critic of the insurrectionary
tradition, Conor Cruise O'Brien.[27] Such *ad hominem* rebukes cannot
be allowed to control the direction of historical enquiry. The purpose
here is not to sanctify either 'Carsonism' or 'Redmondism', but simply
to explain mainstream nationalist and unionist ideologies on the eve of
the rising.

Writing of this epoch in 1960, Conor Cruise O'Brien observed:
'The confusion of the time was rich and explosive . . . it was the man of
action rather than the man of prudence who flourished in it . . . The

---

[23] *Irish Times*, 13–18 July 1991.

[24] As is implied in Professor O'Tuathaigh's fascinating lecture, 'The Irish-Ireland
Idea: Rationale and Relevance', in E. Longley (ed.), *Culture in Ireland: Division or
Diversity* (Belfast, 1991), 63.

[25] 'The Canons of Irish History', *Studies*, 61 (1972), 177.

[26] P. O'Snodaigh, *Two Godfathers of Revisionism: 1916 in the Revisionist Canon*
(Dublin, 1991), 35.   [27] *Phoenix*, 9/6 (22 Mar. 1991).

moderation and inclusive view of a John Redmond came to seem irrelevant or even tarnished virtues. Through the mouths of Carson and of Pearse all Ireland heard ancestral voices prophesying war. Different ancestors and a different war.'[28] Yes, one wants to say, there is much truth in this—Ireland was torn apart in this period. The mobilization of Ulster Protestants in an effort to remain firmly within the United Kingdom lies in stark contrast to the separatist impulse of the Easter Rising. But it is right also to say that from September 1914 until the Easter Rising, unionist and nationalist Ireland was to all intents and purposes—despite those different ancestors—fighting on the same side in a European War. This book is an attempt to reassert the complexity of this experience, 'confused', 'rich', and 'explosive' as it was.

[28] '1891–1916', in id. (ed.), *The Shaping of Modern Ireland* (London, 1960), 22.

I.

The Outline of a Crisis

A violation surely of the most fundamental rights which any
district within the UK now possesses and yet you are recklessly
going not merely to deprive Ulster of her fair share of
representation, not merely to divorce it from the governmental
system of the UK, and not merely to put it under the control of
the majority which it profoundly distrusts, but you are actually
going to take upon yourselves the function of keeping it under the
heel of that majority. . . . You will have to prove . . . that the cause
in which English blood is being spilled in order to coerce Ulster
has got its moral basis deep in the whole history of our country.

Arthur Balfour, *Hansard*, liii. 1303, 9 June 1913

How are you in these days, these democratic days, in this
democratic age, in this democratic country, to force a million of
men into a system which they refuse to join. . . . How are you
going to expel the Irish minority from citizenship of the UK?

Harry Lawson, MP, *Hansard*, xxxvi. 1499, 11 Apr. 1912

In 1885 rumours began to circulate in Belfast Conservative and
Liberal circles that Mr Gladstone was contemplating a major change
of policy. The great leader of the Victorian Liberal party was, it was
said, considering the implementation of a measure of home rule for
Ireland. The reaction to these rumours in unionist Belfast was one of
shock, dismay, and even disbelief. Nevertheless, Gladstone, as Liberal
prime minister, introduced the first Home Rule Bill in parliament in
May 1886. Unfortunately the question of Irish self-government
already possessed a distinct religious or sectarian dimension. The
general election of 1885 revealed the political topography of this
sectarianism. The home rulers won every seat with a Catholic
preponderance, which meant every seat in the three southern
provinces but two (the two Dublin University seats) and half of those in
Ulster. Charles Stewart Parnell, the Protestant leader of the home

rule party, tried to develop a genuinely non-sectarian political rhetoric, but some of his most important cadres found it difficult to maintain such a tone. In the middle of February 1886, the *Freeman's Journal*, the most substantial organ of nationalist opinion in the country, declared all too forthrightly: 'We contend that the good government of Ireland by England is impossible . . . the one people has not only accepted but retained with inviolable constancy the Christian faith; the other has not only rejected it, but has been for three centuries the leader of the great apostasy, and it is to this day the principal obstacle to the conversion of the world.'[1] Such a case for home rule could hardly by definition have appealed to the Irish Protestant and unionist minority—a minority which was in fact a majority in the four north-eastern counties.

With the benefit of hindsight, it is clear that Ulster unionist opposition was to be the major obstacle on which the home rule project floundered. Yet surprisingly, in their discussions leading up to the bill, neither Gladstone nor the Irish nationalist leader Parnell devoted much attention to this problem. They were much more concerned with the resolution of the Irish land question, which they both hoped would allow the Irish gentry to resume a normal and desirable role as leaders of the Irish people.[2] This was a fundamental political error; spurned and enraged, Ulster unionists opened up a campaign which played a key role in blocking for over a generation any concession of self-government to any part of Ireland.

Five years later Parnell was, in effect, to acknowledge that his earlier dismissive attitude towards the Ulster unionist threat had been an error. In a Belfast speech in May 1891 he spoke of relations between the Catholic nationalist majority and the Protestant unionist minority in Ireland:

I have to say this, that it is the duty of the majority to leave no stone unturned, no means unused, to conciliate the reasonable or unreasonable prejudices of the minority (*cheers*) . . . it has undoubtedly been true that every Irish patriot

---

[1] *Freeman's Journal*, 18 Feb. 1886, quoted in Thomas C. Hammond, 'The Religious Question in Ireland', *The Nineteenth Century*, 23/131, (Jan, 1913), 345.
[2] For the intellectual assumption which underpinned this strategy, see J. A. Froude, 'On the Uses of a Landed Gentry', in id., *Short Studies on Great Subjects* (London, 1877), iii. 389–428. On Parnell's personal belief, F. Hackett's very shrewd comment should be noted: Parnell, he wrote, was 'amenable to liberal considerations but utterly immune from liberal sympathies', *Ireland: Study in Nationalism* (New York, 1918), 330. L. G. Redmond-Howard, *Home Rule* (London, 1912), 36, describes Parnell as a 'patriot', but also a 'Tory' and a 'landlord'.

has always recognised . . . from the time of Wolfe Tone until now that until the religious prejudices of the minority, are conciliated . . . Ireland can never enjoy perfect freedom, Ireland can never be united; and as long as there is an important minority who consider rightly or wrongly . . . that the concession of legitimate freedom to Ireland means harm and damage to them, either to their spiritual or temporal interests, the work of building up an independent Ireland will have upon it a fatal clog and a fatal drag.[3]

But when he spoke these words Parnell was a desperately isolated man in the throes of the O'Shea divorce crisis. The mainstream nationalist press stigmatized his speech as the pathetic attempt of an adulterer to curry favour with the Orange lodges.

Rather than respond to Parnell's themes, most nationalists tended to insist on the irrational, supremacist nature of unionism and to reduce it to Orangeism, which was only one component of a wider movement. In fact, two rather different traditions fused in the Ulster unionist movement from 1886 to 1918. The largest force was composed of the traditional conservative and Orange interest; for these people Gladstone's conversion to home rule in 1886 was merely the logical culmination of a career of betrayal of traditional Protestant and established propertied rights in Ireland. The man who had disestablished the Irish Church in 1869 and failed to repress the Land League in 1879–82 had now made his last inevitable capitulation to Irish Catholic nationalism. Even, perhaps at times especially by other unionists, a considerable number of the supporters of this group could be seen as exhibiting, as liberal unionist critic J. J. Shaw was to put it, 'the pride, self-complacency and religious bigotry of a narrow arrogant faction', a description which should not allow us to forget the substantial moderate element to be found in Ulster's conservative gentry.[4]

---

[3] Quoted in Paul Bew, *C. S. Parnell* (Dublin, 1980), 127–31.

[4] *Mr Gladstone's Two Irish Policies* (Belfast, 1888), 20. The collection of letters, *Passion and Prejudice*, ed. P. Bew, K. Darwin, and G. Gillespie (Belfast, 1993), gives a good picture of the attitude of the Tory gentry. Several of the correspondents—Viscount Bangor, Lord Dunleath, Sir Robert Kennedy, the Earl of Kilmorey—were on the military council of the UVF, while others involved—e.g. Lord Charlemont or T. H. Verschoyle—held commands at a lower level, yet all display a certain, and in some cases, a marked liberality of outlook. *The Times*, 22 Aug. 1885, published an insightful article which summed up the dilemma of Irish Tories faced almost simultaneously by the democratization of the franchise (1884) and the threat of home rule (1885–6)? 'Personal feelings, local jealousies, class interests, the strong rough elements of Orangeism, . . . will be more powerful and less manageable in the future. The old responsible Conservatives . . . of more moderate views . . . find they can no longer exercise a

For the important body of liberal unionists, however, matters stood rather differently. In 1880 the Liberals held nine of the Ulster seats as against the Conservatives' eighteen; well represented in the business community, they felt they had good reason to believe that a home rule parliament's economic policy would inevitably jeopardize their hard-won prosperity, dependent as it was on integration with the British market. Before 1886 they had seen Gladstone's reformist projects in Ireland, either in the spheres of religious privilege or landlord–tenant relations, as largely justified. They believed in short in the benign power of the liberal democratic Westminster parliament of the leading country in the world to reconcile or at least arbitrate conflict between fanatical Irish warring creeds and classes. For this Liberal grouping, Gladstone had reversed his earlier proud principles and abdicated from the British state's ineluctable progressive role in Ireland. As one of them, J. J. Shaw, put it in 1888: 'We can not consent to argue for the maintenance of the Union upon any but the broadest principles of Liberal policy. . . . We can not consent to treat the great bulk of our fellow-countrymen as politically, morally or socially inferior to, or as less considered than, their Protestant neighbours. . . . [But] the controlling and steadying influence of the United Kingdom was never more needed in Ireland than at present.'[5]

The existence of this liberal strand was of vital importance to Ulster unionism. In the first place, it helped to ensure the solidarity of the almost entire Protestant community, without which the unionists would have been numerically overwhelmed even in the six north-eastern counties of Ulster. Secondly, it helped to accommodate internal social and class strains, as did the later emergence of unionist 'Labourism'. It should not be forgotten that the pathbreaking Wyndham Land Act (1903) owed almost as much to the discontent of the northern liberal unionist tenantry as it did to the nationalist United Irish League in the south. Thirdly, it ensured that the Ulster unionist case received a better hearing by the leaders and opinion-formers in British life, even outside naturally sympathetic right-wing circles.

controlling influence in elections by virtue of their rank and wealth' only judicious handling 'could hope to make tractable' the 'very uncompromising spirit' of the 'Orange element'. This cutting is the first and dominating item in the political scrapbook of cuttings and letters of R. T. O'Neill, the Antrim Tory MP from 1885 to 1910. The scrapbook is in the possession of Dr Onora O'Neill, Principal of Newnham College, Cambridge.

[5] *Mr Gladstone's Two Irish Policies*, 22.

In fact the leader of the Irish party, John Redmond, had adopted a conciliatory tone throughout the 1890s and early 1900s; this was a deliberate and self-conscious attempt to draw on Parnell's contribution to Irish political debate. Redmond was initially very reluctant to rely on British state pressure to bring the unionists into line, and gave primacy to resolving Ireland's internal division. In 1898 he declared: 'What has been the real stumbling block in the way of the English people granting us Home Rule? It has been the fact that Ireland herself has been divided upon this question of Home Rule into two camps, and that many thousands and ten thousands of the Irish people have held aloof from the national movement or a movement in favour of an Irish nation, which I desire to see, and which if it came into existence would mean the obtaining of home rule within six months—in a movement in which all classes and creeds of Irishmen could unite. (*applause*)'.[6] In 1910 Redmond, in frustration, abandoned this principle in favour of a policy which gave primacy to gaining the support of the British state for the home rule project. Irish unionists were not slow to remind him of his former stand.

Redmond's reputation has suffered from a withering fire from two sides. On the one hand there are those who, sympathetic either to unionism or the conciliatory O'Brienite nationalist faction, castigated him for his failure to mark out a more consistently moderate course. This school argues that such a course might have averted the sectarian polarization of the 1912–14 epoch. William O'Brien believed that it would have averted the partition of Ireland. On the other hand, Redmond has been presented as an essentially spineless Westminster rhetorician by those sympathetic to the revolutionary nationalist tradition. Given these heavy—albeit incompatible—condemnations, it is all the more necessary to attempt to reconstruct Redmond's precise strategy. With respect to the accommodation of Irish Protestant interests, the formal generosity of Redmond's position is striking. He accepted the safeguards against religious discrimination in the Home Rule Bill as a 'humiliating necessity' as long as there were a 'dozen' men in Ireland 'of our race and kin' who entertained honest fears upon the subject. It remains the case, however that he had reneged on his own stated positions as leader of the Parnellite minority in the 1890s. Then he had insisted that an alliance with English 'progressives' to destroy the power of the House of Lords was a snare and a delusion. The House of Lords was too strongly rooted, he had said, to be

[6] *Freeman's Journal* 11 Oct. 1898.

vulnerable to any such attack. Anyway, the correct strategy for Irish nationalists was to win the hearts and minds of the Irish unionists rather than seek outside intervention by the British state against them. After 1900 Redmond reluctantly moderated this stance. Increasingly he regarded the Irish party, for all its obvious deficiencies, as the all-important instrument in the fight for home rule. It had to be kept as united as possible at almost any cost. If this meant that it was sometimes necessary to forego opportunities for conciliation in Ireland—as after the Wyndham Land Act of 1903—then so it had to be. William O'Brien, the ardent conciliationist, found himself side-lined. Yet, despite the formal commitment to the Irish party as an instrument, there was an ambiguity, conceivably a crippling, fatal ambiguity, in Redmond's attitude towards his parliamentary colleagues. Perhaps all the years of unsavoury disputes—culminating in the 'mob rule' methods used to silence the O'Brienite faction at the 'baton convention' of 1909—had left an indelible impression. Redmond often appeared to be the party's captive rather than its chairman. Conor O'Kelly, a North Mayo MP who had a certain sympathy for Redmond, observed:

Mr Redmond is powerless, or thinks he is. He won't attempt to shake off the incubus which he must heartily detest. The leaders of Mr Redmond have taken his measure to the inch, they know their man. They know that he will sacrifice anything to retain his 'leadership'. He abandoned the land conference to do it. He abandoned William O'Brien to do it. He abandoned Tim Healy to do it. In fact, there is nothing he is not willing to abandon save that particular piece of furniture he uneasily sits in. In a word, if Mr Redmond wishes to sit in the chair he must be always content to be sat upon. That is the price exacted. He pays up and looks as pleasant as he can.[7]

Such an experience can hardly have been a pleasant one for a proud man. Redmond was in many ways an unusual leader for the Irish movement; his temperament in many respects appeared to be rather fastidious, lacking in the requisite arts of political enthusiasm. Redmond was born in 1856, a member of a Wexford Catholic landed family; his mother was born a Protestant and she always remained a unionist. Like other leading Wexford Catholic families—the Greenes for example[8]—the Redmonds were not afraid to send their sons to

[7] Letter published in the *Irish Times*, 27 July 1993.

[8] Sir David Goodall, 'Sir John Greene and the Wexford Independent', *The Past*, 18/2, 35. Redmond's second wife was Protestant; see P. Maume, 'John Redmond—Visionary, Statesman or Traitor?' *Irish Times*, 4 Mar. 1993.

universities disapproved of by the hierarchy. After finishing his schooling at Clongowes in 1873, Redmond went on to Trinity College, Dublin. His biographer, Warre B. Wells, noted: 'John Redmond never said a bitter word of Trinity and it was there that he learned to appreciate the quality of Protestant Ireland.'[9] Sean O'Faolain saw Redmond as 'the true Norman type'. He added: 'The mental characteristics are emotional control, conservation of energies, restrained idealism, a certain closeness, imagination well in hand . . . not the list of qualities that one would think of when speaking of the more Gaelic parts of Ireland, where character is so much more ebullient and unpredictable.'[10] Francis Hackett, in similar vein, observes that Redmond 'was for an Irish leader, prematurely conservative: a man of courage and faith and rectitude, he made the one mistake of an agitator. He accepted the established code before the order which he strove for was established.'[11] Serjeant Sullivan was even more pointed: 'There never was a more unIrishman than the new chairman . . . Jack made no figure on an Irish platform, he was too conscious of the facts, and too conscientious to bellow for the conventional and popular falsehoods. He was slow, cautious, cynical with a prejudice in favour of truth that was almost English.'[12]

It may not be surprising, then, that a man of Redmond's temperament was prepared to view the disappearance of the home rule party with some dispassion:

This party was created for one special purpose. We were bound to look for strength in an iron bound discipline to which many of our fellow countrymen refused to submit. We bound ourselves from the start to accept no office in connection with the administration of Ireland, and therefore all Irishmen who had an ambition to take part in the administration, in one shape or another, of the affairs of Ireland were excluded from our ranks. We could not call for assistance from the wealthy classes of our countrymen, or indeed from the most highly educated classes of our country, and great businessmen were, by the very nature of things, excluded from the possibility of coming over to London to take part in a struggle such as we are waging.

After Home Rule is granted all that will change. The Home Rule party, as we have known it, will disappear and I believe you will then have intellect, commercial genius, and patriotism, eager to take advantage for the first time

[9] Wells, *John Redmond* (London, 1919), 35.
[10] *The Irish* (first pub. 1947; repr. Harmondsworth, 1980), 63.
[11] Ireland 246.
[12] *Old Ireland* (London, 1927), 137.

for one hundred years of the gratifying and laudable ambition of serving their country in Parliament.[13]

These remarks pose the obvious question: why was Redmond unable to call for assistance from the 'wealthy classes of our countrymen or indeed from the most highly educated classes of our country'? Their allegiances, it seemed, lay elsewhere. Let us look first of all at the category of wealth: at a glance, the gap between the Irish unionist parliamentary party and the Irish nationalist parliamentary party was immense. By January 1910 no Irish unionist member was recruited from the lower professional and wage-earning ranks, yet those classes provided 46 per cent of the Irish parliamentary party's membership.[14] The unionists had also been expensively educated. Aside from a small grouping who had been educated privately, the nineteen-strong Irish unionist parliamentary party numbered four old Etonians (Peter Kerr-Smiley, Arthur O'Neill, W. J. McCalmont, and the marquis of Hamilton), William Moore (Marlborough), W. Mitchell-Thompson (Winchester), and Charles Craig (Clifton); James Craig (Merchiston) had also been to well-known public schools outside Ireland and Godfrey Fetherstonhaugh had been educated at the Chard Grammar School in Somerset. This was clear proof of the wealth of the families involved. Only two of these men (Moore and Fetherstonhaugh, educated at Trinity College, Dublin, and who became senior barristers) felt the need to go on to higher education in Ireland: only one (Kerr-Smiley) went on to higher education outside Ireland. Substantial or merely ambitious Irish families were in the habit of attempting to give their sons an English accent or, perhaps, important career 'contacts' by sending them to English schools. Irish educationalists, unionist and nationalist alike, argued that this was a futile strategy in the majority of cases (though the friendship formed at Eton between Arthur Balfour and the marquis of Londonderry proved to be of enduring importance). The educationalists claimed that the overwhelming majority of distinguished Irishmen 'all the world over' had received their secondary education in Ireland.[15] The second

---

[13] John Redmond, *The Home Rule Bill* (London, 1912), 66. This volume supplements R. Barry O'Brien (ed.), *Home Rule: Speeches of John Redmond MP* (London, 1910).

[14] See Alvin Jackson's lucid essay comparing the two parties, 'The Rivals of C. S. Parnell', in D. McCartney (ed.), *The Politics of Power* (Dublin, 1991), 78.

[15] Maurice C. Hime, *Home Education: Irish Schools for Irish Boys* (London and Dublin, 1887), 29, 119. This is no sense a nationalist argument—Dr Hime served on the education committee of the Ulster Provisional Government (*Weekly Northern Whig* 27 Sept. 1913).

largest identifiable group in the Irish unionist party had, indeed, been educated solely in Ireland and was rather more intellectually able. The unionist party's KCs—James Campbell, Sir Edward Carson, James Chambers, Fetherstonhaugh, John Gordon, and A. L. Horner— provided the great bulk of the parliamentary brain-power of Irish unionism.

Redmond's reference to the 'wealthy classes' is clearly justified; he was not indeed able to call for assistance from them. But what about the 'most highly educated' classes of 'our' countrymen? The unionists had only one member (Kerr-Smiley) who was educated at the third level outside Ireland; the nationalists, on the other hand, had a decent fringe of such men—for example, three Oxford graduates, two from London, and two from the Scottish universities.[16] But it was precisely the cultured and highly idiosyncratic Darwinian intellectual Arthur Lynch, MP for West Clare, educated outside Ireland at the University of Melbourne, who most fully acknowledged that there was indeed a difficulty in the relationship between nationalism and the most 'highly educated classes'—especially when it came to science. In his passionate work *Ireland's Vital Hour*, attacked as 'objectionable' in the mainstream constitutional national press, he publicly acknowledged the poor Irish record in science and indeed, for good measure, placed the blame on the Irish Catholic Church's attitude towards scientific research,[17] though he also identified Sinn Fein as being part of an anti-scientific outlook in Ireland.[18] 'A chapter on Irish science need but be short. In the whole range of Irish history, there is no event, no calamity, more than this should give us serious thought.'[19]

But what of Redmond's claim that the 'great businessmen were by the very nature of things' excluded from coming over to London to take part in the home struggle? In 1910 there was only one large businessman in the ranks of the Irish parliamentary party—Ulster Presbyterian eccentric Samuel Young. The charge made in the ILPU

---

[16] Jackson, 'Rivals of C. S. Parnell'.

[17] *Ireland's Vital Hour* (London, 1915), 328.

[18] Ibid. 196. Warre B. Wells, an admirer of the 'idealism' of Sinn Fein, admitted: 'For narrowness of outlook many of the less known and some of the best-known figures in the Sinn Fein exceed the worst of the members of the old party.' *Irish Indiscretions* (London, 1922), 43.

[19] Ibid. 322. Recently the Irish president, Mary Robinson (*Irish Times* 28 Sept. 1991), has picked up this theme—long suppressed in Irish public discourse—when in a discussion of the Easter Rising of 1916 she linked the Sinn Fein mentality with the failure to see Anglo-Irish science as part of the 'glory of Irish culture'.

pamphlet, *Union or Separation*, against Parnell in 1886 retained its pertinence. 'If the business energy, if the wealth of catholic Ireland are on the side of the revolution, why are they not to be found among the (Parnellite) members sent to represent that cause in Parliament?'[20] By contrast the Irish unionists were able to attract with negligible effort the linen barons and shipbuilders who together dominated Ulster industry.[21] They were also able to attract men with extensive interests outside Ireland, like the banker J. R. Lonsdale (later Baron Armaghdale) and W. J. McGaw, 'a large businessman in the Middle East and India'.[22] It is difficult to believe that 'great businessmen' in Ireland were by the 'very nature of things' excluded from coming over to London to support the home rule cause; unless by 'the very nature of things' is meant not the inconvenience of travelling but the fact that many of them were unsympathetic to home rule. In short, this group too appears to be anti-home rule or at any rate lukewarm about it. But, when all is said and done, the frank acknowledgement that the home rule party did not represent the 'best of Irish intellect, commercial genius and patriotism' is remarkable enough. It helps to explain Redmond's striking lack of interest—throughout the crisis of 1912–16—in getting his hand on the levers of power. Nicholas Mansergh has described Redmond in this respect 'as blindly dismissive' of a strategy which 'alone could save him'.[23] But this failure of political will—if failure it was—is rooted in a consistent attitude towards the meaning of the home rule project. In Redmond's view, the Irish party would dissolve with the arrival of home rule. The type of skills which had been vital in the past would not be required in a changed dispensation. Redmond preferred to dream about new alignments. All this helps to explain Redmond's ardent personal support for a nominated Irish Senate in his speech at the National Convention:

I want the Irish Second Chamber from the very start to be crowded with men who have not been partisans of the National Party in the past at all. I want to see it crowded by men of business and affairs—men of commerce, men

---

[20] Public Record Office Northern Ireland, *IP* 989C/3/5, cited in P. Buckland *Irish Unionism 1885–1923* (Belfast, 1973), 20.

[21] Jackson, 'Rivals of C. S. Parnell', 77.

[22] M. Stenton and S. Lees, *Who's Who of British Members of Parliament*, 4 vols. (Hassocks and Brighton, 1976–81), ii. 229.

[23] Mansergh, *The Unresolved Question: The Anglo-Irish Settlement and its Undoing* (London, 1991), 86.

representing the professions, the arts and the sciences, and the literature of Ireland, men having large stakes in the country—and although I am quite sure that after a while, when the old lines of demarcation between parties have been obliterated in Ireland, men of this type would be elected in large numbers, still, I doubt if they would be elected at the start, and I want to see them there at the start; and I tell you, if I had in my hands the nomination of the first Senate of the Irish Parliament, I would put into it a large majority, a considerable majority, of men of the type to whom I have referred.[24]

In an interview with J. A. Spender, published three weeks later on 18 May 1912, Redmond was even more explicit: 'I would like to put in men of the type of Lord Dunraven, Lord Castletown, Sir Horace Plunkett and Lord MacDonnell . . . men who, while not agreeing with us, are sincerely anxious to work for Ireland.'[25] Traditionally English unionists argued that the brilliant orators of the Irish party had revelled in the stage provided by Westminster (English disparagement of Irish economic and scientific skills went hand in hand with a high estimation of Irish verbal fluency). Deprived of this exciting metropolitan context, the new representatives at a parochial parliament would be—so men like Arthur Balfour argued—of lower calibre. The Irish genius was essentially a political one; home rule would stifle that genius. Redmond was turning this argument on its head. The Irish party MPs, he implied, were mere political machine men; the party had failed to tap the best talent in Ireland. With the coming of home rule all that would change. Redmond had always shared with Parnell the notion that self-government would lead to some form of reconciliation of creeds and classes, embracing even the former landlords. T. P. Gill, a close friend both of Parnell and Redmond, added the final gloss in a lecture to the mid-Tipperary Farmers' Association at Thurles: 'The landlords', he argued, as had both Parnell and Redmond, 'now that that banner of conflicting interest between them and other classes is thrown down are going to take a high and useful place among the leaders of the new society.'[26] In retrospect, it all appears to be unrealistic; but a Senate nominated in this fashion—in the context of a peaceful home rule settlement—might conceivably have been a force for harmony.

Certainly T. P. Gill's vision was not a purely individual one. It was

---

[24] Redmond's National Convention speech at the Mansion House, Dublin, 23 Apr. 1912, cited in Redmond, *Home Rule Bill*, 85.

[25] *Weekly Freeman's Journal*, 18 May 1912.

[26] *Cork Examiner*, 9 Mar. 1912.

characteristic of Redmond's immediate circle—Hugh Law, the Donegal MP, for example, laid out a vision of home rule: 'That it can itself revolutionise economic conditions I do not believe.' But he did hope for 'a widely diffused comfort and happiness'. Law added that the Irish had an instinct for association: 'Whatever our faults the cold, icy, aloofness of the English upper and middle classes is not found amongst us.' He then returned to a theme which had been integral to the rhetoric or both Parnell and Redmond:

Home rule an accomplished fact and the land question settled is there any reason why Ireland should any longer be deprived of the services of some who have, in recent years, held aloof from the national movement? It was not to be expected that many of them would appear in Irish public life so long as the land war was still raging. The liberation of the tillers of the soil had to be achieved, let who might be offended, because of it. That work is now accomplished thanks to the brave men, some of whom are still with us. What is there any longer to divide .. the younger landlords from their fellow countrymen but the dying embers of a dead controversy? Give to them the opportunity which nationalists, mindful of Parnell's teaching, will not deny them of doing work for Ireland and I warrant they will not fail her.[27]

But if it did not represent the 'best of Irish intellect, commercial genius and patriotism' what did the Irish party represent? William O'Brien's scathing pamphlet *The Party*, published in 1917, did its best to prove that the Redmondite party was a new, but degenerate, creation having little connection with the authentic, heroic 'Parnellite party of the Land League epoch'. This approach seems to have exercised a decided influence on later historians. Their accounts present the party as above all a respectable, stolid, even boring entity. In 1949 F. S. L. Lyons pointed out that in the Irish parliamentary party the 'upper middle-class element (barristers, solicitors, doctors and journalists together with landowners and large businessmen) was larger—albeit only slightly larger—than the lower middle-class' element (local shopkeepers, farmers, labour leaders and salaried workers)—the upper middle-class element having 45 out of 83 MPs in 1910'.[28] As a group, the Irish Catholic upper middle-class was considered by radical publicists not to possess the full measure of nationalist integrity. 'The well-to-do shopkeeper, the gentleman farmer and professional classes

---

[27] *Weekly Freeman's Journals*, 8 Nov. 1913.
[28] Lyons, *Irish Parliamentary Party* (London, 1957), 172.

generally are . . . merely concerned in getting a lodgement, or at least a leg in, amongst the aristocracy, who, as a body are alien to them in race and creed, in national and religious aspiration and belief.'[29] They were keen to participate in charities, and artistic and sporting ventures which were associated with the 'ascendancy', less keen to take part in purely Catholic ventures—some of the leading Catholic colleges were among Trinity College, Dublin's 'best feeders', despite Cardinal Logue's view that Trinity College was 'no place for our people'.[30] Even the existence of a slight majority of such people in the Irish parliamentary party was, for some critics, a cause of recrimination. In 1973, Joseph Lee went so far as to describe the Redmondite party as 'obesely bourgeois'.[31] In 1984, K. T. Hoppen, in a pioneering work, described them as 'men who would readily have declared themselves Whigs or Liberals in earlier days'.[32] In 1986, John Hutchinson described the party as 'bureaucratic, careerist and ossified'.[33] Lyons insisted that 'respectability' had its political advantage: 'whenever home rule came within the realm of practical politics there was inevitably much discussion about the nature of the proposed Irish parliament, and about the type of member who would be responsible for working it. It was obviously in the nationalist interest that English public opinion should be assured that the population of Ireland did not entirely consist, as some seemed to think, of ex-Fenians and lawless tenants, but that there did, in fact, exist a sober and responsible class which was in a position to take over the government of the country.'[34] But precisely how 'sober' and how 'responsible' was it? Let us look first of all at Lyons's category of ex-Fenians and lawless tenants. In fact, the Irish party had a striking number of ex-Fenians within its ranks. These included J. J. O'Kelly (Roscommon North),[35] J. P. Phillips (Longford South),[36] David Sheehy (Meath South),[37] Michael Reddy (King's County),[38] John O'Connor (Kildare North)[39] Michael Meagher (Kilkenny North),[40] and Tom Condon (Tipperary East).[41] William Lundon (Limerick East), who in 1909 was succeeded by his son

---

[29] *Leader* 18 Jan. 1913.   [30] *Weekly Freeman's Journal*, 29 June 1912.
[31] *The Modernisation of Irish Society* (Dublin, 1973), 152.
[32] *Elections, Politics and Society* (Oxford, 1984), 485.
[33] *Dynamics of Irish Nationalism* (London, 1986), 284.
[34] Lyons, *Irish Parliamentary Party*, 172.
[35] Bew, P., *Land and the National Question* (Dublin, 1978), 242.
[36] *Longford Leader*, 7 Apr. 1917.   [37] *Drogheda Independent*, 24 Dec. 1932.
[38] *Midland Tribune*, 2 Aug. 1919.   [39] *Kilkenny People*, 21 Dec. 1927.
[40] Ibid.   [41] *Weekly Freeman's Journal*, 27 Sept. 1913.

Thomas until 1918, was also a Fenian.[42] Also an ex-Fenian was P. A. Meehan, MP for Leix. Of all these men, Meehan's break with his radical past was the most complete. Though he turned down a baronetcy in 1907, Meehan became an ardent advocate of Irish reconciliation with the British empire.[43] All the other ex-Fenians traded at times on their past efforts and certainly did not engage in any denigration of the men of '67.

Even more important than the party's Fenian heritage was its Land League heritage: since 1879 the Irish parliamentary party membership had reflected (*pace* William O'Brien) an intimate involvement with agrarian agitation. Arthur Lynch, the West Clare MP, correctly insisted on this in his novel *O'Rourke the Great*, when he offered a 'composite' picture of the Irish parliamentary party's rank and file. In his memoirs, he made the same point: 'most' of the Irish party membership won their seats 'because they had done good work in the strenuous days of the Land League'.[44]

There was a group of pure Parnellites–Land Leaguers: the leading figures were the Redmond brothers, John and Willie, John Dillon, and T. P. O'Connor. The dissidents William O'Brien and Tim Healy—also of this school—stood formally outside the party's ranks. But others imprisoned during the Land League crisis also included the congregationalist William Abraham (Dublin Harbour).[45] William Doris (Mayo West) was a lawyer who had been secretary of the first Land League's legal affairs department and actually issued the No Rent manifesto of 1881.[46] Peter Ffrench (Wexford South),[47] a son of evicted tenants, originally a school teacher who evolved into an 'extensive' farmer, had been an active Leaguer. Playwright and businessman William Field, MP, had been 'closely identified' with the Land League and one of its 'most popular orators'.[48] John Hackett, MP (mid-Tipperary), had been the secretary of his local Land League branch.[49] Richard McGhee, the Presbyterian MP for mid-Tyrone, had been a close ally of Michael Davitt in the 1880s.[50]

After the Phoenix Park murders of 1882 a number of key Land

---

[42] *Limerick Chronicle*, 3 Oct. 1951; *Limerick Leader*, 3 Nov. 1951.
[43] P. F. Meehan, *The Members of Parliament for Laois and Offaly 1801–1918* (Portlaoise, Leinster, 1972), 72.   [44] *My Life Story* (London, 1915), 328.
[45] *Freeman's Journal*, 3 Aug. 1915.   [46] *Mayo News*, 19 Sept. 1926.
[47] *Free Press*, 9 Nov. 1929.   [48] *Irish Independent*, 30 Apr.1925.
[49] *Tipperary Star* 3, Oct. 1914.
[50] Conor Cruise O'Brien, *Parnell and his Party* (Oxford, 1957), p. 245.

League officers—notably Patrick Egan, Thomas Brennan, Malachy O'Sullivan, and P. J. Sheridan—had fled to the United States. Undoubtedly, but for this prudent evacuation, the Land League presence in the Irish party leadership would have been even greater. Also, the split with William O'Brien kept a number of notable ex-Land League MPs such as Tim Healy, Eugene Crean (Cork South-East),[51] and Lawrence Gilhooly (Cork West)[52] outside the ranks of the Irish party. During the Plan of Campaign (1887–9) three new leaders emerged—all incidentally from very prosperous backgrounds—and later found seats: John Fitzgibbon (Mayo South),[53] John Roche (Galway East),[54] and Dennis Kilbride (Kildare South).[55]

Fitzgibbon was the son of an 'extensive' businessman, who became in turn one of the 'largest commercial men in the west of Ireland'. After John Dillon, he was the most important nationalist in the region. Roche was an 'enterprising' farmer and miller in Woodford.[56] Dennis Kilbride inherited a large holding from his father.[57] Fitzgibbon took on Lord de Freyne; Roche made the marquis of Clanricarde his obsession, while Kilbride challenged Lord Lansdowne. John Cullinane (Tipperary South) also emerged as the paid organizer of the Plan.[58]

Then there was an even larger group, who emerged on the land reform platforms of the United Irish League, founded in 1898. These included J. P. Farrell (Longford North), Richard Hazleton (Galway North), John O'Dowd (Sligo North), Joe Devlin (Belfast West), J. M. McKean (Monaghan South), auctioneer T. F. Smyth (Leitrim South), draper P. J. O'Shaugnessy (Limerick West), Tom O'Donnell (Kerry West), L. Ginnell (Westmeath), J. P. Hayden (Roscommon South), W. J. Duffy (Galway South), and successful local businessman M. Flavin (Kerry North).[59] Lyons has pointed out that after 1906 there was a significant rise in the farming element in the party's ranks—sixteen as against eight in the 1892–5 epoch.

There was yet another associated category, a type perhaps pioneered by William Doris and Tim Healy, who have already been mentioned

[51] *Cork Examiner*, 13 June 1939.   [52] Ibid., 17 Oct. 1916.
[53] *Roscommon Messenger*, 28 Sept. 1929.
[54] *Galway Observer* 29 Aug. 1914.
[55] *Nationalist and Leinster Times*, 1 Nov. 1924.
[56] L. Geary, *The Plan of Campaign* (Cork, 1986), 27.
[57] *Nationalist*, 1 Nov. 1924.   [58] Geary, *Plan of Campaign*.
[59] For the activities of this grouping see my *Conflict and Conciliation* (Oxford, 1987), 35–70, 122–202.

and best characterized as Land League lawyers.[60] J. J. Clancy (Sligo North),[61] J. C. R. Lardner (Monaghan North),[62] and J. Muldoon (Cork East)[63] all specialized explicitly in matters of land law and land purchase to a degree which gave them a high local profile. None of these figures was quite so much in the thick of the fight as the first rank of activists, but they were all well known for their influence on the detail of land reform and their role in the transfer of estates in their constituencies. The party's identification with the land issue is indisputable. If there was a difficulty here, it lay in the fact that by 1910 the returns from the land question were both diminishing and ambiguous.

There were other ways of gaining access to the ranks of the Irish party. Some members were notionally representatives of sections of the Irish diaspora: Dr Charles O'Neill (Armagh South)[64] was based in Scotland, as was the barrister Thomas Scanlan (Sligo). Alderman Daniel Boyle (North Mayo), who had started out as a railway clerk, ended up as President of the Ancient Order of Hibernians in England.[65] Fluent Gaelic speaker Matthew Keating (Kilkenny South)[66] emerged out of the world of London Irish business and politics. The Irish Australian Lynch partly belonged to this group, but is probably more correctly placed amongst the journalists and littérateurs—the Liverpool/Irish-based T. P. O'Connor and his brother-in-law William O'Malley, MP for Connemara, a decided moderate on agrarian matters. O'Connor, Lynch, and O'Malley all published autobiographies which throw light on the party's history.

Then again one might be a grandee. There was certainly a category of useful, wealthy, or well-connected Protestant home rulers—scathingly described by William O'Brien as a 'little group of tame Protestant Home Rulers maintained for obvious reasons at Westminster as nominees of a "hibernian" party to whose inner rites their religion forbade their admission'.[67] (The comparison might be made with Sir Denis Henry, Catholic Ulster unionist parliamentary candidate

---

[60] For a discussion of this activity see *Kerryman*, 22 Mar. 1958.

[61] *Irish Independent*, 26 Nov. 1928.

[62] *Democrat and People's Friend*, 9 May 1925.

[63] *Wicklow People*, 26 Nov. 1936.

[64] *Frontier Sentinel*, 19 Jan. 1918; *Armagh Guardian*, 18 Jan. 1918.

[65] S. Fielding, *Class and Ethnicity: Irish Catholics in England 1880–1935* (Buckingham, 1993), 83; *Weekly Freeman's Journal*, 22 Feb. 1913.

[66] *Kilkenny People*, 27 May 1937.

[67] *The Irish Revolution* (London, 1910), 118.

and MP after 1916). These included the Sandhurst-educated Chief Whip Captain A. J. Donelan, the son of Colonel Donelan (Wicklow East) and Hugh A. Law (Rugby, Oxford, and son of an Irish Lord Chancellor), who sat for Donegal West. Both Donelan and Law actually converted to Catholicism before their deaths. Here there was a marked contrast with Parnell, whose eyes 'blazed with indignation' when an Irish party MP foolishly suggested that he would prefer to die a Catholic.[68] Also significant here was Stephen Gwynn (Galway),[69] son of a Trinity College, Dublin, Professor of theology (interestingly, Gwynn's wife also converted to Catholicism). Two other Irish Protestant members with profound Trinity connections were the writer Edmund Haviland Burke (King's County), a descendant of Edmund Burke, and Professor J. G. Swift MacNeill (Donegal South),[70] also educated at Christ Church, Oxford, a descendant of Jonathan Swift, and the son of a well-known Dublin evangelical clergyman. Finally, there was the ancient and venerable Sam Young (Cavan East), a wealthy Presbyterian Belfast distillery businessman who had supported every 'popular' Irish cause in Ireland since the days of O'Connell: the 'father of the house'. Young died in Parliamentary harness at the age of 97 in 1918. Commenting on Young's idiosyncratic politics for a man of his religion and class, T. P. O'Connor noted: 'Even in this Mr Young was typically Ulster, for belonging to a minority at variance with the overwhelming majority of his fellow provincials and co-religionists he brought to his views the characteristic dourness and inflexibility of the Ulster temperament.'[71] O'Connor added: 'He did not always agree with his colleagues. On questions that involved Capital and Labour he took the side of Capital, and was an avowed enemy of any legislation that he thought Socialist in tendency'.

Undoubtedly, most of these useful Protestants owed their place to the distinction or wealth of their families—Parnell himself had been the greatest example of this. It was clearly felt that some of this distinction might rub off on the party. But there were Catholic grandees too: the moderate Sir Walter Nugent (Westmeath South), who heroically devoted himself to the complicated financial affairs of

---

[68] *Wicklow People*, 20 Sept. 1924, for an account of Donelan. For Law see *Donegal Democrat*, 10 Apr. 1943. For the Parnell incident, see John Valentine, *Irish Memories* (Bristol, 1928), 10. I owe the Parnell reference to Dr Patrick Maume.

[69] *Irish Times*, 17 June 1950.

[70] Ibid. 25 Aug. 1926.   [71] *Anglo-Celt*, 27 Nov. 1918.

the *Freeman's Journal* newspaper, and Sir Thomas Grattan Esmonde (Wexford North), papal chamberlain under four popes, of whom it was appreciatively said 'his friends ranged from Pope Leo XIII and King George to Indian trappers in the Arctic wastes and South Sea cannibals'.[72]

There were other politicians who grew out of the world of Dublin municipal politics. P. J. Brady, MP for Stephen's Green, was a solicitor with an extensive practice; he was also known to be an active social welfare worker, particularly with the St Vincent de Paul Society.[73] J. P. Nannetti, (Dublin College Green), son of an Italian sculptor,[74] had devoted himself to labour concerns; W. F. Cotton (Dublin County South)[75] was a pioneer of gas lighting in the city. The eldest son of one of the leaders of a successful group of Dublin iron founders, Cotton developed multifarious business interests himself. Municipal politics also threw up J. D. Nugent,[76] the key figure in the Dublin operation of the Ancient Order of Hibernians. Even small centres like Tramore could produce figures like hotelier M. J. Murphy (Waterford East),[77] whose key claim to fame was in the development of local amenities. Murphy was a close personal friend of John Redmond, as was barrister John Mooney (Newry), who acted both as Redmond's parliamentary secretary and the party's treasurer.[78]

The party naturally had a place for northern nationalists, for example Devlin's henchman J. T. Donovan (Wicklow West), who had formerly edited the United Irish League newspaper *Northern Star* in Belfast.[79] Jeremiah MacVeagh (Down South) was also a close associate of the Redmonds.[80] Philip O'Doherty (Donegal North), a Derry solicitor was, however, a sharp critic of Redmond's alleged lack of support for the northern minority.[81]

All told the phalanx of fifty agrarians, which constituted well over half the Irish party's parliamentary strength, gave the party its specific *persona*. The sophisticated nationalist intellectual Francis Hackett rejected the Ulster unionist view of the Irish party as 'too ferociously unfriendly', but even he conceded that 'the failure of the party has been principally due to its agrarian preoccupations' and argued: 'The

[72] *Free Press*, 24 Sept. 1935.   [73] *Irish Independent*, 21 May 1943.
[74] *Weekly Freeman's Journal*, 27 Apr. 1915.
[75] Ibid., 9 June 1917. His brother was in charge of the lighting in the Kremlin.
[76] *Irish Independent*, 19 Mar. 1940.   [77] *Waterford Star*, 6 Sept. 1919.
[78] *Frontier Sentinel*, 4 Apr. 1934.   [79] *Wicklow People*, 2 Jan. 1922.
[80] *Irish Times*, 18 Apr. 1932.   [81] *Derry Journal*, 10 Feb. 1926.

parliamentary party never had a genuine economic policy outside land purchase. Its one ambition was to haggle for and to boast about state aid.'[82] Other small groupings clearly existed—Protestants, northern Catholics, municipal worthies, journalists—but they were too small to affect the party's broad image. These categories were, of course, overlapping: Stephen Gwynn and Haviland Burke, 'useful Protestants', were frequent speakers on agrarian platforms. Some of those who came from comfortable families—such as Gaelic enthusiast, Olympic lawn tennis winner, and captain of the Christ Church, Oxford, cricket team, John Pius Boland; keen yachtsman, Alderman Cotton, or even V. P. Kennedy (Cavan West),[83] son of the Crown solicitor for the county and nephew of a tobacco magnate—might have considered themselves to be in the grandee category. (Bridget Boland's memoir brilliantly evokes her father's comfortable and slightly dreamy world: 'Industry there must be, my father felt, and he tried everything. It must be admitted that in his efforts to establish it he was spectacularly unsuccessful.'[84]) The Irish party also had some bright former university scholarship or exhibition boys in its lower ranks—men like the barrister John Muldoon, or J. C.R. Lardner. At the margins—more typically amongst northerners or *émigrés*—it had a few spectacular examples of upward mobility, such as Joe Devlin, the ex-Belfast barman, who had made himself into one of the best speakers in the House of Commons. The greatest example of all was Dr Charles O'Neill. O'Neill had left Antrim as a youth with absolutely no resources, started selling tea on a post round in Coatbridge in Scotland, and gradually acquired a small lodging house and then a public house. At this point he decided to enter politics; when he was sneered at on account of his lack of educational attainment, he responded by successfully taking a medical degree at Glasgow University.

This was John Redmond's parliamentary party. It was regularly accused by its radical critics of corruption, venality, and jobbery. A total of sixty jobs was listed in the *County Cork Eagle's* definitive list of 6 June 1914 as having been extracted from the Liberal government for Irish party cronies. *Freeman's Journal* writers did particularly well: Ignatius O'Brien, a *Freeman* editorial writer, became Lord Chancellor;

---

[82] Hackett, *Ireland*, 331.

[83] For Kennedy, see *Anglo-Celt*, 27 Nov. 1943.

[84] For Boland, see Bridget Boland, *At My Mother's Knee* (London, 1978), 48. I owe this reference also to Patrick Maume.

another *Freeman* writer, George McSweeney, became Serjeant at Law, a step on the road to becoming Irish Solicitor-General. Three other *Freeman* writers, M. Bodkin, D. Lenehan and R. Adams, became judges. Valentine Kilbride, Denis Kilbride, the MP's brother, became Irish Taxing Master at £1,000 a year; Thomas Scanlan, MP for Sligo, acted for the government in the *Titanic* inquiry. It did not help matters that Justice W. H. Dodd, once Liberal MP (1906–7) for North Tyrone, sent a Clare ranch 'warrior', Patrick Arkins, to gaol for seven years for breaking down a wall—because the Irish party had helped to get Dodd elected. John Redmond had one charge against him: his son-in-law (Max Green) became chairman of the Prison Board. There is no doubt that this is a significant list; but some of the *County Cork Eagle*'s claims can be challenged. Tom Kettle, for example, had considerable academic ability, and his appointment to a chair in the National University need not be placed at the door of political influence. A list of sixty appointments is in any case hardly startling given that the Irish party was the largest party in the country and a sympathetic Liberal regime was in power; even the Tories spoke of governing Ireland according to 'Irish ideas', and this inevitably meant the appointment of nationalists to key positions.

If not exactly austere in its ethos, the Irish party was fairly honest. The overwhelming impression is that it was representative of the mass of the nationalist population and its sentiments. The poorest farmers were not directly represented, it is true, but Fenians and Land Leaguers, who sympathized with them, certainly were. On matters of 'national principle', Redmond had every reason to regard his followers as reliable, and certainly had no occasion to doubt that they could be used as a unified voting bloc when the subject of home rule suddenly became the central issue in British politics. As in the mid-1880s, this had much to do with the competition between the two main parties. The context is clear: the 1909 budget crisis, combined with the Conservative use of blocking tactics in the House of Lords. The election of 1910 gave Redmond the balance of power at Westminster: the second election of that year in December confirmed this position of strength. Many leading Liberals remained unenthusiastic about the prospect of an Irish alliance, but the political realities left them without any other option. The Parliament Act of 1911 reduced the veto of the Lords to a delaying power, and in 1912 the Home Rule Bill for Ireland was introduced. The Conservatives were furious. Many Tories thought that the Liberals were using a temporary parliamentary majority to alter the constitution in a quite unacceptable way. Some even believed that the normal rules of the game had been suspended and that they were themselves no longer obliged to play by them. It was not simply that some Conservatives felt that the Liberal leadership was tamely accepting Redmond's dictation, and that behind Redmond lay an appalling coalition of Irish American separatism, rural thuggery, and Catholic exclusivism. It was also the case that 'thinking' Conservatives believed that, in proposing home rule for the whole of Ireland, key Liberals were acting against at least some of their own inclinations.

It was already apparent that the opposition of the unionist minority in Ireland to a measure of home rule was likely to be fierce. The anti-home rule campaign in Ulster was officially launched on 25 September 1911 at Craigavon, the home of James Craig. The start of the meeting had to be delayed because of the length of the procession composed of the Orange lodges, the unionist clubs and the County Grand Lodge of Belfast. The Conservative press placed the attendance at 250,000; the Liberal press at 100,000. With typical insouciance a delegation of prominent Liberal politicians from the Eighty Club did not deign to view the proceedings, although they were in Ireland on a 'fact finding' visit. The earl of Erne, Imperial Grand Master of the Orange Order, took the chair as a family bereavement meant the duke of Abercorn was unable to attend. Abercorn also sent a message to the meeting, stressing the financial difficulties of the home rule project and arguing that 'England' was now subsidizing Ireland to the tune of £5 million per annum. Deprived of such resources, an independent Irish parliament would be forced to tax heavily the thriving industries of the north, thus bringing about their collapse. In support, R. M. Liddell pointed out in his speech that one thousand of the leading Ulster manufacturers and merchants had signed an anti-home rule pledge.[85] Carson's words at Craigavon were intended to attract attention. He was determined, he said, to 'defeat the most nefarious conspiracy that has ever been hatched against a free people', and concluded: 'We must be prepared . . . the morning Home Rule passes, ourselves to become responsible for the government of the Protestant province of Ulster.'[86] The intellectual basis for this position had been outlined in a long letter to the meeting from the Antrim man, Provost Anthony Traill of

---

[85] *Irish Times*, 27 Sept. 1911.
[86] A. T. Q. Stewart, *Sir Edward Carson* (Dublin, 1981), 73.

Trinity College, Dublin. Traill denounced nationalist sectarian discrimination and the way in which the mood of conciliation generated by the 1903 Wyndham Land Act had been destroyed by the cattle drivers. Thus far Traill had said nothing which could not have been accepted by nationalists of the William O'Brien hue or the 'constructive' wing of southern unionism. But he went on to insist that there were 'two Irish nations', both having an equal right to be entrusted with legislative powers. Gladstone had been prepared to offer such a parliament to Ulster, he said, and if the offer were repeated it might have to be accepted 'in the last resort'. Southern unionist opinion was deeply alarmed, suspecting that Traill merely spoke Carson's secret thoughts. Carson, the *Irish Times* noted, was 'dogged and determined', but 'may not be a great strategist', while Traill's proposal would be a disaster. Traill believed that the existence of two neighbouring parliaments, one with a Catholic minority, the other with a Protestant minority, would force both to be generous to their respective minorities. In practice, however, the *Irish Times* was sure that it would not work in this benign fashion. With some prescience, it noted: 'Two parliaments in Ireland would perpetuate in the worst forms our unhappy difficulty. They would invite persecution of the minority in each division in Ireland.'[87] There would be 'endless bickering and retaliation'. In short the opinion-formers within southern unionism, while admiring the 'narrow, passionate negation' of the north's attitude to home rule, also feared the early emergence of explicit partitionism in the anti-home rule movement. They wished to use Ulster as an obstacle to prevent home rule for Ireland, but already Sir Edward Carson, a southern unionist himself, appeared to be abandoning this notion in favour of a strategy which would lead to the establishment of a northern parliament. Carson was undoubtedly suppressing his personal convictions;[88] more to the point, the use of extreme language damaged the unionist cause. Unionist policy remained formally unchanged, but a significant conceptual slippage had begun; a slippage which was linked to a reordering of priorities. The abstract case for continued equal citizenship within the UK gave way to a regional case for Ulster Protestant self-determination. Thomas Sinclair, the leading Presbyterian liberal unionist issued a

---

[87] *Irish Times*, 27 Sept. 1911; for Gladstone's late change of mind on Ulster, see Hansard, 5th ser., liii, 1321, 9 June 1913.
[88] George Boyce, 'Edward Carson (1845–1935) and Irish Unionism', in C. Brady (ed.), *Losers in the Game* (Dublin, 1989), 148.

statement on behalf of the unionist leadership at the beginning of 1912 which clarified matters definitively: 'Ulster's claim in the disastrous event of Home Rule being imposed upon Ireland is plain and intelligible. It is not a request for a distinctive Ulster Parliament, it is simply a demand ... that our northern province shall continue to possess the exact constitutional privileges and rights which in common with her British fellow-citizens she enjoys today as an integral part of the UK, and that she shall continue to be represented on equal terms with Great Britain in the Imperial Parliament.' But Sinclair added ominously: 'Should this claim be refused, the only alternative consistent with our rights as subjects of the King is the Ulster Provisional Government, to come into operation on the appointed day; and this once established, we are resolved we shall see it through.'[89] The Ulster unionists felt strongly that they could rely on powerful friends in the rest of the United Kingdom if they took such a course of action. They also had the confidence which came from economic strength. Any form of Ulster independence would, of course, have presented ideological difficulty, but a solution was produced to deal with it: 'The intention was that if the home rule bill became law, Ulster should be held in trust in the King's name, until the Act was repealed.'[90]

As Roy Foster has concisely expressed it:

The removal of the Lord's veto in 1911, and the subsequent Home Rule Bill, were presented in Ulster as issues that could not legitimately be decided by party votes at Westminster; support for this argument came from a wide spectrum of opinion ranging from the respectable to the great, including George V ... the Ulster question arrived in Britain as the issue upon which the landed and plutocratic interests decided to confront Lloyd George's welfare policies.

For many Conservatives in Britain, Ulster was an appropriate area for exerting political energy, given the conditions of liberal hegemony and reckless reform. An assault on property and Empire had been conspiratorially planned by a minority interest: this legitimised separatist threats of Unionist Ireland. And 'Unionist Ireland' increasingly meant Protestant Ulster, ostentatiously left unmentioned on Asquith's bill. The question of whether Ireland was one nation or two hung in the air.[91]

---

[89] *Irish Times*, 4 Jan 1912. In a possibly symptomatic error, the *Irish Times* report rendered 'distinctive' Ulster parliament as 'destructive' Ulster parliament.

[90] *Dictionary of National Biography 1931–40* (Oxford, 1949), 200; entry by John Andrews for Sir James Craig.

[91] *Modern Ireland 1600–1972* (London, 1988), 465.

There is no question that some Conservatives—frustrated by divisions over tariff reform in particular—turned to the Ulster issue with an undiscriminating enthusiasm. It has to be said, however, that Conservative leaders also contributed some serious reflections on the implications of the home rule project.

In truth, while the Conservatives tended towards energy on the Ulster question, the Liberals tended towards lethargy. Two important members of the cabinet, David Lloyd George and Winston Churchill, submitted a formal exclusion proposal to the cabinet in February 1912, but they were overruled by the majority, led by the prime minister, H. H. Asquith. For almost eighteen months the government, in the words of one modern authority, having insufficiently examined the Ulster issue in the first place, then gave it 'scant' attention.[92] Instead it allowed an inevitable polarization of Irish opinion to develop as uncertainty, with wild hope on one side and fear on the other, fuelled sectarian antagonism. It may even be that Asquith saw no other way to wean Redmond from his sentimental commitment to Irish unity. Unfortunately, however, Asquith's failure to consult in a significant way with Ulster unionist opinion undermined the base of those within that community who sought to compromise. British Liberal ignorance of Ulster unionists and their case was a cause of fury: Augustine Birrell, Asquith's Irish chief secretary, was felt to be particularly culpable. 'Are there half a dozen men in Ulster whom Mr Birrell knows even by face?'[93] The Presbyterian *Witness* noted the existence of a constituency which 'would have been willing on any fair or reasonable terms to have considered some arrangement for satisfying the demands of the Roman Catholic Nationalists that would not sacrifice the liberties of Ulster and Irish Protestants. But the government paid no attention to the opinion or feelings of the Ulster Unionists and Protestants; never asked their opinion or consulted one of their representatives as to their wishes or views.'[94]

Instead, those who favoured the use of force increased their hold on events: a Hibernian attack on Presbyterian schoolchildren at Castle-dawson was rapidly followed by a mass expulsion in early July of Catholic workers from the Belfast shipyards and other factories. In

---

[92] Jalland, 'Irish Home Rule Finance, 1910–14', in *Liberals in Ireland* (Brighton, 1980), 69, 157. For powerful support of many of Jalland's key arguments, see Bentley B. Gilbert, *David Lloyd George: A Political Life*, ii: *The Organisers of Victory 1912–16* (London, 1992), 93–106.   [93] *Witness*, 3 July 1914.

[94] Ibid., 12 June 1914.

September 1912 some 250,000 signed the Solemn League and Covenant. In January 1913 the Ulster Volunteer Force was formed, and by September of that year—with the support of many in high places—the elements of a provisional government were established. By October Asquith was belatedly offering an implicit acceptance of partition, but by this point the tensions unleased in Ireland were almost out of control. The Curragh 'incident' of March 1914 revealed that the British army could not effectively be used to force Ulster Protestants into a united Ireland. The unionists further attempted to strengthen their position by a defiant massive importation of arms at Larne on 24–5 April 1914.

Nationalist Ireland was inevitably stirred to react. On 25 November 1913 the Irish Volunteers were founded; Redmond had resisted their formation for at least one very powerful reason. He knew that unionists would claim that the formation of a force which it could be said was designed to coerce a community into accepting home rule made a mockery in their eyes both of professions of moderation and the rhetoric of self-determination. But he was powerless to prevent these new developments and had to reach instead an uneasy accommodation with them, eventually forcing them to accept Irish party leadership. But in July 1914 three Dubliners were killed following the nationalist gunrunning at Howth. All shades of nationalist opinion bitterly contemplated this tragedy and compared it savagely with unpunished Ulster unionist defiance of the law. On 25 May 1914 the Home Rule Bill finally passed the Commons; it had twice been defeated in the Lords: on 30 January 1913 and 15 July 1913, but now it seemed to have overcome all parliamentary obstacles. On 8 July 1914 the Lords made its last stand on the Irish question: it altered an amending bill which allowed temporary exclusion of parts of Ulster to make the exclusion permanent and to cover all of Ulster. The unionist leader Sir Edward Carson had repeatedly made it clear that mere temporary exclusion was unacceptable. The nationalist leadership had equally indicated that this was the limit of its concession. The Buckingham Palace Conference of 21–4 July 1914 failed to reach a compromise.[95]

---

[95] See David Trimble, *The Foundation of Northern Ireland* (Lurgan, 1991), 7–9, for the most recent unionist treatment of the Buckingham Palace Conference. But see also Alan J. Ward, *The Easter Rising: Revolution and Irish Nationalism* (Arlington Heights, Ill., 1980), 90–4. Ward concludes: 'The excluded area would have included a substantial Catholic minority, but it would have been protected by the United Kingdom Parliament and by explicit guarantees of religious freedom. The real turning point for Ireland then,

But this failure, and the anger generated by the deaths at Howth, was rapidly overshadowed by the outbreak of war between the United Kingdom and Germany. A major historian of British Liberalism in this epoch, Professor Trevor Wilson, has noted: 'at the time the Great War intervened, time had not run out on the question of home rule'.[96] He adds: 'Each of the major parties in Britain was freely accusing the other of bringing Ireland to the brink of bloodshed. It does not quite follow that they were prepared themselves to invoke bloodshed rather than attempt a last minute closing of what, between the sides within Britain had become a pretty narrow gap.' War, in fact, was to provide a context which at first appeared to have determined the shape of an Irish settlement: home rule was placed on the statute book in a suspended form while Asquith now asserted—as Ulster Protestants joined the British forces in large numbers—that the coercion of unionist Ulster was now 'unthinkable'.

may well have been not the failure of home rule but the failure of the Liberal government to devise and impose a plan of partition in 1914. The significance of this missed opportunity must not be underestimated.'

[96] Review of P. Jalland's *Liberals and Ireland* (Brighton, 1980), in *Historical Studies*, 20 (1982–3), 131.

2.

The Case against Home Rule

There are people in Belfast who are destitute of religious bigotry. There are leaders of the Ulster party who are free from it and I am glad to name the right honourable gentleman opposite [Sir Edward Carson] as being as free from religious bigotry as any man can possibly be. But the pulse of the machine is religious bigotry.

Augustine Birrell, *Hansard*, lii. 1579, 10 June 1913

I am sincerely and passionately attached to Ireland as the honorary member for Galway or any of his friends. I share their love for Ireland's soil, for her scenery, her people, her history, her poetry and her romance . . . but this is a matter of citizenship.

Ronald MacNeill, *Hansard*, liii. 1522, 10 June 1913

There is no doubt as to the intensity of communal feeling during the home rule crisis. All serious journalists commented on it. W. F. Monypenny's classic *The Two Irish Nations*, published in London in 1913, was the greatest evocation of the prevalent mood. Monypenny stressed the presence of distrust and even hatred: all the various animosities of 'race', 'religion', and 'class' were involved in the crisis, he argued. Commenting on the Ulster unionists, Monypenny added: 'Grant even that in their very fears there may be an element of unreason, the unreasonableness of a community is a political fact like any other, it can not be got rid of, as radical newspapers seem to think, by scolding and vituperation.'[1] R. H. Murray echoed one of Monypenny's themes when he noted: 'Why then is the Belfastman more attached to the union than the Corkman? The answer is plain: they belong to different races, with different traditions and ideals. No doubt the southern race is numerically greater than the northern. The race, however, that produced Lord Lawrence, the saviour of India,

[1] *The Two Irish Nations: An Essay on Home Rule* (London, 1913), 65–7.

Earl Cairns, the greatest judge of the nineteenth century, Lord Kelvin, the uncrowned king of science since Darwin, is not one to be jeered or despised.'[2]

The word Irish itself became for some almost a term of abuse. William Beach Thomas recalled in his memoirs: 'The atmosphere was one of sheer war especially among the farmers. There was one whose face and utterance remain as clear in my memory as Lord Carson. His family had been two hundred years in Ulster but he was Scottish to the bone and he said "Irish" as if it meant enemy. "What the Irish want to do" he said, "is to drive out the capitalist just as they have driven out the landowners, and we want to keep the capitalist".'[3] It was a nice implicit distinction. Many thousands of the Ulster unionist supporters in the 1912–14 crisis had in the recent past supported the anti-landlord attitudes of both the Ulster Liberals in the 1880s and the Russellites in the 1900s.[4] This had meant a tacit co-operation on this issue with nationalists in both epochs. Belfast's Lord Mayor and MP for South Belfast, was the successful businessman R. J. McMordie (successful enough to be featured on the front page of the *Financial Times* on 28 March 1914), who had, for example, been closely identified with Liberal land reform politics, founding the *Daily Post* (with his brother Hans) in the 1880s in order to further these principles.[5] Interestingly, R. J. McMordie's cousin, a former Presbyterian Moderator, William McMordie, stood out against the denial by Ulster unionists of an Irish identity: 'Unionists are Irishmen too. We love our country and work for its good. We do not wish to be separated from our fellow countrymen.'[6] McMordie opposed the partition of Ireland, but even his proposal that home rule be delayed for a generation in order to allow O'Brienite moderation to gain ground in the south was obviously unacceptable to mainstream nationalism.[7]

Most unionists felt that their case would have been weakened if the nationalist side had been capable of operating a consistently more tolerant line. One unionist MP told D. D. Sheehan, an O'Brienite MP: 'My friends and I have always marvelled at the vacuity of the Irish

---

[2] R. H. Murray, 'The Evolution of the Ulsterman', *Quarterly Review*, 220/438 (Jan. 1914), 115.   [3] *Traveller in News* (London, 1925), 51.

[4] 'The old tenant righters who voted for King-Kerr and a good many of those who voted for Beddoes are members of the East Antrim Unionist clubs by now.' *Weekly Northern Whig*, 8 Feb. 1913.   [5] *Northern Whig*, 26 Mar. 1914.

[6] *Witness*, 17 Jan. 1914.

[7] J. B. Armour to W. S. Armour, 8 Jan. 1914, Public Record Office Northern Ireland, D 1792/A3/5/5.

party in throwing over the member for the city of Cork [William O'Brien] when he had all the cards in his hands.'[8] It is interesting to note that Sir Edward Carson always took care to make generous reference to the O'Brienite tendency. Speaking to Liverpool Conservatives, for example, Carson wished to show that he was not devoid of generosity towards his fellow countrymen, when he said that he had seen 'with great gratitude a movement within the past few years in Ireland, in which men like Mr O'Brien and Healy, great enemies of his own politically, had been trying . . . to bring about a feeling of friendship throughout all classes and religions and they had been scouted and outlawed'.[9]

One of the best unionist pamphlets of the home rule crisis, *Ulster's Protest*, made a point of listing only 'industrial, political and imperial' reasons for refusing to submit to home rule. It angrily denounced the leading Liberal politician, the Earl of Crewe, who had argued that the 'only sentiment involved' in Ulster unionism was 'that of hatred to the Church of Rome'. (It may have given the pamphleteer some comfort to see the earl of Crewe's daughter, in open rejection of her father's analysis, marry Arthur O'Neill, the unionist MP for Antrim.)[10] But, *pace* the author of *Ulster's Protest*, there really is no denying the specifically religious or sectarian tone of much of the controversy: though, of course, *Ulster's Protest* was correct to deny that the 'only sentiment' involved was 'hatred of the Church of Rome'. The Presbyterian journal, the *Witness*, declared in an editorial: 'But the central and outstanding feature of Ulster Unionism is its vitalising avowal of FAITH IN GOD. The Ulsterman may in this respect be but a lonely survival of an age of faith or he may be the prophetic herald of a coming time when faith shall return to the earth.'[11] There was plenty of open hostility directed towards the Catholic priesthood too. As a 'Southern Presbyterian' put it for a northern audience: 'I stood in St Peter's yesterday and witnessed the attitude of practised priests going through their elaborate forms of worship like a complicated piece of machinery, all those hard, cruel-looking men appeared to me to turn towards the setting sun. Why should they be called in to cast a blight over the energetic and progressive population of Ulster?'[12] Even

---

[8] P. A. O'Siochain, *Ireland: Journey to Freedom* (Kells, 1989), 36.

[9] *Northern Whig*, 1 Oct. 1912.

[10] The angry home rule Liberal, J. B. Armour, commented: 'She has lost all sense of the proprieties of civilised life and ought to be tarred and feathered.' J. R. B. McMinn (ed.), *Against the Tide* (Belfast, 1985), 93.　　　　[11] *Witness*, 17 *July* 1914.

[12] Ibid.

economic arguments tended to have a religious dimension, which is not to deny that economic fears were not of great importance—fears, in particular, that home rule would destroy the prosperity of Belfast. Peter Kerr-Smiley, MP, speaking to the Antrim Orangemen at Mosside, argued the economic case against home rule: 'Already the shadow of Home Rule has had a most depressing effect on Irish securities, and if that was the case now what might they expect once they have experienced the reality?' But he had also made it clear that the economic consideration was not the dominant one: 'The whole education of the country would be placed in the hands of the teaching orders of the Church of Rome and Protestants, whether they like it or not, would be compelled to contribute towards the teaching of doctrines of which they did not approve. He put the religious aspect of the case first for, after all, it was the most important one. (*cheers*)[13] His unionist parliamentary colleague, J. H. M. Campbell (Dublin University), agreed: 'He would not be candid with them nor fair to himself if he did not say that he believed that there was at the root of all this terror of Home Rule, permeating the law-abiding people of this great province, a deadly apprehension of religious intolerance in the future.'[14] Scottish businessman Hugh T. Barrie, MP for North Derry, told an Edinburgh audience: 'In it [a home rule parliament] all social advancement would be subordinated to the political machine which had behind it the immediate object—namely, the harassing by taxation of rich and prosperous Ulster.' But he then added immediately: 'It would take its orders on religious matters from Rome, and these orders would never be remarkable for their fairness or for the recognition of individual conscience.'[15] Sir Robert Kennedy (Harrow and University College, Oxford), a retired senior UK diplomat who had also served on the Military Council of the provisional government, was one of the most sophisticated of the Ulster unionist leaders. But even he was prepared to say: 'It is evident that the political struggle in which they were engaged was to a great extent a religious question. It was a struggle not against the doctrines and teaching of any particular church, but for the maintenance of civil and religious liberty. . . . If Protestant ascendancy was bad, Roman Catholic ascendancy would be ten times worse.'[16]

The economic case, real as it was, was usually inextricably linked to

---

[13] *Ballymoney Free Press*, 18 Jan. 1912.   [14] Ibid.
[15] Ibid., 14 Mar. 1912.   [16] *Weekly Northern Whig*, 24 May 1913.

sectarian sentiment. As J. H. Stirling put it: 'We are no stupid bigots who fear that the tragedy of Scullabogue Barn—where, in 1798, Protestant women and children were penned in and burned alive—may be re-enacted. Even in Catholic Ireland the world has moved too far since then. But we know that the same result—the extermination of the loyal Protestant minority—can be effected just as surely by the taxation of their property and the ruin of their industries.'[17]

Nationalist politicians in the home rule party went out of their way to avoid saying anything which would give any credibility to such views. By and large, they were successful in this enterprise. But they could not control all their supporters; in particular, they could not control Father Gerald O'Nolan, who gave a tactless millenarian address in December 1912 to the sodality of the Catholic students at the Queen's University, Belfast: 'We shall have a free hand in the future. Let us use it well. This is a Catholic country, and if we do not govern it on Catholic lines, according to Catholic ideals, and to safeguard Catholic interests, it will be all the worse for the country and all the worse for us.'[18] O'Nolan's blistering diatribe against 'poisonous Anglicizing influences' in favour of that 'dear faith for which our fathers bled and died' played no insignificant role in strengthening unionist resolve; but the most significant instance was the *Ne Temere* ruling and the McCann affair. The *Ne Temere* decree, promulgated in 1908, laid down that any marriage to which a Roman Catholic was a party, if not solemnized according to the rites of the Church of Rome, should be treated as invalid from a canonical point of view. This had major implications for mixed marriages in Ireland where, up to this point, an ambiguous but possibly more humane set of understandings had been allowed to exist. In particular, the religious identity of the children of mixed marriages now become a serious issue, as Protestants feared that they would, in effect, 'lose' all the children of these marriages. One particular case proved to be the focus of all these fears. As Stephen Gwynn recalled: 'The case of an unhappy marriage [the McCanns] in Belfast was exploited with fury on a thousand platforms.'[19] It was a critical moment for Catholic Ireland—even the most liberal Protestants felt, for example, that German Catholics had handled the issue raised by *Ne Temere* with greater sensitivity than their Irish counterparts. The Irish parliamentary party, in theory so voluble

---

[17] *Ballymoney Free Press*, 14 Mar. 1912. [18] *Witness*, 20 Dec. 1912.
[19] *John Redmond's Last Years* (London, 1926), 49.

in defence of Protestant rights, lapsed into silence and casuistry, yet a
key issue of religious equality was clearly at stake. Listen to the solemn
tones of Bishop D'Arcy:

The recent Papal Decree, termed *Ne Temere*, regulating the solemnisation of
marriages, has been enforced in Ireland in a manner which must seem
impossible to Englishmen. According to the Decree, 'No marriage is valid
which is not contracted in the presence of the [Rome] parish priest of the
place, of the ordinary, or of a priest deputised by them, and of two witnesses at
least.' This rule is binding on all Roman Catholics.

It is easy to see what hardship and wrong must follow the observance of this
rule in the case of mixed marriages. As a result, it is now the case, that in
Ireland, marriages which the law of Ireland declares to be valid are declared
null and void by the Church of Rome and the children of them are illegitimate.
Nor is this a mere academic opinion: such is the power of the Roman Church
in this country that she is able to enforce her laws without deference to the
authority of the state.

The celebrated McCann case is the most notable illustration. Even in the
Protestant city of Belfast we have seen a faithful wife deserted and her children
spirited away from her, in obedience to this cruel decree. And we have seen an
executive afraid to do its duty because Rome had spoken and justified the
outrage.[20]

The McCann case became the subject of a set-piece parliamentary
debate. Unionists—led in the debate by R. J. McMordie, MP, insisted
that Mrs McCann had lost her children (who were taken out of the
country by Mr McCann) thanks to the connivance of the Catholic
clergy; more particularly, the inactivity of the police under a Liberal
administration was taken as a presage of future oppression under home
rule. The nationalists, led in this by Joe Devlin, insisted that there was
no such implication—simply the story of an unhappy marriage. Indeed,
according to Joe Devlin here was a mere propaganda tactic designed to
hide capitalist oppression in Belfast. It was a guilty diversion from the
class struggle:

When the McCann's case came on there was a crowded meeting in the Ulster
Hall. Who were on the platform? The crushers of the poor, the manufacturers
who sweated women, and the responsible agents for the pinched faces. These
were the men who came there for wretched political capital, and had not a
single voice to raise on behalf of the toiling women who were doing so much to
build up the greatness of the city and advance the material interests of the

masters of Belfast. . . . They thought they have switched off discussion and examination of all these crimes against democracy by catching at an isolated domestic incidental instance to prevent light being cast upon the economic conditions they impose.[21]

The fact is that only one Liberal Presbyterian was not deeply shaken by *Ne Temere* and the McCann affair, and that was Armour of Ballymoney. But Armour, it should be noted, was an opponent of mixed marriage.[22] At least one Irish party MP, Arthur Lynch, remained unimpressed by Devlin's case: 'The notable McCann case was debated in the House of Commons, but as usual in that assembly the duty of eliciting the truth became secondary to the play of party politics. A charge which made a considerable impression was followed by a speech which swept the matter out of sight to the stirring music of applause. I was far from satisfied myself.'[23] Another ordinance, issued on 9 October 1911, was construed as seeking to establish immunity for the clergy from proceedings in civil courts. Unionists claimed that this decree lifted the Catholic clergy above the civil law, despite certain benign interventions by senior Catholic clergy on this point.[24] The interventions of the Catholic Church in these sensitive areas greatly complicated the home rule project. Augustine Birrell, Liberal chief secretary in Dublin, felt that there was a real danger that Liberal commitment to a Dublin parliament could be undermined by displays of clerical high-handedness. On 19 December 1911 Birrell wrote to Dillon: 'That was an odd marriage case in Galway. Yours is a very funny church. What was the Bishop about? It would be an odd thing if the marriage laws upset home rule.'[25] He continued to concern himself with the problem. In some anguish, Birrell wrote to Dillon on 15 January 1912: 'Papal decrees seem inexplicable. Perfectly harmless

---

[21] *Hansard*, 5th ser., xxii. 174, 7 Feb. 1911.

[22] McMinn, *Against the Tide*, 88. Armour felt that the general opinion among those who knew the woman and her family history was that she was 'no great shakes and to use her case for purely political purposes shows the straits to which the Ulster Tories are reduced'.

[23] Arthur Lynch, *Ireland's Vital Hour* (London, 1915), 142. For the debate see *Hansard*, 5th ser., 176–7, 7 Feb. 1911, for McMordie, and esp. col. 174 for Devlin. For Lynch's view of Devlin, see his novel *O'Rourke the Great: A Novel* (London, 1921): 'Joe had something of O'Connell, something of Tom Sawyer and something indeed, however small, of Tom Thumb.'

[24] *Weekly Freeman's Journal*, 6 Jan. 1912. Letter from His Grace the Archbishop: 'Misrepresentation Exposed: What Rome's Latest Aggression Amounts To'.

[25] Trinity College, Dublin, Dillon Papers, 6759/152.

in themselves. *Bombinans in Vacuo.* To issue them *now* in Ireland looks like malice.' He added icily: 'I am perfectly *certain* that unless *withdrawn* or otherwise effectively dealt with it will be absolutely necessary to introduce into the Home Rule Bill words especially designated to the Marriage Laws and the new Papal bulls.'[26] This is precisely what happened. In the end, the third clause of the Home Rule Bill contained a new section: 'the Irish Parliament shall not make . . . any religious belief or religious ceremony a condition of the validity of any marriage'. This was a provision which is not to be found in the bills of 1886 or 1893. Asquith explained:

These words, as the House will see, are chosen especially to exclude the possibility—I have never thought it myself even a possibility—of legislation on the part of the new Irish Parliament to make any attempt to give effect to either of those recent papal pronouncements which go by the name of the *Ne Temere* and *Motu Proprio* decrees, in other words, to establish any privileged status of clerical persons before the tribunals of this country, or in any way to interfere with the validity of mixed marriages between persons of different religious beliefs.[27]

Birrell continued to fret over this problem. Increasingly, he hoped that Irish home rule politicians would themselves resist the power of the Catholic Church. In November 1913 he told his North Bristol constituents: 'Neither Liberals nor Tories wish to quarrel with the authority of the religion of the great majority of the Irish people; but if you want to see an independent Ireland, place responsibility in the hands of the people, and you will see they are not so frightened of the priests as some of us are.'[28] The forced and contorted tone of this comment inevitably provoked derision on both sides in Ireland.

The religious–ideological gulf between the two communities had its counterpart in a material–economic one. Beach Thomas noted: 'Did ever two communities live in so different an atmosphere as Belfast and Dublin?'[29] Beach Thomas was essentially a unionist, but the same point was made by an ardent home ruler, Sydney Brooks: 'Anyone who makes the tour of Ireland feels on reaching Londonderry and Belfast that he is for the first time in contact with the atmosphere and problems of a modern manufacturing city.' Brooks added with even greater clarity of expression:

---

[26] Trinity College, Dublin, Dillon Papers, 6579/182.
[27] John Redmond, *The Home Rule Bill* (London, 1912), 6.
[28] *Ballymoney Free Press*, 4 Dec. 1913.   [29] *Traveller in News*, 57.

The two towns in tone and spirit, in their social structure and instinctive way of looking at things, and their economic formation, stand in a category of their own and have little or no affinity with Limerick, Cork, Waterford or even Dublin; while the gap that separates them from the smaller urban centres, that except in Ireland would not for a moment aspire to the name of towns, is the gap of the entire industrial revolution.[30]

There is no question, for example, that economic factors played a key role in the generation of unionist opposition to home rule. The economic dangers were stressed in key pamphlets such as those by Peter Kerr-Smiley, MP,[31] and J. C. Davidson.[32] Some of these fears may appear to be exaggerated—*Ulster's Protest* argued: 'Irish Nationalists not only despise industry: they hate it and envy it.' But unionists always insisted that the industrial progress of Belfast depended on complete economic integration with the UK and imperial market. A significant strand of mainstream nationalist opinion was attracted by the idea that a policy of Irish protection might redress the industrial underdevelopment of the rest of the island. There was therefore a latent tension on this point, but it was also the case in 1912 that the Redmond leadership was prepared to dilute economic nationalism in the pursuit of home rule. In 1910 Redmond had accurately told a newspaper reporter: 'We are willing to abide by any fiscal system enacted by the British government.'[33] There were also nationalists who were ardent in their desire to retain access to British markets,[34] but unionists felt that they might in the end lose the argument within the nationalist camp. Anyway, the unionist economic case was a broader one; their fears existed whether nationalists embraced protection or not.

Here it is worth looking at the views of Thomas Sinclair (1838–1914), one of the leading lights of both liberal unionism and the Belfast business community. Educated at the Queen's University in the days when there were 'giants among the professors',[35] he was taught by, amongst others, James McCosh, later to be president of Princeton. Like the 'great majority of Belfast merchants' in the 1860s and 1870s, Sinclair was a Gladstonian liberal. By 1912 he was considered to be the most important liberal unionist in Belfast. To the

---

[30] Brooks, 'The Problem of Ulster', *North American Review*, 88/5 (Nov. 1913), 617.
[31] *The Perils of Home Rule* (London, 1911).
[32] *Northern Whig*, 3 Oct. 1912. [33] *Nationality*, 6 Apr. 1918.
[34] J. P. Boland, *The European Crisis and Ireland's Domestic Interests* (Dublin, 1915).
[35] *Northern Whig*, 16 Feb. 1914.

end, it was said, 'his leadership made for moderation and calmness and the avoidance of bitterness and all evil speaking'.[36] In the years preceding the home rule crisis, Sinclair happily worked alongside Catholic nationalists on official committees,[37] yet when the crisis emerged he became one of the key figures on the Ulster provisional government, effectively drawing up its constitution.[38] Sinclair was convinced that home rule would be an economic disaster: 'The root of the evil will be in the want of credit of an Irish Exchequer in the money markets of the world. Now, a fundamental condition of commercial and industrial well-being is financial confidence. If the Public Exchequer of a country lacks confidence, it is a truism to say that consequently commercial confidence must be gravely impaired ... already, since the present home rule crisis has become acute, the handwriting on the wall has been made evident in the depreciation of leading Irish stock to the extent of 15 to 20%.'[39] Fully to understand such sentiments, it is necessary to grasp the self-confidence of the business community in Belfast. As J. L. Garvin has noted: 'Former industries expand, new ones are continually added: nowhere is business intercourse more incisive and decisive—economical of time.' Belfast, he adds, 'had never been more prosperous, more progressive, more proud of itself'.[40] The *Financial Times* of 28 March 1914 ran a special Ulster supplement which glowed with praise for the 'premier shipbuilding centre of the entire world' and the fine quality of its 'captains of industry' devoted both to the technical education and cultural development of the city.

Sir Edward Carson often picked up on these themes in his speeches. Commenting on a suggestion by Redmond that the government would acquire the Irish railway system—a proposal which, as Carson pointed out, was one of Redmond's very rare indications to the distinctive nature of the likely activity of a Dublin Parliament—Carson asked:

[36] *Northern Whig*, 16 Feb. 1914.
[37] St John G. Ervine, *Sir Edward Carson and the Ulster Movement* (Dublin and London, 1915), 71.
[38] Little is known of the work of Sinclair's Constitutional Committee, but it did recommend female suffrage; see Vivian Kelly, 'Irish Feminists: Britons First, Suffragists Second, and Irish Women Perhaps a Bad Third: An Examination of the Difficulties Facing Suffragists in Ireland at the Time of the Home Rule Crisis' (M.Sc. thesis, Queen's University, Belfast, 1992), fos. 29–30.
[39] Rosenbaum, *Against Home Rule*, 178.
[40] *Northern Whig*, 30 Oct. 1912.

Where is he going to get the money? Where is he going to get the credit? I have asked this question over and over again—'If you withdraw Imperial credit from this country, at what rate of interest will you borrow money to carry out any improvement for our people?' and I have never had an answer. I have asked men in London, I have asked great financiers. What rate would you fix? and they say, 'We could not fix any rate, because people would not lend money at all ... not merely upon sentimental grounds, not merely upon religious grounds, but putting it at the lowest upon economical and financial grounds, we find no hope in these proposals at all'.[41]

Speaking to the 500–600 delegates of the Ulster Unionist Council in September 1913, Carson declared: 'To tell me that the small farmers and the labourers engaged in their own occupation, purely agricultural, of the South and West of Ireland are in a position to frame Acts of Parliament for the guidance and governance of this great community of the North of Ireland, is really to turn Parliament into a pantomime and nothing else.'[42]

But the problem in Sydney Brooks's view lay not simply in the gap between north and south, Belfast and Dublin, but also in the gap within Belfast itself. The home ruler Brooks argued rather surprisingly: 'My personal observations when last in Belfast confirmed the impression that the Catholics there are not the equals of the Protestants; they have not the same toughness of fibre; they live in a squalor that no Protestant would tolerate for a moment, anybody who passes from the Catholic to the Protestant quarters in the city is conscious of a different social atmosphere and the local inhabitants can usually tell by a mere glance at each other's appearance ... which of the two rival communities to which he belongs.'[43] J. A. Rentoul, an ex-unionist who, like Brooks, supported home rule, noted: 'It is a remarkable fact that there are many people in Ulster who have never sat at a table with, or met on equal terms, a Roman Catholic and who know Catholics, if at all, only as domestic servants.'[44]

This problem, of course, was not confined to Belfast or the north. Katherine Tynan observed that the Mayo Protestant gentry—admittedly the most exclusivist in Ireland—deprived themselves of the company of men like Canon D'Alton of Ballinrobe and his 'fine stately presence, his scholarly mind, his abounding kindness and hospitality'.

[41] Speech at Ramore Hill, Portrush, reported in the *Ballymoney Free Press*, 7 Aug. 1913.   [42] Ibid. 2 Oct. 1913.
[43] Brooks, 'The Problem of Ulster', 622.
[44] *Stray Thoughts and Memories* (London, 1921), 202.

The Mayo Protestant gentry, she notes, were unaware 'socially at least' of the existence of such men.[45] Perhaps this sense of exclusion may lie behind D'Alton's vigorous and contemptuous dismissal of the Ulster unionist community as a 'peculiarly foul deposit'[46] on the soil of Ireland. One interesting anecdote from Lord Ernest Hamilton's memoirs gives us a hint of the opportunities for reconciliation which were lost through lack of social contact. Father O'Conologue, the Irish party's election agent, was regarded by the Hamiltons as the 'bitterest Nationalist in North Tyrone. He would invariably cross himself and spit when he passed any member of my family on the road.'[47] However, in the flush of his election victory in 1886 Lord Frederic (Lord Ernest's brother) invited the defeated opponent to a champagne party. After much quaffing, Father O'Conologue delivered the toast: 'And, I declare to you gentlemen, that there is no man on God's earth I would rather see representing North Tyrone than Lord Frederic Hamilton.' Lord Ernest enthusiastically remarked: 'Great indeed are the powers of Moet and Chandon.'

But there was not enough champagne in Ireland to bridge the gulf between the two northern communities. It is necessary to comment here on a neglected point. In Ireland as a whole, the period 1861–1911 saw a substantial *embourgeoisement* of the Catholic population. Despite a slight fall in the percentage of Catholics in the total population of Ireland between 1861 and 1911, the percentage of Catholic doctors, lawyers, and engineers steadily grew, as, of course, did the percentage of schoolteachers. In 1861 34 per cent of Ireland's barristers and solicitors were Catholic; by 1911 this had risen to 44 per cent; the percentage of Catholic medical practitioners rose from 35 to 48 per cent in the same period.[48] But in the north-eastern counties there was rather less Catholic advance. Nationalist writers attributed this to various forms of discrimination—the reluctance of Protestants to be treated by Catholic doctors, for example. There was, however, another dimension to the problem. The process of agrarian reform in the period 1870–1909—which had involved a shift of national resources in favour of the Irish farming classes and their children—had opened up major professional opportunities for the children of the Irish Catholic middle-class farmer throughout most of the island. This group had

[45] Tynan, *The Wandering Years* (London, 1922), 34.
[46] *Mayo News*, 25 Aug. 1914.
[47] Ernest William Hamilton *Forty Years On* (London, 1922), 213–14.
[48] J. Hutchinson, *The Dynamics of Cultural Nationalism* (London, 1987), 262.

also benefited from the gradual displacement of the landed Protestant ascendancy. But in the north-east the same process had worked out differently. Here, the main beneficiaries had been the Protestant farming classes and their offspring. Owing in part to the inherited advantages of capital and land, they had been in the decisive position to take advantage of new educational opportunities. In Antrim, for example, Catholics constituted one-fifth of the population, yet they were seriously under-represented in the professions: there were two Catholic doctors, as against sixty-five Presbyterians/Methodists and sixteen Episcopalians. In law, matters were only slightly better: there were nine Catholic legal figures (barristers or solicitors) as against twenty-two Episcopalian and sixty-two Presbyterians/Methodists.[49] This social gulf contributed to a Protestant tone of hostility mixed with obscure fears of Catholic revenge. One *Witness* leader is a good example:

We are continually hearing that if there is a mansion or a country residence vacant in Ulster, agents of the Roman Catholic Church have an eye on it to secure it for some conventual, educational or ecclesiastical purpose. There is hardly a farm vacated by a Protestant that the agents of the Church are not on the watch to secure for a Roman Catholic. The reason why we say agents of the Church is that we have been so informed, and that many farms, especially in Down and Antrim, have fallen into the hands of Roman Catholics whose previous position and circumstances would not have suggested the necessary capital.[50]

There is another telling example of such pessimistic fearfulness. The distinguished commentator Beach Thomas consulted with the Revd John McDermott, a Presbyterian ex-Moderator, in the garden of his manse: 'A more splendid figure it would be hard to imagine—tall, indeed, almost of a giant stature, straight and dignified, with the head of a prophet or philospher, with every sign and symbol of the thinker in his guise and his language.' McDermott was a decidedly non-Orange figure—in some ways a typical liberal unionist not without a sympathetic interest in '98,[51] yet even he felt sure that Ireland under home rule would experience a new phase of agrarian agitation, 'a demand for land appropriation and no rent'. McDermott added:

[49] T. Galloway Rigg, *Leader*, 26 Apr. 1913.
[50] *Witness*, 6 Feb. 1914.
[51] See his son's memoir, *J. C. McDermott: An Enriching Life* (privately printed, Belfast, 1979), 38.

All oppressed people hug to themselves the memory of past wrongs and the hope of future vengeance. Such memory and such hope are their solace and their refuge. I know of peasants even in Antrim who possess carefully treasured maps, as much as 200 years old, on which are marked the lands that are still theirs. The lands may have been confiscated for rebellion, they may have been sold for a good price, they may have passed from class or family to another according to any of the common and natural chances and changes. But these later incidents are wiped out. All that is remembered is the old ownership. This recording spirit exists in the people all over Ireland; and there are churches and buildings marked down in the same way as the plots of land. It is certain that out of this feeling trouble will proceed.[52]

These comments already indicate the existence of a considerable depth of Protestant suspicion of Catholics. Yet there was also, in the early phase of the home rule crisis, a very definite effort made to place limits on the public expression of such sentiments. This was particularly so within the Presbyterian community, the largest and best educated of the Protestant denominations. In February 1912 the *Ballymoney Free Press* prided itself: 'Not a word of sectarian bitterness has been heard from Presbyterian platforms.' Indeed at the 25,000-strong Belfast Presbyterian convention in that month—in many respects the greatest and most remarkable demonstration of determined resistance to the government's promised home rule measure—the same point was frequently made. One commentator on the convention observed in the same issue: 'Very many of them are old enough to have shared in the alliance of 1870–85 which made true liberalism a beneficent northern force to promote the farmers' wrongs and to promote the common good, but they refused to continue it when they believed the object of one party to the alliance was an ascendancy likely to become a tyranny.'[53]

This was allegedly the nub of the matter. A 'Southern Presbyterian' explained: 'We did not suspect that Rome would, as soon as she had the power, enter upon so foul an outrage as she has inflicted on Mrs McCann, nor marshal her forces for establishing herself as the ruling power of the State. We did not suspect that Rome would demand the right to measure out to us our civil and religious liberties. Our attitude of conciliation has changed into one of defiance.'[54] The liberal Presbyterian tradition lived on in the form of a more polite, less

[52] *Ballymoney Free Press*, 18 Apr. 1912.   [53] Ibid., 8 Feb. 1912.
[54] *Witness*, 30 Aug. 1912.

aggressive, almost mawkish political rhetoric. T. G. Houston's words at the Presbyterian convention are an example. Houston was a renowned Headmaster of Coleraine Academical Institution, and he provided a classic example of this sort of polite, almost soothing language, while, none the less, remaining firmly within classic unionist parameters:

We do not agree with the Roman Catholics in many of their doctrines, but we recognise them as Christians. Have we not a warm corner in our hearts for another ecclesiastic whom many of us have known in the flesh—

> The powerfullest preacher
> The tenderest teacher
> The kindliest crater in all Donegal
> Father O'Flynn, the flower of them all

... In another and better world, where we trust all such barriers are broken down, we do desire their better acquaintance. When I say this I feel sure that I am speaking the mind of all educated Irish Protestants and I think it is of the utmost importance that here and now this declaration of our sentiments should be openly and publicly made.

The attitude of the Presbyterians of Ulster at this great crisis of our history ... should be one of grim, determined, inflexible opposition towards any and every form of Home Rule, it should be one of unshaken trust in God and loyalty to his laws, it should be one of chivalrous courtesy to our opponents, the rules of civilised warfare (*applause*), Queensbury rules, shall I say always being observed.[55]

The leader of Irish unionism, Edward Carson, always retained a certain qualified liberal unionist reputation. In fact, as his most recent biographer, Alvin Jackson, has pointed out,[56] Carson applied for membership of the National Liberal Club during the passage of the first Home Rule Bill in 1886, an act which led George Bernard Shaw jokingly to describe himself in 1913 as an 'old Dublin home ruler like Sir Edward Carson'. Carson explicitly told the *Northern Whig* on 1 October 1912 that 'referring to the religious aspect of the question ... he would not be in this movement if he thought in any way there was any single privilege taken from any man who differed from him in no matter what religion'. The fact that Catholics tended to be nationalists and Protestants tended to be unionists was a consequence of a history

---

[55] *Ballymoney Free Press*, 8 Feb. 1912. Houston repeated this language precisely in the *Weekly Northern Whig*, 20 Sept. 1913.

[56] Alvin Jackson, *Sir Edward Carson* (Dublin, 1993), 94. *Weekly Freeman's Journal*, 8 Nov. 1913.

which could not be changed. The United Kingdom was opposed to any form of religious discrimination; the UK parliament could overcome any difficulties by a policy of justice.

Certainly Provost Anthony Traill of Trinity College, Dublin, felt perfectly happy in 1908 when he wrote to Carson to denounce the 'backward' 'Orange' advocacy of other unionist MPs[57] on educational matters: 'pandering to the lowest class of Orangeman instead of instructing them'. Stephen Gwynn, a nationalist MP close to the Redmond leadership, devoted an interesting and thoughtful passage to the topic:

Sir Edward, as everyone knows, is not an Ulsterman, and the chief of many advantages which Ulster gained from his advocacy was that Ulster's case was never stated to Great Britain as Ulstermen themselves would have stated it. It is not true to say that Ulstermen by habit think of Ireland consisting of two nations, for all Ulstermen traditionally regard themselves as Irish and have always described themselves as such without qualification. But it is true to say that Ulster Protestants have regarded Irish Catholics as a separate and inferior cast of Irishmen . . .

It does not express the truth to say that Sir Edward Carson was adroit enough to avoid putting this view of the case to the electors of Great Britain or to the House of Commons. Temperamentally and instinctively, he did not share it. He was a Southern Irishman who at the opening of his life held himself, as not one Ulsterman in a thousand does, perfectly free to make up his mind for or against the maintenance of the Union. As citizens of the United Kingdom, he held, they were more honourably situated than they could be as citizens of an Irish state within the Empire. This was an attitude which Ulster could endorse although it did not fully represent Ulster's conviction.[58]

Gwynn is here offering a shrewd insight into Carson's characteristic approach to the home rule crisis. But it should not be pressed too far. It does not quite catch the toughness at the centre of the later Carson's political being. This may be seen when Carson is compared with J. A. Rentoul. At first glance, Carson and Rentoul shared much common ground. In October 1889 Rentoul gave a lecture in Belfast on the 'British empire', the themes of which were international and cosmopolitan in dimension. Eleven days later he was offered the safe unionist seat of Down East, which he held as James Craig's predecessor from 1890 to 1902. Rentoul, who hailed from local liberal Presbyterian

---

[57] 2 May 1908, Public Record Office Northern Ireland, D 1507/A/2/10.
[58] *Redmond's Last Years*, 96–7.

stock, was entirely free from any sectarian feeling. He insisted on the
'equality' of Catholics. He was not an Orangeman: 'I have seldom seen
an Orange procession and was present only once at an Orange
demonstration.' His defence of the union owed nothing to any spirit of
hostility towards Catholic Ireland: 'I defended the union because I
believed it was better for Ireland to be a section of a great prosperous
Empire than to be a small self-governing country.'[59] But Rentoul
could not stomach Carson's course in the home rule crisis, let alone
undertake it himself. The young St John Ervine, then in an anti-
unionist mode which contrasted sharply with his later opinions,
described Carson 'as a stage Irishman . . . no other Irishman speaks
with so deliberate a brogue . . . chosen to lead because he could be
trusted not to go too far'. But one of Ervine's friends who read his
book in manuscript disagreed: 'He is not an attractive personality, this
Carson, but he has a kind of power and character, big in a way in
resistance though not concrete statesmanship.' Ervine conceded some
interesting ground in response: 'I will willingly concede that there is a
powerful negative force in Sir Edward's character; indeed, I will go
further and add that if I had to choose between Sir Edward and Mr
John Redmond, I would prefer Sir Edward to be my leader. He has
force of some sort and even a certain degree of dignity of utterance,
whereas Mr Redmond has no force at all, but is merely an imaginative
orator.'[60] The reluctant tribute won from a sharp, even contemptuous
commentator, conveys much more sense of Carson's contribution to
the anti-home rule cause than any amount of unionist platform
hyperbole.

   Critics of the Ulster unionist movement naturally laid great and
negative stress on the role of the Orange Order, portrayed usually as
an organized force of religious bigotry *par excellence*. Unionists were
fully aware of this ideological onslaught and sought to combat it. The
Liberal leadership was thought to be guilty of a 'shocking attempt to
portray the whole Irish Unionist movement as simply an outbreak of
Orangeism, and therefore, a species of wild fanaticism which ought to
be put down by the forces of the Crown'.[61] The *Witness* declared:
'[this] is wrong in fact and brutal in policy'.[62] The strategy for dealing
with anti-Orange taunts was the three-pronged one. In the first place,
unionists insisted on the limited role of Orangeism within the Irish

[59] J. A. Rentoul, *Stray Thoughts and Memories*, 212.
[60] *Sir Edward Carson*, 49–50.   [61] *Witness*, 30 Aug. 1912.   [62] Ibid.

unionist coalition. A 'Southern Presbyterian' stressed: 'I understand that the whole strength of Irish Orangeism amounts to not more than 30% of all Irish Unionists. The other 70% of Irish Unionists are outside the craft altogether.'[63] It was angrily pointed out that the reform Presbyterian church was still, in 1911, expelling members who joined the Orange Order and yet the entire church bitterly opposed home rule. Perhaps surprisingly the Orange Order itself happily offered its support to his argument. On 2 February 1912, the Ulster Unionist Council, strongly supported by the Orange leader Colonel Wallace, issued a telling statement published the next day in the *Whig*:

That we, the Standing Committee of the Ulster Unionist Council, desire to call public attention to the gross mis-statements that are constantly being made by members of the Government and their supporters in the Press, in which they assert that our opposition to Home Rule proceeds solely from the Orange Order. We consider it right to point out that the Ulster Council is representative of every shade of Unionist opinion, and includes not only the Orange Society, but every other Unionist organisation in Ulster—Conservative, Constitutional, and Liberal Unionist—all of whom send duly elected delegates to the Council.

We have, in addition, the support of large numbers of men who hold Radical views on general politics, but who are determinedly opposed to the imposition of Home Rule upon our country.

The second element of the strategy lay in an insistence that Presbyterians, at least, had a tradition of co-operation with Catholics and of a certain coolness towards Orangeism. A 'Southern Presbyterian' recalled: 'It so happens that I am not an Orangeman. I was brought up in a home and at a time unfavourable to the organisation.'[64] He added: 'In the middle of the last century the Presbytarian Church in Ireland entered upon a policy of conciliation towards Irish Roman Catholics and deemed it best to do nothing that might keep alive historic hatreds or make it difficult for our countrymen to work together for the common good.' The third element of the strategy—and probably the most important and revealing one—claimed the Orange Order was in any case basically a positive force in Irish society, at any rate when compared with the heartless activities of nationalists. The whole apparatus of rural intimidation—from boycotting to outright murder—

---

[63] *Witness*, 30 Aug. 1912.   [64] Ibid.

was referred to here with a righteous shudder. A 'Southern Presbyterian' asked:

When did Orangemen forfeit their rights as citizens? Are not Orangemen worthy of being heard in Irish affairs? It is true they are a secret society: but they have never been charged with hanging horses or cutting the udders of milch cows. They have never blackened their faces and butchered on a winter night peaceful households around the family hearth. They have never organised boycotting, hounded lonely defenceless women to death, refused persons of a different faith the necessities of life, and prevented the village carpenter from providing a coffin for the dead. No, Orangemen may have their faults but these faults lie in an excess of loyalty to the Crown and Constitution, lie in too vivid a memory of the glories of Derry and the Boyne, in too sincere a devotion to the Dutch William who at the Revolution established our liberties and gave us our present Royal House.[65]

No career is more evocative of this change of mood than that of Peter Kerr-Smiley, MP, an Eton and Trinity Hall man who emerged in politics under the tutelage of Professor Richard Smyth, MP, one of the most gentle, scholarly, and intellectual adherents of traditional Ulster Presbyterian liberalism.[66] By 1913 Kerr-Smiley, chairman of the liberal unionist *Northern Whig* newspaper, was endowing Orange halls. As the *Ballymoney Free Press* noted: 'Unionist Protestantism is making its way when we find the new hall at Bushside dedicated with a memorial slab having this worthy inscription: "Kerr-Smiley Orange Hall, 1912". One event clearly emerges in the present cross-currents, the progress of home rule has greatly stimulated the Orange Order . . . The Rev J. P. R. Breakley indicated that Mr Smiley had been a liberal subscriber to the building—a fact which itself shows the tendencies of history, past and present.'[67]

In 1906 a mere seven Irish unionist MPs were in the Orange Order.[68] Within a few years the power of the Order had dramatically increased at this level. The Revd J. P. R. Breakley concluded happily at a Bushmills demonstration: 'there was not a single member of the

---

[65] Ibid., 1 May 1913.

[66] Finlay Holmes, *Our Presbyterian Heritage* (Belfast, 1985), 125. See, more generally, Professor Holmes's excellent essay, 'Ulster will Fight and Ulster will be Right: The Protestant Churches and Ulster's Resistance to Rule 1912–14', in W. F. Sheil (ed.), *Studies in Church History*, xx: *The Church at War* (Oxford, 1983).

[67] *Ballymoney Free Press*, 27 Mar. 1913.

[68] James Craig to R. H. Wallace, Public Record Office Northern Ireland D 1889/6/6; 5 Dec. 1906, Craig counted seven Orange Irish Unionist MPs.

Irish Unionist party in Parliament but owed his seat largely to the influence and practical support of the Orange society, nor were there any who more sincerely acknowledged that practical help than the members of that party themselves.'[69] Between 1908 and 1913 the Orange Order's membership in Belfast more than doubled, rising from 8,834 to 18,800; other unionists insisted, however, on the equally remarkable growth of the more socially upmarket unionist clubs movement.[70]

Misinformed taunting about the role of Orangeism was just one cross which Ulster unionists felt they had to bear. It helped to fund a profound sense of betrayal, particularly when the role of English nonconformist liberalism was considered: 'stripped of all claptrap about the rights of democracies and the rights of majorities, this is really the common bedrock position from a religious point of view: let Irish protestantism fall if we can destroy the anglican church in England, is the cry of English nonconformists.'[71] There is no question that the theme of British treachery is to be found in unionist rhetoric. It was often linked with a notion of moral decline at the centre. Even the most liberal of the unionist newpapers was capable of expressing such sentiments: 'the amazing aspect of this case is that England, to which Ireland belongs by right of conquest, is grandly indifferent to how the battle may end. Nothing more illustrative of the decadence of England could be adduced.'[72] The Presbyterian *Witness* employed an analogy with the American civil war to make a similar point:

The Southern States of America demanded in practical effect what the Irish are demanding—separation from Great Britain. The North went to war rather than submit to it. The British Government in regard to Ireland represents the Northern States of that day. But they do not fight; they surrender; and with their surrender sacrifice all the interests, all the feelings, all the traditions of their loyal friends in Ireland. It is asking too much of these men to submit to the rod and the lash.[73]

The inevitable result was a decline in traditional pro-union political theory and a tendency, instead, to argue for Ulster Protestant self-determination. It was regularly said that all the arguments in favour of Catholic nationalist self-determination were also arguments in favour

---

[69] *Ballymoney Free Press*, 18 July 1912.
[70] P. Bew, P. Gibbon, and H. Patterson, *The State in Northern Ireland 1921–72* (1979), 70; McDermott, *An Enriching Life*, 39.   [71] *Witness*, 19 July 1912.
[72] *Ballymoney Free Press*, 8 Aug. 1912.   [73] *Witness*, 2 Aug. 1912.

of some form of Ulster Protestant self-determination. This idea came to be linked to the concept of an Ulster parliament, which emerged in 1912, with a certain appeal not to the reactionary, but to the liberal element, of Ulster unionism. 'The statement of Unionist Ulster is that it merely wants to be let alone . . . unfortunately since Satan entered the Garden of Eden good people will not be let alone.'[74] In other words there was a need to formulate a policy which in some way made concessions to the broad metropolitan view of the Irish question. The *Ballymoney Free Press* in the same editorial stated: 'We have during the past few years taken up an attitude favourable to the specific claims of Ulster. Lord John Russell proposed we think, in 1866, to give each of the Irish Provinces a special Parliament.' Some months later, it was declared, with an explanatory gloss: 'Lord John Russell, one of the most moderate of English Premiers . . . was consistently in favour of Irish local self-government being subordinate to the Parliament of the Empire.'[75] Russell's ideas had been formed in an epoch so different from that of 1912–14 that it was doubtful if they were an adequate guide to action. An ardent opponent of home rule, he had, however, been in favour of 'lightening the labour of Parliament', and had proposed a 'project' of 'provincial corporations'[76] springing from 'popular origins . . . invested with local power'.[77] The renewal of interest in Russell's vague proposal at this junction was patently revealing. As the *Quarterly Review* wryly and sadly summarized: 'The Unionists have fallen unconsciously more and more into the mental habit of advocating not the principles of Unionism against a divided kingdom, but the principles of home rule in favour of a divided Ireland.'[78] Carson himself had asked: 'what argument is there that you can raise for giving home rule to Ireland that you do not equally raise for giving home rule to the protestant minority in the north-east?'[79]

But it is important at this point to make a distinction between the case the unionists made and the unionist case, particularly as it was perceived from London. It is interesting to look at those who combined Ulster family roots with intimate involvement in the British power élite, notably Andrew Bonar Law, leader of the Conservative and unionist opposition in the House of Commons, James Bryce, former

---

[74] *Ballymoney Free Press*, 8 May 1912.   [75] Ibid., 19 Sept. 1912.
[76] John Russell, *Recollections and Suggestions 1813–73* (London, 1875), 391.
[77] Ibid., 390.
[78] 'The Home Rule Crisis', *Quarterly Review*, 221/441 (July 1914), 278.
[79] *Hansard*, 5th ser., xxxiv. 1440, 26 Mar. 1912.

Irish chief secretary and celebrated UK ambassador to the United States, and Baron MacNaghten, Lord of Appeal. Despite their common North Antrim roots, all three tended to argue in a different way from that of mainstream Ulster-based unionists. None of them placed unionist or Protestant fear of ill-treatment at the hands of Catholic–nationalist Ireland at the centre of their reasoning. Bryce, in particular, believed that these fears were exaggerated. Rather, all three believed that a coherent, reasonably large community which was content with its existing political institutions had a right not to be disturbed. In Bryce's view, Gladstone should have left the north-east counties out of the Home Rule Bill of 1886. He believed that it would have been possible to win Parnell's acquiescence to this; in 1914 he had come to the conclusion that Asquith should also follow a policy of exclusion. But he noted sadly 'Gladstone's failure to appreciate one of the great obstacles in his path in the resistance of the protestants to the north-east corner of Ireland—because his ignorance of that part of Ireland was shared by his colleagues and by most English politicians'.[80] The result of Gladstone's ignorance was to drive Ulster's liberal unionist Presbyterian community 'into the hands of the Orangemen'. For Bryce, the Presbyterians were the key group in the conflict; they had sympathy and support from English and Scottish non-conformity, so the English Tories, by latching on to their cause, gained a popular resonance they would not otherwise have had. Bryce was keenly admired in his native Antrim; in the spring of 1913[81] he had retired as British ambassador to the United States and by the autumn of that year he had returned to his 'fatherland'. It was openly speculated that he had prepared a lengthy and confidential report for the premier. One liberal unionist observed: 'Whether or not the great diplomatist lent his influence in the way of caution may be merely guessed at; but if he did, the service was one for which all friends of peace and good order will feel devoutly grateful.'[82] In a discussion of the Presbyterian clergy who opposed home rule, the *Witness* insisted, 'what political sympathies they have are with old and true liberalism.[83] We do not suggest that they are either socialists or syndicalists or could accept all the policy of the present government, but we do say that so far as liberalism as they and we understand it, and so far as it is represented by the government they would all be found on its side.'[84] For Bryce it was the decisive

[80] H. A. L. Fisher, *James Bryce, Viscount Bryce of Deechmont, OM* (London, 1927), 218.
[81] *Ballymoney Free Press*, 19 May 1913.   [82] Ibid., 16 Oct. 1913.
[83] *Witness*, 10 Apr. 1914.   [84] Ibid.

tragedy of Gladstone's and Asquith's policy that such a resource had in effect been handed over to the Tories.

Bonar Law was, of course, a reassuring figure for Ulster unionists. He had regularly visited the province during his father's last years: as the *Ballymoney Free Press* put it, he was 'a scion of a highly respected Ulster family enshrined in the memory of North Antrim folk'.[85] Some of his extremist public rhetoric in defence of Ulster unionism has been sharply criticized; it contrasts, it should be noted, with a much greater degree of private moderation and also with some notably diffident parliamentary performances.[86] Frans Coetzee has recently presented him as an 'icy Presbyterian, warming to the task of turning the Conservative party into an anti-home rule instrument'.[87] In fact, matters are more complex. Bonar Law, unlike Walter Long, was never a serious opponent of 'Irish self government';[88] his aim was always to secure some form of Ulster exclusion, and he was heavily influenced by a major security concern:

But what is there in the previous history or in the present action of the men who will control [an Irish] parliament to give us the right to believe, to give us the right even to hope, that it will be always friendly? Why, even now, when smooth words are the order of the day, when the only chance of carrying Home Rule is to allay the suspicion of the British people, the presence of the British flag, your flag and ours (*cheers*)—within sight of a Nationalist demonstration has been branded as an intolerable insult. If we were ever engaged in a great war, and if that Parliament were unfriendly, what then?[89]

Law argued that home rule was not in the real interests of nationalist Ireland. The British state had proven that it could deal with all Catholic grievances while creating the framework for greater freedom than that which existed in Catholic countries. The tragedy of the home rule project at this time was that it reopened old sectarian sores. Then he explained the nub of the Irish unionist case as he saw it:

---

[85] *Ballymoney Free Press*, 1 Feb. 1912.

[86] David Dutton, *His Majesty's Loyal Opposition: The Unionist Party of Opposition* (Liverpool, 1992), 225; see also *Cork Examiner*, 5 Feb. 1912.

[87] Frans Coetzee, *For Party or Country: Nationalism and the Dilemmas of Popular Conservatism in Edwardian England* (Oxford, 1990), 154. See also, and interestingly, Jeremy Smith, 'Bluff, Bluster and Brinkmanship: Andrew Bonar Law and the Third Home Rule Bill', *Historical Journal*, 36/1 (1993), 161–78.

[88] Richard Murphy, 'Faction in the Conservative Party and the Home Rule Crisis', *History*, 40/232 (1986), 222–34; John Kendle, *Walter Long, Ireland and Union 1905–1920* (Dublin, 1992).

[89] *Ballymoney Free Press*, 8 Apr. 1912.

You say that under Parliament and Government composed of men whose ways are not your ways, whose standards are not your standards—the men who run the Irish League and the Molly Maguires—you say that under such a government all industrial prosperity will be ruined, but there is something more than industrial prosperity. It is not for that that free men will give their lives. You say that neither civil nor religious liberties will be safe. . . . You make no claim except that you should not be deprived of your birthright; you make no claim except that you still enjoy the protection of the British law, that you should not be driven out of the empire that your fathers have done so much to build up and to sustain. That is your claim. (*cheers*)

His private comments are also of some interest. He wrote to Lord Riddell: 'It may seem strange to you and to me, but it is a religious question. These people are prepared to die for their convictions.'[90] But for Bonar Law himself the substance of the Ulster unionist case lay elsewhere. As he wrote to Ninian Crichton Stuart on 7 October 1912:

The real reason why in my opinion the Ulster question should be kept to the front is that, whether the cause be religious (or not), and I do not think it greatly matters, the population there is homogeneous and determined to be treated in the same way as the citizens of the United Kingdom. In my opinion, from every point of view, they have the right to take that attitude. . . . Perhaps the clearest way in which I can show how I feel in regard to the matter would be by reversing the picture. Suppose three quarters of Ireland were of the exact class of which the Ulster minority is composed and suppose that there in the rest of Ireland were one quarter of the population who looked with horror upon the idea of being governed by Orangemen and demanded the right to continue under the control of the British parliament. In that cause, whatever the reason, I should think their claim was just, and in the same way whether the reasons which activate the people of Ulster are sound or not, I think their claim is one which this country can not without dishonour, disregard.[91]

This is an important passage: at root, it explains Bonar Law's conviction, a conviction which did not leave him when other 'imperial' considerations of security were apparently satisfied.

For a similar view, it is possible to turn to another distinguished Ulsterman. The Rt. Hon. Lord MacNaghten, Lord of the Appeal, spent a portion of every year at his Irish seat, Runkerry, Bushmills,

[90] F. M. Gollin, *The Observer and J. L. Garvin 1908–14* (Oxford, 1960), 389.
[91] Robert Blake, *The Unknown Prime Minister* (London, 1955), 126. J. Bardon, *A History of Ulster* (Belfast, 1992), 435, argues that Bonar Law saw home rule 'as a deadly threat to Empire', but this is in fact only one element in his argument.

situated in close proximity to the Giant's Causeway. A superb sportsman as well as a formidable legal mind, MacNaghten linked the world of the Ballymoney Cricket Club (of which he was an active member) to that of the Colquhoun Sculls at Cambridge in 1851—which he won—and the Diamond Sculls at Henley in 1852, when he was also the victor.[92] Despite his aristocratic and Tory connections, he had, as an Ulster Tory MP, supported Gladstone's 1881 Land Act, in a speech which won warm praise from the Liberal premier. When the Church of Ireland bishop C. F. D'Arcy, who was considering the home rule issue, sought MacNaghten's advice, he was told—in terms reminiscent of Bonar Law—that 'to deprive a community, against its will of the citizenship and liberties into which its members were born would be a political outrage'.[93] MacNaghten himself was one of the Law Lords to sign the Ulster Covenant.[94] In short, he thought the Home Rule Bill exceeded the bounds of legitimate government action, especially when the Liberal government sought to dictate the future political status (in an all-Ireland context) of the community so affected.

As A. J. L. Morris puts it in his analysis of metropolitan unionist political theory:

The Home Rule Bill in this view was no ordinary piece of legislation. It was a *fiat* affecting the very status of citizenship. The right of insurrection which writers like St Loe Strachey invoked had as its premise the Lockean argument that, by rejecting the claims of the northern Unionist to the maintenance of their constitutional position, the government was severing the bonds of consent which linked the Ulstermen to Westminister, so returning them to a pre-political state of nature. With the termination of Ulster's constitutional obligation to the sovereign power a right of resistance rose against the illegitimate coercion of the government. Put simply the argument amounted to this proposition: 'though I must obey the Captain of the Boat while I am on the boat, I think I have a moral right to resist being thrown out of the boat'.[95]

This was the core of the 'establishment' unionist case. It might talk of 'two Irish nations'. It might flirt, as a debating point, with the notion that it might be right to expel a community—but certainly not to tell it where it must go. But, at heart, mainstream British unionism was

[92] *Ballymoney Free Press*, 20 Feb. 1913.
[93] Charles Frederick D'Arcy, *Adventures of a Bishop: A Phase of Irish Life. A Personal and Historical Narrative* (London, 1934), 65.
[94] *Weekly Northern Whig*, 1 Mar. 1913.
[95] A. J. L. Morris, 'A Study of John St Loe Strachey's Editorship of the Spectator 1901–1914', (Ph.D. thesis, University of Cambridge, 1986), fos. 202–3.

convinced that no government could legitimately end (or seriously dilute) unionist Ulster's citizenship within the United Kingdom.

Joseph Chamberlain, for example, insisted that he had fought against ascendancy all his political life. But he remained wedded to the Ulster unionist cause until his death in 1914. Why were Ulster Protestants so widely criticized, he asked. 'Why, because they are proud to belong to a greater country; because they take their share in the autonomy of the UK in which they take a part; because they cling to the traditions and history of the United Kingdom, which is just as much their possession and heritage as it is ours; because they refuse to be cast adrift and cut away from the hopes and resources which they have hitherto cherished.'[96]

The greatest constitutionalist theorist of the epoch, Albert Venn Dicey, fully supported this thesis. This leading exponent of parliamentary sovereignty insisted that there were none the less limits to the power of a parliamentary majority. He offered a particularly forceful analogy in support of this case.

Suppose that for the sake of drawing closer the *entente* with France, an English Premier were to bring in a Bill to transfer the Channel Islands and their inhabitants to the French Republic. Let us suppose further that the inhabitants of Jersey and Guernsey proclaimed their determination to remain part of the British Empire and to retain the position which they at present occupy. I doubt whether any Englishman of weight or character would maintain that the Parliament at Westminster had a moral right to carry out a plan when the supposed circumstances might well be called infamous.[97]

Dicey's advocacy was of immense benefit to the unionists.[98] All of

---

[96] *Northern Whig*, 8 Jan. 1914. For a critical view, see J. P. Loughlin, 'Joseph Chamberlain, English Nationalism and the Ulster Question', *History*, 77/250 (June 1992), 202–20.

[97] *Northern Whig*, 11 Mar. 1914.

[98] Dicey's thought on these questions is now deeply unfashionable; for broad context see Jose Harris, *Private Lives, Public Spirit: A Social History of Britain 1870–1914* (Oxford, 1993), 11–13. More directly and explicitly, see Ferdinand Mount, *The British Constitution Now* (London, 1992), 54–6. Mount describes Dicey's sentiments as 'inflammatory', 'brutish', and 'cowardly'; he is, however, clearly unaware of Dicey's highly moderate Irish interventions in the crisis—on the occasion of Churchill's visit and on the eve of the Curragh 'mutiny'—nor does he directly refer to the nub of Dicey's case as expressed here. We do not, however, have to accept Lord Chief Justice McDermott's later analysis that Dicey 'warned that if the Home Rule Bill of that time passed into law, resistance to it would then become unlawful and might even amount to treason' (J. C. McDermott: *An Enriching Life*, 42). In fact Dicey, in *A Fool's Paradise* (London, 1913),

these noted figures—Bryce, Bonar Law, MacNaghten, St Loe
Strachey, Chamberlain, and Dicey—agreed on one essential point.
They all denied the right of the government to force the unionists to
fall under the sway of a polity other than the UK parliament. It is a
notable fact that the Liberal government itself lacked thinkers who
were prepared to argue the contrary case and vigorously assert that the
government has such a right, in part, of course, because the Whig
tradition in Britain had, at least since 1832, encouraged a greater
inclusiveness *within* the constitution.[99] There was, of course, no
shortage of writers who were prepared to denounce the bigotry of the
Ulster party, but this is not quite the same thing as a refutation of the
opposition's principal thesis. The phrase 'minorities must suffer' was
attributed to Birrell but he was never happy with it. This was the
symptomatic silence of Asquithian liberalism: attacks—often exaggerated in tone—on the record of Irish landlordism[100] or Dublin
Castle[101] took the place of a substantive argument on the key point.

116, is silent on this key point: 'I will not give an opinion . . . that will depend upon
circumstances which I cannot foresee.' Mount's use of the term 'evasive' is surely
justified. Brendan Clifford, in his introduction to *Lovat Fraser's Tour of Ireland in 1913*
(Belfast, 1992), comments drily: 'In the absence of a written constitution with an
apparatus of enforcement—or indeed even when such exists—social opinion functions
as a constitution. In Britain, the constitution is entirely a matter of opinion. And Dicey,
who was by far the most influential opinion former on the constitution, justified rebellion
against the Home Rule Act on constitutional grounds. He did this not only in letters and
pamphlets—but in the *Introduction to the Law of the Constitution* (8th edition)—a work
which has never been superseded and remains in print to this day.' (p. 5)

[99] See Jonathan Parry, *The Rise and Fall of Liberal Government in Victorian Britain*
(Yale, Conn., 1993), for the most sensitive recent treatment of Liberal discourse.

[100] Harold Spender, *Home Rule* (London, 1912), which has a preface by Sir Edward
Grey, describes Irish landlords as 'a class' in the 1830–70 period as being motivated by a
'career of hostility towards their tenants . . . little else than a passion for revenge'.
(p. 107)

[101] Robert Harcourt, MP, in his introduction to L. G. Redmond-Howard, *Home Rule*
(London, 1912): 'Dublin Castle, when it reflects Irish opinion at all, reflects only the
opinion of those Irishmen who despise and vilify Ireland.' (p. vi)

3.

Churchill, Castledawson, and the Covenant

Protestants and Catholics in Ireland have, especially in Northern Ireland . . . a spirit of collective antagonism, not personal hatred to one another. There is no danger of religious persecution. There are little weaknesses in human nature, which we must be prepared for in all countries but they do not amount to oppression or persecution.

Lord Bryce, Hansard, lxiv. 551, 1 July 1914

Unionists are bound to respect, even to the extent of scrupulosity, freedom of speech and freedom of meeting. Many English Unionists will feel that a blunder was committed in raising any difficulty about holding an Assembly of Home Rulers even in Ulster Hall . . . a Home Ruler has as good a right to advocate home rule at Belfast as a Unionist has to advocate Unionism in Dublin . . . I dread the violence of Unionists, who, in crushing freedom of debate, strike at the strongest reasons for the maintenance of the Union . . . Let no one urge in reply to my strenuous denunciation of lawless violence that I maintain the doctrine that no circumstance whatever can justify rebellion against a Sovereign Parliament. I am too sound a Whig to maintain any such absurd dogma of servitude. What I do assert is that at the present moment no circumstances have arisen which go near to the justification of rebellion or lawlessness.

A. V. Dicey, The Times, 27 Jan. 1912

The Home Rule Bill was introduced in the House of Commons on 11 April 1912. The government remained formally committed to the principle of Irish unity. Over the next few weeks, however, some ministers—in particular Winston Churchill—sent out conciliatory signals in the direction of the Ulster unionists. The background is of some interest. On 3 October 1911 Churchill had referred contemptuously to the 'frothings of Sir Edward Carson'. He offered to address a pro-home rule demonstration in the Ulster Hall in Belfast on 8

February 1912, a venue where his father had once delivered a famous loyalist speech. The Irish unionist leadership, considering itself to be grievously provoked, openly committed itself to preventing such a meeting in the Ulster Hall, though not elsewhere in the city and the hall was aggressively double-booked. The message was clear: at this early stage in the crisis, Sir Edward Carson, a former Law Officer, was prepared to support irregular proceedings which might well lead to violence.[1] He also revealed himself as being increasingly 'Ulsterized' in his political instincts, for the exposed minority of southern unionists were worried by this apparent lack of respect for the principle of free speech. In the end, Churchill moved his meeting to Celtic Park and a very tense day passed off peacefully, except for a 'rush of irresponsible rowdies' towards Churchill's car.[2] But, as the *Irish Times*, which had disliked the methods employed 'on ethical grounds', noted, the strength of Ulster unionist sentiment had been made clear: 'Churchill's visit had merely served to emphasise facts which the Radical and Nationalist leadership were desperately anxious to conceal.'[3] Sections of the Liberal leadership began to take Sir Edward Carson and his movement a good deal more seriously.

At the end of March 100,000 nationalists attended a pro-home rule demonstration in Dublin. 'As decent a crowd of its kind' that could be 'found anywhere in the empire', the *Irish Times* charitably claimed on 1 April. Joe Devlin declared that, in comparison with this demonstration, 'the march past of the awkward squads in Belfast would be as a farthing candle in the sunshine'. John Dillon proclaimed: 'The work of Oliver Cromwell is nearly undone.' John Redmond struck a more positive note: 'The true purpose of [home rule] . . . is to put an end . . . to the disastrous and ruinous war which has gone on between Ireland and the Empire.' In early April the awkward squads gave their reply in Belfast: 100,000 unionists were present at Balmoral. Carson introduced Bonar Law, who was accompanied by seventy MPs from English and Scottish constituencies. According to the *Irish Times* on 10 April: 'The most important feature was the turn out of the Unionist clubs. The Orangemen are accustomed to processions . . . there were thousands of others standing witness to their determination of their adherence to the cause of the union. [This is] . . . a direct answer to

---

[1] *Irish Times*, 25 Jan. 1912.
[2] Ibid., 9 Feb. 1912. One of the 'rowdies', William Grant, was later to be a minister in the Government of Northern Ireland. *The Autobiography of Terence O'Neill* (London, 1972), 31–2.   [3] Ibid.

any taunting allegation that resistance to home rule is a fanatical movement fostered solely by the Orange Order.' On 11 June T. G. R. Agar-Robartes, a Cornish Liberal MP, suggested in the House of Commons the desirability of excluding the four heavily Protestant counties: Antrim, Down, Armagh, and Londonderry. The unionists supported the Agar-Robartes amendment, but it was defeated on 14 June by 69 votes. This indicated a certain fall in government support. Carson chose to regard the defeat as 'a declaration of war', others felt that a reluctant government had been forced to act against its most profound inclination. The *Irish Times* noted simply: 'It has been compelled to change its mind by Mr Redmond.'[4] This was the context of a most dangerous development—a slide into large-scale sectarian communal violence in Ulster. The unionists, albeit reluctantly, had been prepared to offer serious consideration to a scheme of partition: the government, or some of its members and supporters, had flirted with the idea and then turned away from it.[5]

On 29 June, a serious affray at Castledawson, County Londonderry, initiated a marked deterioration in the intercommunal relations. A Presbyterian Sunday School excursion party largely composed of women and children and numbering about 500, was attacked by one William Craig, a member of a Hibernian band which unluckily happened to be returning from a Maghera demonstration. (At Maghera, ironically, there had been Protestant home rulers on the platform and much non-sectarian oratory.) Craig dashed into the excursion party and seized a small Union Flag, attempting to drag it from a small boy who held on to it. The local RIC officer, Sergeant Burchill, pushed Craig back, and was struck by several of the Hibernians. A general row ensued, the excursion party was thrown into a confused mass, and blows were struck on both sides. The violence escalated: there was large-scale stone-throwing and many of the Protestants armed themselves with forks, shovel shafts, and sticks. The police decided to take decisive action: they brought out their rifles and fixed their swords. Ruefully, the two antagonistic crowds decided to disband, but not before many of the children were terrified out of their wits.

Tales of the incident soon spread. Inflamed Protestants regarded this attack upon children as an indication of the baseness of nationalist

---

[4] *Irish Times*, 14 July 1912.
[5] A. T. Q. Stewart, *The Ulster Crisis* (London, 1912), 58–9; Montgomery Hyde, *Carson* (London, 1953), 313–14.

intent. Catholics felt that the incident had been greatly exaggerated by local Protestants; in particular, they criticized the role of the Revd Robert Barren, who had been superintending the Presbyterian excursion. The Belfast presbytery indignantly repudiated charges of exaggeration. The *Witness* declared of Castledawson: 'Its real importance lies in the view that it points to the difference between the Hibernians and other nationalists and their professed leaders. . . . We have said that it did not matter what the leaders said: it was what the rank and file thought and said which should be the dominating factor.'[6] At the same time there was undoubtedly a certain exploitation of the Castledawson affray. When the Revd J. D. Craig Houston told the Presbyterian assembly that they should not use the outrage for political purposes, 'So we do!' cried the ranks of this normally staid body.[7] For offences connected with Castledawson twenty-three Hibernians and seven Protestants were subsequently brought to trial. At the Ulster Winter Assizes, held in Londonderry, all twenty-three Hibernians were convicted and each sentenced to a term of three months' imprisonment with hard labour for riot and unlawful assembly. The seven Protestant defendants in the same case were acquitted.[8] For Protestants this verdict proved where the responsibility lay; for Catholics it proved merely the partiality of the judiciary. On 8 January 1913 a Memorial praying for remission of the unexpired period of the sentence imposed on the Hibernians was signed by a large number of Castledawson residents of all classes and professions— unionists, Conservatives, nationalists, Orangemen, Liberals, and clergymen of all denominations—and sent to the Lord Lieutenant. Amongst the signatories were the Revd Mr Tarleton, rector of Castledawson, the Revd Mr Lindsay, rector of Magherafelt, and Alexander Clarke, JP, the proprietor of the large linen factory at Castledawson. The signatories were surprisingly representative on a cross-community basis: there were six Catholic clergymen as against three Protestants, but, on the other hand, there were ten unionist professional men as against nine Catholics. Given the immense bitterness occasioned by the incident in the Protestant community, it is important to note that the spirit of harmony and conciliation was by no means extinguished. The complete synopsis[9] of the signatures to the Memorial in the table below makes interesting reading.

[6] *Witness*, 5 July 1912.   [7] Ibid.
[8] Public Record Office, CO 903/17/6–8.   [9] Ibid.

TABLE I. *Signatures to Memorial, 8 January 1913*

	Catholics	Unionists	Total
Clergymen	6	3	9
Magistrates	9	3	12
Professional men	9	10	19
Bank officials	—	4	4
Clerk of Union	—	1	1
Chairman District Council	1	—	1
Commissioner for Oaths	1	1	2
Merchants and others	70	36	106
County and District Councillors	4	2	6
TOTAL	100	60	160

Mr Justice Wright, who presided at the trial, in reporting on the Memorial, expressed his opinion that there could be no doubt of the righteousness of the verdict, adding that he had carefully considered the case before passing sentence and that he saw no reason to recommend any reduction of the sentence of three months' imprisonment with hard labour which he had imposed. This was not a sentiment which was shared at the highest level in Dublin Castle. On 4 February the Lord Lieutenant, with the support of the Chief Secretary, made an order that the twenty-three prisoners convicted and sentenced should be released on 5 February;[10] they had served only half their sentences. The *Weekly Northern Whig* bitterly noted in an editorial of 15 February 1913: 'Stripped of all casuistry the plain fact remains that the Government is under the thumb of the Hibernians.' The pamphlet *Ulster Protest* added: 'Such is the meaning of Mr Redmond's perfectly true statement that Mr Devlin is the real Chief Secretary of Ireland.'

Few, however, believed that the government had acted purely out of considerations of abstract legality. The political context is all too clear: the by-election in Londonderry City on 30 January 1913 was narrowly carried by the Scottish Presbyterian Liberal, David Clegthorn Hogg, a large local employer, over Lt. Col. Hercules Arthur Pakenham

---

[10] Public Record Office, CO 903/17/6–8.

(unionist) by 2,699 votes to 2,642. Not surprisingly, the Irish party presented the victory and the choice of a Presbyterian candidate as great proof of the non-sectarianism of Catholic politics. At Hogg's celebratory dinner, Redmond offered a limited olive branch to unionists—he was prepared to offer them an influence in an Irish parliament greater than their numbers warranted. Such rhetoric was soon to be undermined by allegations in the *Pall Mall Gazette* concerning the inner history of the Derry election. It was claimed that the Hibernian factions in the city had made a deal with the government before they consented to vote for the Liberal candidate.[11] Patrick Arkins, a Clare peasant sent down for seven years by Justice Dodd for an agrarian offence (knocking down a wall), was to be set free after three months; also to be freed were the Castledawson prisoners. The government kept the bargain—shortly after the Derry result Arkins and the Castlesdawson men were released. Perhaps Birrell had not entirely suppressed his memory of these events when he referred drily in his memoirs to the 'near impossibility' of any English government dispensing 'even handed justice'[12] in Ireland.

But long before their eventual release the behaviour of the Castledawson nationalists had rebounded negatively on the nationalist minority in Belfast. As the stories of Castledawson reached Belfast, loyalists contemplated savagely the attack on their women and children: some of the children at Castledawson were those of Belfast shipyard workers.[13] Inflamed, some at once turned to violence and revenge. From July onwards, at the shipyards and in their immediate vicinity, assaults were committed on Catholics and also on Protestant liberals and home rulers. These assaults were so serious and there was such a degree of intimidation of Catholic workers that about 2,000 of them left their employment at the shipyards. When the July holidays (the 'Twelfth') started, not more than a hundred Catholics remained in the shipyard.[14] Southern unionists were embarrassed by the events. They felt themselves to be in 'a sense outsiders',[15] confronted by such 'inflexible contempt of opponents'. 'It is not for us to live as vividly in the past or map the future with such arrogant confidence.'[16]

It was hoped that passions would diminish over the July holidays,

---

[11] Quoted in the *Roscommon Herald*, 8 Feb. 1913.
[12] Augustine Birrell, *Things Past Redress* (London, 1937), 216.
[13] *Weekly Freeman's Journal*, 18 Jan. 1913.
[14] Public Record Office, CO 903/17/2.   [15] *Irish Times*, 12 July 1912.
[16] Ibid.

but this did not happen. By the end of July Harland and Wolff (whose owner Lord Pirrie was a recent convert to home rule from the ranks of liberal unionism) felt compelled to act; it threatened to lay off its entire 17,000-strong workforce unless the Catholic workers were re-admitted.[17] George Clark, the managing director of Workman and Clark, which employed 9,000, appeared to be less sympathetic to the plight of the Catholic workforce: they had been 'easily frightened'[18] he declared tactlessly. This provoked the *Leader* to a bitter attempt at verse in mid-February 1914:

> The senior director of Workman and Clark
> This lack of true grit in the Papists did mark
> He deemed that each Papist in courage was slack
> Who left with a murderous mob at his back.

Workman and Clark was not the only firm to attract such critical comment. The Sirocco engineering works appeared to be equally culpable.[19] A South Bucks. working man's delegation reported eighteen months later:

On Thursday [29 January] our first visit was to the Sirocco Works, where we were received by Mr Davidson, the proprietor. He remarked that only about fifty Catholics were employed, and explained that in consequence of the shipyard and other disturbances in 1912, he made an arrangement with the Protestants that if they agreed to work with the older hands among his Catholic employees he would employ no more in the future. The unionist workmen, Mr Davidson assured us, kept him regularly to this bargain.[20]

Both George Clark and S. C. Davidson were to serve on the Financial and Business Committee of the Ulster provisional government: on the other hand Lord Pirrie's threat cooled passions and led to an improvement: many Catholic employees felt able to return to work. But as late as 28 September 1912 the *Weekly Freeman's Journal* noted sadly: 'It must be remembered, however, that none of the expelled Catholics and Home Rulers have been taken back at Workman and Clark's. Some time ago it was rumoured that some had gone back

---

[17] Public Record Office, CO 903/87/356. See also Henry Patterson, *Class, Conflict and Sectarianism* (Belfast, 1981), 89–91. For Pirrie's politics see Herbert Jefferson, *Viscount Pirrie: Belfast* (Belfast, 1930), 133–41.

[18] *Weekly Freeman's Journal*, 1 Feb. 1913.

[19] Public Record Office, CO 904/87/38.

[20] *Leader*, 21 Feb. 1914. See also A. Morgan, *Labour and Partition* (London, 1991), 134.

there but it appears the rumour was groundless.' There was to be a messy and unsatisfactory aftermath in the courts. The police noted: 'The various cases for the disturbance at the shipyards and other places during the summer of 1912 were heard at the Assizes this month. Notwithstanding that the judge charged strongly in each case for a conviction most of the defendants were acquitted.'[21] Unsurprisingly many nationalists contrasted this leniency with the fate of the Castledawson Hibernians.

Both sides, nationalist and unionist, were keen to establish their own definitive interpretation of these tragic events. The most famous unionist effort came from a *Belfast Telegraph* journalist, John A. Watson, employing the pen-name *Flambeau*. Watson insisted upon the direct causal role of Castledawson. 'A man went into Workman and Clark's to have revenge upon another man for something in connection with the Castledawson affair and the row began.'[22] He tended to minimize the scale of loyalist violence. 'He would agree that there was ruffianism and that there was a grave situation in Belfast before the 8th of July but he would not say that more than 100 people altogether had been kicked during the month of July.'[23] He insisted on the spontaneous and uncontrolled nature of this activity. 'It was never organised by any responsible body. It was the fruit of the works of the irresponsible camp followers of unionists, boys who are not to be held responsible for any act they commit and who don't read the newspapers.'[24]

Against this, nationalists dismissed entirely the role of Castledawson. Such a view was a mere 'pretence'.[25] There was instead a pronounced tendency in the Irish party leadership and its liberal allies to stress the role of élite manipulation. The *Weekly Freeman's Journal* insisted that those who carried out the expulsions were mere 'dupes':[26] 'One would be tempted to be strongly humorous about the horrors of Orange ruffianism in Belfast'[27]—were it not for the fact that the demagogic leadership of loyalism would thereby escape just censure. The prominent Belfast priests who issued an appeal on behalf of the expelled men to the 'Catholics of Ireland' declared: 'At the instigation of certain well known political firebrands, the Unionist clubs . . . have

---

[21] Commissioner's Report to the Inspector-General of the RIC, March 1913, Public Record Office CO 904/89/410.
[22] *Weekly Freeman's Journal*, 1 Feb. 1913. The report covers the libel action which *Flambeau*'s article provoked. [23] Ibid. [24] Ibid.
[25] Ibid. [26] Ibid., 20 July 1912. [27] Ibid.

fomented disturbances . . . leading to the expulsion amid scenes of brutal violence of almost 3,000 Catholic working men.'[28] Despite this 'brutal violence', Joe Devlin, nationalist MP for West Belfast, symptomatically declared rather generously that 'if left alone' the shipyard workers were 'good and sincere and honest men'.[29] Instead emphasis was laid on malign leadership. It was alleged, for example, that Bonar Law sniggered openly when the issue was discussed in the House.[30] The liberal *Daily Chronicle*, referring explicitly to Bonar Law and Carson, spoke of 'eminent statesmen' who had 'deliberately worked up the murderous passions of simple men in order to regain office and power'.[31] An apparently irresponsible interview (hinting at or possibly even encouraging violence), given by George Clark to the *London Evening News* was much discussed.[32] (The Clark 'interview' was followed by fierce unionist denials of its authenticity.) In part, this desire to stress the role of evil demagogues was a consequence of the widespread desire amongst both the Liberal and nationalist leaderships to suppress the true extent of the divisions within the Irish masses. There was a great fear that the violence would be used as proof of the existence of 'two nations' in Ireland. For this reason, delegations of expelled workers were bitterly disappointed by the low-key attitude of both Birrell—who after all had ultimate responsibility for law and order in Belfast—and Redmond, who 'apparently did not think the situation was serious'.[33]

The idea of one Irish nation was to define Asquith's response to the growing crisis. In the immediate aftermath of the expulsions, Asquith coincidentally received a deputation from the Belfast Chamber of Commerce; the deputation of 'betrayed' and 'anguished' businessmen to a British Liberal prime minister had become almost one of the more distressing rituals of British public life during home rule crises.[34] But while Gladstone had treated this group dismissively, Asquith had 'assured the deputation that he himself had never spoken with any disrespect of the conscientious opposition of the large number of those who, in Ulster and Belfast in particular, have been captains of industry and have conducted with so much success and with such large results

---

[28] *Weekly Freeman's Journal*, 1 Feb. 1913.   [29] *Witness*, 12 July 1912.
[30] *Weekly Freeman's Journal*, 3 Aug. 1912.
[31] *Daily Chronicle*, 12 July 1912, quoted in *Weekly Freeman's*, 18 Jan. 1913.
[32] *Witness*, 12 July 1912.
[33] *Weekly Freeman's Journal*, 26 July 1912.
[34] J. P. Loughlin, *Gladstone, Ulster and Home Rule* (Dublin, 1986).

the commercial and industrial development of this great community'.[35] As one London unionist source, the *Daily Telegraph*, noted: 'This in itself was a remarkable admission for it practically acknowledged the basis of the Ulster cause not merely against the present Home Rule scheme, but any disturbance whatever of Ulster's position in the United Kingdom.'[36] The prime minister not only admitted its strength, but he added: 'It is a factor—and an important factor—in the case, and I can assure you that it has given to myself and my colleagues very serious ground for reflection.'[37]

Despite all the politeness, however, Asquith managed to convey an air of being out of touch. At this meeting, when the Belfast group explained one of their fears 'with regard to the question of the Gaelic language in the exams for public bodies they could suffer', Asquith intervened, in an amazed tone: 'Are you really apprehensive as to that?'[38] Yet within a few months of this interview John Dillon—the Irish party leader with perhaps the least reputation for tolerance of unionist fears—was to speak openly of 'gross oppression'[39] of the 'Protestant boy' arising out of mainstream nationalist language policies. Asquith offered to look into the question of safeguards here only to find that the deputation did not think that safeguards could be of any avail. This seems to have exasperated the premier, who was within a few days of an important Irish visit. Introduced by a benevolent Redmond on 19 July, Asquith attempted a major speech in Dublin. The prime minister insisted: 'Ireland is a nation, not two nations, but one nation.' But, having promised in his speech to deal with the 'very clear issue' of Ulster unionism, he lamely concluded with a reference to the 'supposed opposition of Ulster'.[40] The *Irish Times*, shortly before exasperated with northern unionist intransigence, was moved to anger: 'He is doing his best to make civil war inevitable.'[41] In almost desperate tones, the southern unionist organ insisted that, unpleasant though it was, Ulster unionism was implacable. A week later Bonar Law gave his reply in what has recently been described as a 'highly provocative speech'.[42] Addressing 30,000

---

[35] See *Witness*, 19 July 1912, for an account of the Birrell meeting and subsequent reactions.   [36] Ibid.   [37] Ibid.

[38] *Irish Times*, 14 July 1912.   [39] See Ch. 4 below.

[40] *Irish Times*, 20 July 1912.   [41] Ibid.

[42] Catherine B. Shannon, *Arthur J. Balfour and Ireland 1874–1922* (Washington, DC, 1988), 176. Cf. also P. Travers, *Settlements and Divisions in Ireland 1870–1922* (Dublin, 1988), 127.

British unionists at Blenheim, Bonar Law asked rhetorically: 'Does anybody imagine that British troops will be used to shoot down men who enjoy no privilege which is not enjoyed by you, whose only offence is that they refuse to surrender the rights which none of you would surrender?' He answered his own question: 'The thing is unthinkable.'[43] This, rather than rhetoric about a 'corrupt parliamentary bargain' or even the 'two nation theory',[44] was the nub of Bonar Law's case—though he held sincere and convinced views on both topics. This sets the context for his impassioned declaration that he 'could imagine no length of resistance to which Ulster can go in which I should not be prepared to support them'. Clearly he was thinking of resistance to a forcible attempt to impose home rule; there is no question of any support for the shipyard violence. There is no doubt that Bonar Law's rhetoric, which contains the ominous if truthful phrase 'there are things stronger than parliamentary majorities', has alarmed even sympathetic historians[45] ever since. It even alarmed normally sympathetic contemporaries. *The Times* of London fully supported Bonar Law's espousal of the 'two nations' theory; it even believed that there were limits to the power of parliamentary majorities—'if conventions are strained too far against realities the system will break down'[46]—but it felt that his warning was more 'explicit than necessary'. After all, the Home Rule Bill would take two years to become law. (Bonar Law was stung by this criticism and replied in the House of Commons: 'Nothing seems to me more certain than that the state of tension which now exists can not continue for two years from this time.'[47]) More generally the mood at Blenheim was optimistic. The government's defeat at the recent Crewe by-election had encouraged the hope that normal political methods would effectively defeat home rule. F. E. Smith, perhaps determined to lighten the platform mood, insisted that the Liberal government simply did not have the resolve to face the Ulstermen down. The *Irish Times* expressed a similar spirit: 'We believe . . . that the great day of Ulster's

---

[43] *Irish Times*, 29 July 1912

[44] See F. S. L. Lyons, *Ireland Since the Famine* (London, 1971), 302–3, for this interpretation, which is based on a rather partial reading of the Blenheim speech.

[45] See, most recently, John Ramsden's entry in K. Robbins (ed.), *The Blackwell Biographical Dictionary of British Political Life in the Twentieth Century* (Oxford, 1990), 255–8.

[46] *The Times*, London, quoted in the *Irish Times*, 29 July 1912.

[47] *Hansard*, 5th ser., xli. 2135, 31 July 1912.

trial will never come. The trial of the Liberal government by the democracy of the United Kingdom will come before that.'[48]

The difficulty with the mainstream nationalist and Liberal interpretation is clear enough: unionists were still concerned to win the battle for British public opinion, and the shipyard expulsions could only weaken such a strategy. As Carson put it in the House of Commons: 'These attacks . . . are to be deeply deprecated and, even to put it on the very lowest grounds, do not and cannot further anything in the nature of a political cause.'[49] This is partly why the Orange Order and the Ulster unionist leadership quickly condemned the expulsions. A letter from Carson to Colonel Wallace, leader of the Belfast Orangemen, dated 11 July and published that evening in the *Belfast Evening Telegraph*, urged 'self-control and discipline and the preservation of the peace'.[50] The *Witness* editorialized: 'We are ashamed of them [the expulsions] and have no desire to minimise them', but news reports in the same issue referred to the incidents in the shipyards as being 'comparatively slight'.[51] At first sight Carson was equally ambiguous: on 21 August he wrote to Craig: 'I am very distressed about the men who are being prosecuted for the rows in the shipyards. Do you think they or their families ought to be assisted in any way? You know how much I feel about others suffering when I don't, and they received great provocation.'[52] Nevertheless, it should be noted that at a private meeting a year later Carson urged the unionist business class to protect the interest of Catholic workers. An informer's report commented that 'amongst other things dealt with by Sir Edward was the present position of Roman Catholic workers in places where the workers were mixed and he strongly advised every other precaution be taken in order to ensure that such workers be not interfered with, and it was suggested by some present that this was the right course to adopt, that a good amount of harm had been done to the cause in the past by the neglect of this.'[53] Yet within a few days of this private meeting Carson was to proclaim publicly at Ramore Hill: 'I cannot see how men differing in a matter, not of politics but of the elementary rights of citizenship, and of the method of government,

---

[48] *Irish Times*, 25 July 1912.
[49] *Hansard*, 5th ser., xli. 2111, 31 July 1912.
[50] Morgan, *Labour and Partition* 132.
[51] *Witness*, 12 July 1912.
[52] Montgomery Hyde, *Carson*, 318.
[53] Conference of businessmen with Edward Carson, 25 July 1913, Public Record Office, CO 904/27/2, pt. I.

how they can go on living side by side in this great industrial community of Ulster.'[54] Carson specialized in an awful frankness: this is but one rather pointed example of his refusal to fudge unpleasant issues; his open admission of the anarchic consequences of his position was another. Replying to a liberal critic, he said:

He says that my doctrines and the course I am taking lead to anarchy. Does he not think I know that? Does he think that after coming to my time of life and passing through the various offices and responsibilities I have accepted, I did this like a baby without knowing the consequences? . . . all this chopping of logic is so much nonsense. We are prepared, if we fail, to take the consequences. The whole of this matter is to be one of the gravest responsibilities I have ever had in my life. I am no thoughtless lad, trying to inflame bigoted passions. I loathe them. I know what I am dealing with.[55]

These words should not, of course, be treated as an abject admission of guilt or acceptance of an opponent's case. Carson felt that the Liberals were in no position to lecture him on the subject of legality. In an open letter published in the *Weekly Freeman's Journal* on 24 August 1912, Carson recalled bitterly the late 1880s when 'Liberal members of parliament thronged the Courthouses of Ireland with a view to encouraging those who were being prosecuted, and intimidating the magistrates'. Nevertheless, despite Carson's public contempt for 'bigoted passions', it is hardly surprising that his highly charged language would anger nationalists. And even if Carson personally was not a bigot, could this honestly be said of some of his close political allies in the leadership of Ulster unionism?

The key text in the nationalist interpretation of the expulsions was a speech given by the Orange Grand Master, Colonel Wallace:

What keeps Ireland going now? Protestant money and English subsidies. What keeps the mills going and employs the workers? Protestant money. What pays the wages of thousands of Roman Catholic workers? Protestant money. What would happen if the Protestant men of wealth realised what they could and left the country? If the Protestant employers of labour shipped their works to the other side of the water, if the Protestant employers refused to employ anyone who was not a Protestant, do you think the wretched Roman Catholics who were starving would be shouting for Ireland a nation then?[56]

---

[54] *Ballymoney Free Press*, 7 Aug. 1913.
[55] Quoted in G. Peel, *The Reign of Sir Edward Carson*, (London, 1914), 79. Speech at Glasgow, 1 Oct. 1912.
[56] Quoted in the *Leader*, 27 June 1914.

Speaking in Carlow on 26 October 1913 John Dillon gave the conventional nationalist assessment of this remarkable oratorical effort: 'There could not be the slightest doubt that this savagery could at any moment have been stopped by the leaders of the Ulster Unionists but for a long time it was winked at and encouraged.' Referring to Wallace's speech on 12 July 1911, Dillon continued: 'that infamous language had never so far has as he knew been repudiated or condemned by Sir E. Carson or any of the responsible leaders and long after the shipyard atrocities Colonel Wallace was described by the *Daily Mail* as one of the heroes of the Ulster movement.' He concluded cynically: 'How was the brutish policy of driving Catholics and Home Rulers from their work in Belfast stopped? It was stopped because the leaders of the Unionist party in Great Britain sent word that these proceedings were ruinous to the Unionist party in England and must stop.'[57]

It is obvious that Wallace's speech—a year earlier—was not the immediate trigger for the Belfast expulsions; it belonged to a long and not especially distinguished unionist tradition of decrying the wealth-creating capacities of nationalist Ireland. This was linked to a view that Catholic nationalists did not display sufficient admiration for the productive labours of Protestants and unionists. It was a theme vigorously articulated by English unionists such as Chamberlain,[58] who had assured Carson of his total support. It was bitterly opposed by Catholic nationalists, who stressed, in particular, the farming wealth of parts of Leinster and Munster. Wallace's speech worked by proposing a contrast between the generous employment-creating Protestants and the narrow-minded, boycotting Catholics; it stresses the potential power of Protestant employers, not employees. There is absolutely nothing to suggest that workplace expulsions played any part in the political strategy of the unionist leadership. The immediate trigger for the shipyard expulsions was not Wallace's speech but the Hibernian attack at Castledawson.

Nevertheless, it is reasonable to argue that Wallace's remarks helped to create a climate of contempt for the Catholic Irish which made such expulsions more likely. More critical is Dillon's claim that this 'savagery could at any moment have been stopped by the leaders of Ulster Unionists but for a long time it was winked at. It was winked at

---

[57] *Leinster Leader*, 1 Nov. 1913.
[58] Paul Bew, *C. S. Parnell* (Dublin, 1980), 64.

and encouraged.' In fact, the mainstream unionist leadership and press condemned the expulsions immediately. Carson, in particular, opposed them, in part no doubt because of the effect on English unionist opinion; but it is also true to say that he regarded the Liberal government as having created a context which made them inevitable.

Partly in order to relieve such 'popular feelings, which desired some medium of expression',[59] Carson and James Craig evolved the strategy which led to the mass signing of the Ulster Covenant on 'Ulster Day', 28 September.

Being convinced in our consciences that Home Rule would be disastrous to the material well being of Ulster as well as the whole of Ireland, subversive of our civil and religious freedom, destructive of our citizenship and perilous to the unity of the Empire, we, whose names are underwritten do hereby pledge ourselves in solemn Covenant throughout this time of threatened calamity to stand by one another in defending for ourselves and our children our cherished position of equal citizenship in the United Kingdom and in using all means which may be found necessary to defeat the present conspiracy to set up a Home Rule Parliament in Ireland.[60]

On Ulster Day some 237,368 men signed a similar declaration; nationalist Ireland looked on with a mixture of suspicion and contempt.

The *Irish Times* reported Ulster Day with a sense of awe but also a note of reserve: 'The Unionist citizens of Belfast—heads of great industries, and makers of prosperity, leaders of Churches, men of thought and science—took this irrevocable step with an overwhelming consciousness of their responsibilities.'[61] The religious services had been 'charged with an almost painful emotion'; Belfast displayed 'a civic harmony and passion as the world has hardly seen since Athenian or medieval times'. 'The spirit of the city', it was said, took 'material form'. But the whole operation had its worrying facets: 'The outstanding feature of Ulster Day is the part which religion played in it. ... We have always assumed that the Churches historically connected with Ireland are resolved to continue their work under any circumstances and therefore ought not to identify with any particular form of government.'[62] But it appeared that this assumption was not so widespread in Belfast: in particular, Dr William McKean, the Presbyterian Moderator, seemed not to share it at all. In his sermon at

[59] A. T. Q. Stewart, *Sir Edward Carson* (Dublin, 1981), 78.
[60] *Irish Times*, 30 Sept. 1912.   [61] Ibid.   [62] Ibid.

the Ulster Hall, McKean claimed for his church 'a right to lay the divine measuring rod on every attempted form of legislation bearing on the character, the freedom and true well being of the people'.[63] The *Irish Times* commented with a resignation verging on exasperation: 'We think that this is a very dangerous claim for churches which denounce the doctrine of infallibility. But Ulster is Ulster.'[64] It was little wonder that Sir Edward Carson 'seemed oppressed with the responsibility of his act. His face was drawn, indeed haggard and ghastly pale.'[65]

Nationalists professed themselves to be unimpressed. T. P. O'Connor gave a brief interview to the *London Evening Standard*:

I do not believe that the Ulster campaign has done any harm in England to the Home Rule cause. It has proved that the main source of the objections in Ulster is sectarianism, and sectarianism no longer makes any appeal to the English mind. Accompanied as it was by gross acts of ill-treatment, and the driving out of Irish Nationalists and English Liberal workers in the dockyards, this sectarian campaign has shocked people of all classes, but especially of the working classes, and has revealed to every body the lie underneath the Orange declaration in favour of civil and religious liberty.[66]

The expulsions had none the less made a deep impression on nationalist Ireland. Many in the south began to feel that they could not abandon northern Catholics to an Orange tyranny. As Jasper Tully put it: 'they [the Orangemen] would banish all the Catholics out of Ulster and make it a preserve of their own sort, and the rest of Ireland could only look helplessly on as England has to look at the Boers doing as they like in Transvaal at the present time.'[67] A new and complicating factor had been added to the political debate. In June 1912 the nationalist leadership found it impossible to concede the abstract principle of Irish unity by allowing some form of county option. But to this broad theoretical consideration was now added on a rather more concrete concern about the possible mistreatment of the northern Catholic minority under any such arrangement.

Belfast had no monopoly of intolerance: appalling mob scenes followed in Limerick when George Wyndham gave a vaguely eccentric but warm-hearted unionist speech which commended the virtues of Tory paternalistic schemes of rural reconstruction as opposed to the

[63] Ibid.   [64] Ibid.   [65] Ibid.
[66] Reported in the *Cork Examiner*, 19 Oct. 1912.
[67] *Roscommon Herald*, 27 Feb. 1914.

application of liberal *laissez-faire* dogmatism in Ireland.[68] Nevertheless northern nationalists were understandably deeply disturbed by events which directly and negatively affected the long-term economic prospects of their community.

The Belfast Catholic newspaper the *Irish News* insisted on the existence of 'well organised and carefully selected bands' with recognized leaders, leaders who repaired at night to the unionist clubs and who, it was said, were putting into effect the policies advocated by Sir Edward Carson. They were particularly contemptuous of unionist references to 'irresponsible young blackguards'—'grown responsible men' were as much involved.[69] 'We have now quietly, almost silently, arrived at a state of affairs which may be described as absolutely intolerable'. A personal reference to a 'Carsonite pogrom' may have been unfair. J. L. Garvin was one of many experienced observers who felt that Carson was actually a 'safety valve'. Commenting on the Covenant ceremonies, Garvin declared: 'even the sectarian note, formerly so shrill and corrosive, was more restrained than ever I have known it.' Speaking of Carson personally he said: 'what even Unionists do not realise is the note of restraint, even of magnanimity which he is impressing upon the Ulster controversy.' But it remains the case that a logic of confrontation flowed from Ulster Day. It was an act from which in its nature there could be no retreat. 'Men do not deliver themselves to perpetual shame by signing a public vow of courage and sacrifice which they do not mean to keep.'[70]

[68] *Northern Whig*, 14 Oct. 1912.   [69] *Irish News*, 26 July 1912.
[70] *Northern Whig*, 3 Oct. 1912.

4.

The National Response: Ascendancy, Land, and Language

They are a primitive and in some respects an old fashioned community. They have been taught to fear God and honour the law. . . . They lead strenuous and frugal lives and they have made the district in which they live, through the Union, and they believe, under and by the Union, an example to your empire of industry, of enterprise, of obedience to the law and of loyalty and devotion to your King, your country, your Empire. They desire to live on terms of perfect equality with their neighbours. They have not, nor do they claim, any ascendency of any sort, kind or description.

J. H. Campbell, MP, Hansard, lv. 155–6, 7 July 1913

As to the claim of Ulster, we are told that all they want is to be left alone. This is the stock expression . . . they want no ascendancy. Let us examine, for a moment, what is really the claim of Ulster. I take first of all an extract from a pamphlet of Captain Craig, MP for East Down. 'In dealing with the Roman Catholic Church, two things must be remembered—first there can be no such thing as equality, for if you are not top dog she will be.' This is the spirit of Ulster Unionism. They want to be top dog.

John Dillon, Hansard, liii. 1365, 9 June 1913

Nationalist Ireland reluctantly began to register the extent of the unionist threat to the home rule project. The *Cork Examiner* noted: 'History repeats itself; and despite the threats of the Ascendancy class, Home Rule is as certain as Church disestablishment, land reform and franchise extension.'[1] The same journal added a month later: 'The National organisation must be strengthened and England may in all friendliness be made to recognise that the danger of conflict with the

---

[1] *Cork Examiner*, 19 Feb. 1912.

Orangemen of Down and Antrim is a trivial concern as compared with the certainty of Nationalist outbreaks in case of the frustration of the national will.'[2]

Much of the comment in the mainstream liberal media encouraged this mood of easy optimism. The tone of writing about Ulster unionism was predominantly one of exasperation. J. A. Spender, editor of the *Westminster Review*, provided a typical response: 'The racial and religious feuds of northern and southern Ireland seemed more to resemble a Balkan blood feud than the political contests to which Englishmen were accustomed and they threatened to spread from Ireland to England.'[3] Exasperation sometimes gave way to contempt. Aston Hilliers was a master of the conventional sneering phrase: 'The lurid imagination of the Loyalists seems wrong inside the skins of roadside asses.'[4] The mixture of contempt and exasperation was enlivened by the occasional dramatic volte-face. The editor of the nonconformist *British Weekly*, Sir William Robertson Nicoll, had once claimed: 'Even if English and Scottish Presbyterians were to betray their Irish brethren the latter would fight to the death against a tyranny so monstrous that the most enslaved creatures under its rule have made their protest.'[5] But in 1912 Robertson Nicoll walked away from the unionist cause, claiming to regard their fears as exaggerated. In similar vein the liberal periodical *Truth* replied airily to an Ulster Liberal correspondent who stressed the depth of religious antagonism within Ulster:

English liberals are firmly of the opinion that this extremity of sectarian bitterness is the direct outcome of the past history of English rule in Ireland, that the present state of things tends to perpetuate it, and that the 'education' best calculated to efface it is that which will come of having to row in the same boat and work together for common national ends, as people of different religious views have to do in other countries. These are two quite irreconcilable opinions and there is really no use in arguing about them for neither side can ever hope to convince the other.[6]

Within the broad liberal media, there was one significant exception, the *Daily News* (with H. V. Massingham) and its evening organ, the *Star*. According to the *Star*:

[2] Ibid., 9 Mar. 1912.
[3] *Life, Journalism and Politics*, 2 vols. (London, 1927), ii. 2.
[4] *Contemporary Review*, 102 (Oct. 1912), 521.
[5] *Witness*, 10 Aug. 1912, cited in T. H. Darlow, *W. Robertson Nicoll: Life and Letters* (London, 1925) 224.   [6] Quoted in the *Cork Examiner*, 15 Feb. 1912.

We have never yielded to the temptation to deride or belittle the resistance of Ulster to Home Rule. It has been, it is, and it will be the capital crux of the Irish problem . . . The subjugation of Ulster by force is one of those things that do not happen in our politics. The Ulster Protestants have too many reserves of sympathy on this side of the channel to make policy of naked coercion possible . . . If coercion failed to break the spirit of the Irish Irishman, it is not likely to break the spirit of the Scottish Irishman. It is we know a popular delusion that Ulster is a braggard whose words are empty bluff . . . We are convinced that Ulster means what she says . . . We earnestly hope that Liberals will not be driven by Tory bigotry into an attitude of bitter hostility towards the Ulster Protestants. We have too much in common with each other . . . We are their friends and we can not allow the Conservative party to enjoy a monopoly of good feelings towards the Protestants of Ulster.[7]

This argument was a serious and significant one. Here, after all, was Massingham, the doyen of the radical press, insisting there was a good case for an election on the Ulster issue, which had inevitably been overshadowed by the issue of parliamentary reform in the previous election. But this was not typical of the tone of liberal analysis. There was no real effort made to encourage Irish nationalists to think seriously about the north. In general, liberal rhetoric on the Ulster question was designed to minimize the difficulty. Nationalist allies were to be reassured at all costs. It was hardly surprising that the nationalists found this a comfort. They too tended to adopt a dismissive attitude on the subject of unionist resistance. Edmund Haviland Burke summed up: 'He refused to consider the question of compromise, and he thought if the Nationalists of Ireland extended a compromise now they would be like a victorious army in a strong position that abandoned that position and left its fortified and its entrenched heights to come down to lose itself and be cut up in an undiscovered country.'[8]

Tom Kettle was one of the most generous and intellectually able of the Redmondites. Passionately interested in European ideas, he was always 'to some extent in revolt against the theories of the Gaelic League whom he thought tended to make Ireland insular, morally as well as intellectually.'[9] His wide sympathies did not, however, extend

---

[7] *Star*, 9 Apr. 1912, quoted in the *Irish Communist*, 57 (Sept. 1970), 13–14. For Massingham's role, see *Northern Whig* 1 Oct. 1912. Massingham, interestingly, had been a friend and ally of Michael Davitt; see B. B. Gilbert *David Lloyd George, the Organiser of Victory* (London, 1992), 25, 53, 57.   [8] *Leinster Leader*, 30 Aug. 1913.
[9] Stephen Gwynn, *John Redmond's Last Years* (London, 1926), 186. Cf. also T. M. Kettle, *Ways of War* (Dublin and London, 1917), 27.

to Ulster unionists—in short, they infuriated him. 'Nationalists had always been the real unionists of Ireland', he told a crowd at Newbridge, Kildare, 'as between England and Ireland they [the Nationalists] were the Unionists and not the separatists.'[10] As William O'Brien has pointed out, Tom Kettle was capable of some wild language on the topic. At Skibbereen, he demanded that 'the imperial forces and the police force of the nation should be drawn aside and that Ireland should be left to fight it out with north-east Ulster', and at Kildare he predicted, without any appearance of a joke, that such of the Orange dogs as might have survived should be 'shot' or 'hanged' or sent to penal servitude.[11] Such dire visions rather undermined the force of John Dillon's attempt to conjure up a more benign future for unionists: 'He could assure them that after it was all over these unionists would feel much the better and be extremely thankful that they had been compelled to accept a position of equality with their fellow-countrymen, and in their new lot as part and parcel of the Irish people they would soon find their position in Ireland far stronger and happier than ever it had been.'

Dillon felt able to offer such an agreeable scenario because some nationalists had convinced themselves that they were epitomes of tolerance. As Haviland Burke put it:

The record of the Catholic County Councils—the National County Councils—throughout the Catholic provinces and districts of Ireland was an honour and a glory to them. (*applause*) They did not boycott and exclude non-Catholics from employment by the County Councils and he remembered well staggering an English meeting where a Tory got up to heckle him and cross-examine him on this question when he told him that he (Mr Burke) in common with his friend and colleague, Mr Michael Reddy, represented the Kings County in which 7/9 of the people were Catholics and in which 40% of the employees of the County Council were non-Catholic. (*applause*) And he told them to contrast that with the Orange-based local bodies in the north where the Catholics were treated as serfs and helots in their own country.[12]

Certainly, the record of northern unionist employment in local government was said to be deplorable. According to the Revd Bernard Maguire, speaking at Rock Hall, Ballyshannon:

There was not a single Catholic employed under the Ballymoney Rural Council, Antrim District Council, Antrim Town Commissioners, Portrush

---

[10] *Leicester Leader*, 14 June 1913.
[11] W. O'Brien, *The Irish Revolution* (London, 1920) 181.
[12] *Leinster Leader*, 30 Aug. 1913.

Town Commissioners, Cookstown Urban Council, Aughnacloy Town Commissioners, Coleraine District Council or Bangor Urban Council. Out of £11,000 disbursed by the Belfast Harbour Board in salaries, Catholics received the munificent sum of £200. Fancy the cool audacity of anyone, in face of all these astounding facts and figures, taxing the Catholics with intolerance. (*applause*)[13]

The Burke–Maguire argument was widely accepted on the nationalist side. William O'Brien, with his uncomfortable insistence that Burke was merely one of a small minority of 'tame' Protestant MPs in a party dominated by a secret oath-bound society (the Ancient Order of Hibernians), was regarded as an eccentric. Yet by 1913 unionists regarded the AOH as a more important body than the Irish parliamentary party. This was partly due to a masterstroke by Joe Devlin—he had registered the AOH as a friendly society under the National Insurance Act of 1911. This meant that in many areas of rural Ireland it became the most convenient way of dealing with matters such as medical treatment and burial expenses, and membership rose dramatically, from 13,000 in 1905 to 125,000 in 1914. Where AOH influence was strong, the implications for employment practices tended to be subtantial. In Monaghan, for example, all thirty-seven jobs in the gift of the council went to nationalists; this, in a county with a substantial unionist minority.[14] Outside the ranks of the O'Brienites, ranks which were increasingly weakened as the Liberal government appeared to be willing to accept the mainstream nationalist agenda, few nationalists were willing to respond sympathetically to such concerns. On Ulster Day, the *Weekly Freeman's Journal* insisted that the AOH had only a 'fractional representation' in nationalist conventions and that 'no assembly that ever assembled would submit to the absolute control of any such section'.[15] It was also pointed out that unionist opposition to home rule had 'been as strong in 1886 and 1893 as it is today',[16] in other words, the strength of unionist opposition to a Dublin parliament had long predated the emergence of the AOH as a serious force.

It was an article of faith for Irish party speakers, to insist upon the selfish 'ascendancy' spirit of unionism. Patrick White, MP, told the

---

[13] *Weekly Freeman's Journal*, 13 Jan. 1912.
[14] Foy, 'The Ulster Volunteer Force: It's Domestic Development and Political Impact in the Period 1913–20' (Ph.D. thesis, Queen's University, Belfast, 1986), fo. 51.
[15] *Weekly Freeman's Journal*, 28 Sept. 1912.   [16] Ibid.

South Meath United Irish League: 'The Irish Unionists in the North
of Ireland have had an ascendancy in Ireland since the Act of Union.
They are now under Home Rule about to lose that and it is for their
own material selfish interests that they are fighting at the present time
and it is not for the benefit of Ireland or the glory of the empire, of
which they sometimes profess to be loyal subjects.'[17] Redmond shared
the view that the spirit of ascendancy was the core of the matter. In an
elegant essay for a Canadian academic periodical, he provided a classic
formulation of this case, citing a resolution adopted by the Synod of
the Reformed Presbyterian Church of Ireland which runs: 'It will be
forever impossible to fight Home Rule successfully so long as it is
contended or admitted that the Romanists and other open enemies of
the true religion ought to have political power. We regard the so-called
Catholic Emancipation Act as the first "plague spot" of Home Rule
evil. From the time of the passing of the Act, which gave the Romanists
the franchise, dates the beginning of their power to threaten the
liberties of the Protestants of Ireland.' The Reformed Presbyterians
were a small group, but Redmond insisted: 'More dextrous politicians
express the same sentiments in another form'. He admitted that the
unionists avoided the expression of such sentiments in parliament:
'This argument is not heard in the House of Commons.'[18] In other
words, despite all the pious unionist commitments to equality of
citizenship, nationalists insisted that unionism remained an ideology of
ascendancy. In another such article, published in *The Review of Reviews*,
Redmond was able to declare, with some fatuity, that there was 'no
Ulster question'.[19] Arthur Lynch, the Clare MP, never made this
error, but he agreed that the unionist case was in essence one for some
form of ascendancy: 'In the House of Commons even the most stalwart
of the Ulstermen deny that they are merely fighting for Ascendancy.'
But, as Lynch also pointed out, 'the Revd F. W. Austin, Rector of St
Columbas, Knock, has rushed in where Capt. Craig and William
Moore have feared to tread.'[20] This was a reference to a letter in the
Belfast Newsletter in which the indiscreet Austin had declared: 'We
Irish Covenanters are still treated to sermons and speeches in which
we are frequently told that "we seek no ascendancy". How then is the
Church of Rome to be kept at bay? Why are we such strong Unionists?

---

[17] *Leinster Leader*, 26 July 1913.
[18] The complete text of Redmond's reply to Balfour appears in the *Weekly Freeman's
Journal*, 20 Dec. 1913.   [19] Ibid., 23 Nov. 1912.
[20] *Ireland's Vital Hour* (London, 1915), 161.

If we are not aiming at the Ascendancy of Protestants in some corner of Ireland what are we aiming at?'[21] The garrulous clergyman had blurted out the real truth in Lynch's view. John Dillon agreed: 'When one of these "Unionist" gentlemen goes to England no lamb can bleat so mildly. They declare the last thing they think of in Ireland is ascendancy. They want equality.'[22] But the sentiments to be found in the *Newsletter* represented the true spirit of the Orangemen of the north.

In a particularly able speech at Moate, Sir Walter Nugent, MP, dealt with unionist themes in the same way. His tactic was to acknowledge unionist disavowals of ascendancy but to argue that these old unregenerate notions still lurked subliminally in unionist discourse. 'Sir Edward Carson had said—and he [Sir Walter] did not for a moment question his absolute good faith—that he did not seek ascendancy but only equality, but yet every line of his speeches and every argument used by him was based on the old ascendancy idea of one law for the minority and another for the Catholic majority.'[23] At this point Nugent introduced a historical dimension to the argument. 'Dealing with Sir Edward's assertion that there was no right to deprive a man of the rights as a citizen which he had enjoyed', Sir Walter pointedly asked whether Sir Edward was to be taken as forgetting the Act of Union and that through it men were deprived, by the grossest forms of bribery and corruption, of the rights of citizenship, and that their descendants were subsequently denounced as rebels and shot and hanged for attempting to get these rights restored by the very methods which the unionist leader was now advising the Ulster minority to employ to prevent the will of the majority prevailing.[24] According to the *Westmeath Examiner* this 'splendid point' against 'Carsonism' was 'loudly applauded'.[25] Against this, Irish unionists insisted—it was their article of faith—on the benign nature and impact of the Act of Union: progress and economic development had replaced instability. In any case, Walter Nugent's speech did not constitute a case for an all-Ireland measure of home rule; it was, rather, a critique of the way Ireland had allegedly been treated in the past by Britain. Nugent was himself clearly aware of this, hence his willingness to argue that, in any case, there was

---

[21] *Belfast Newsletter*, 7 Jan. 1914.
[22] *Weekly Freeman's Journal*, 6 Sept. 1916.
[23] *Westmeath Examiner*, 9 Feb. 1914.　　　　[24] Ibid.　　　[25] Ibid.

no question under Home Rule of driving Ulster Unionists from the protection of British law, but there is a question of admitting five-sixths of the Irish people for the first time in history to participate equally with Ulster Unionists in the benefits of the British constitution. Under Home Rule the supremacy of the Imperial Parliament will be as supreme as it is today over every inhabitant of Ulster and Ireland. Ulster will continue to return representatives to the Imperial Parliament, and the whole power of that Parliament will be free to defend the slightest attempt at wrong to the humblest Protestant in Sandy Row or the slums of North Belfast.[26]

In some ways, Nugent almost seems to be describing the strengthening of the union rather than its weakening.

Replying to him, George Reid, a member of the literary committee of the Ulster provisional government, pointed out that it could be argued that Ireland already had all these benefits—so why change at all?[27] Walter Nugent's line of argument contained an enthusiastic acknowledgement of the Westminster link, and even of the supremacy of the imperial parliament; this was a peculiarity of the group of MPs who were closest to John Redmond, and genuinely reflected Redmond's own views. William O'Brien portrayed the Irish party under Redmond's leadership as being dominated by Joe Devlin's Ancient Order of Hibernians. Again and again O'Brien stresses its essentially sectarian nature: 'a squalid bunch of Catholic place-seekers'. But the reality is more complex: there is no question that Redmond failed to create an environment which could keep William O'Brien and his followers within the parliamentary party ranks. There is no question either that Redmond felt it necessary to treat Devlin as a favoured lieutenant: but Devlin himself was a complex figure, sectarian in so far as his role in the AOH went but also socially progressive, and able even to attract some Belfast Protestant working-class votes. Nevertheless, there is no doubt that Redmond had major reservations about many of the tactics with which the Ancient Order of Hibernians was associated—in particular, the continuance of agrarian radicalism and the practice of cattle-driving after 1903. Most of the MPs closest to Redmond by the time of the home rule crisis—Nugent, J. P. Hayden, William O'Malley, and Stephen Gwynn—were clearly outside the nexus of the AOH–cattle-driving activists who had played a key role in silencing William O'Brien at the 1909 baton convention. Redmond liked to present himself as the last word in non-sectarian

---

[26] Ibid.
[27] *Weekly Freeman's Journal*, 22 Feb. 1913.

tolerant nationalism: William O'Brien's critique demonstrates that this
was not so. But it fails to comprehend the way in which Redmond
retained a commitment (albeit a compromised one) to some notion of
reconciliation of creeds and classes in Ireland. It was, at least, partly for
this reason that he and his closest allies eschewed a narrow, insular
path of Irish development and stressed instead a continued involvement in Westminster and imperial concerns. But, unionists asked, how
far did moderate Redmondism represent the real beliefs of Irish
nationalists? How far did he and his party colleagues control the
broader movements within Irish society? As Francis Hackett wisely
explained in this context: 'The powerful bourgeois element in Belfast
. . . retains an impression, refreshed by the AOH, of cliques that keep
alive the old unrest of Fenianism and agrarian *jacqueries*.' He added
shrewdly: 'Plain lack of acquaintance has a good deal to do with
Ulster's scepticism.'[28]

John Redmond's ability to convey moderate and reconciling themes
depended in large part on the nature of Irish nationalism as a mass
movement. The Irish party vigorously condemned radical leader James
Larkin during the Dublin 'lock-out' of 1913. The *Weekly Freeman's
Journal's* multilayered headline of 8 November 1913 conveyed all the
requisite messages:

> The New Evangel
> The Priests of Dublin
> Insulted and Attacked
> Anti Home Rule Move
> Socialist Display
> Russell's Sneers: Shaw's Insults: Lapworth's Threats
> Dublin Workers Pawns
> in Monstrous Game

The parliamentary party was clearly anti-socialist, but its record on
agrarian radicalism was more ambiguous. Questions about the party's
commitment to peace in the countryside were regularly raised, even by
sympathetic liberal audiences in England. For all shades of Irish
unionism, and even large sections of British liberalism, the Wyndham
Land Act of 1903 had been an act of beneficent imperial generosity
towards Ireland: the Treasury had in theory (if not always in actual
practice) agreed to bridge the gap between the price at which the
landlord could afford to sell and the peasant afford to buy. It had been

[28] F. Hackett, *Ireland: A Study in Nationalism* (New York, 1918), 335.

preceded by a process of dialogue linking landlord and peasant leaders. The sudden return to themes of agrarian class conflict, especially after 1906 with the start of a new ranch war, came as a shock and a disappointment. A great deal of unionist parliamentary comment reflects precisely this fact. Some unionists feared that this was a grim portent of a disturbed future. The Revd John McDermott had told Sir William Beech-Thomas that home rule would be followed by an epoch of intensified agrarian agitation. When agrarian radicalism was the matter under discussion the *bête noir* of the unionists was John Fitzgibbon, after John Dillon 'the leading nationalist politician in Connaught'.[29] The Irish Chief Secretary had reacted by attempting to 'co-opt', by offering Fitzgibbon an official position in the Congested District Board. Birrell spoke of Fitzgibbon as 'quite the statesman now', though in 'moments of excitement' he was inclined to throw off the shackles imposed by a government appointment and return to the wilder shores of oratory, Fitzgibbon's career was an apposite symbol. In effect, in the 1912–14 epoch we are dealing with the confused side-effects of the stabilization of revolutionary fervour. The broad picture was one of an increasingly conservative and stable countryside as the progress of land reform became more and more marked. As the Clare RIC reported: 'In agrarian matters, there was hope for improvement as the number of cases likely to cause friction and lead to outrage was diminishing by reason of the purchase and division of lands here and there throughout the county.'[30] Most of the usual indices of agrarian militancy showed a decline. The number of unlet farms from which tenants had been evicted fell from 1,009 to 703 in the 1910–14 period, and the total number of evictions from 147 to 85.[31] The number of those requiring police protection fell from 316 to 249 in the same period, and the number of cases of boycotting dropped from 128 to 26.

All these figures are indications of the decline in the 'traditional' landlord-versus-tenant phase in the Irish land war. But one feature still gave cause for worry: cattle-driving. While showing no signs of reaching the heights of the classic ranch war (1906–10), there was no diminution in the period 1911–14 of the agitation against the grazing system.[32]

[29] *Irish Times*, 3 Jan. 1912. See Bew, *Conflict and Conciliation* (Oxford, 1987), chs. 5 and 6, for Fitzgibbon's role in the ranch war.

[30] Clare report, Public Record Office, CO 903/17/12.

[31] Public Record Office, CO 903/18/69.

[32] Public Record Office, CO 903/18/71.

TABLE 2. *Return showing the results of agitation against the grazing system, 1902–1914*[a]

Year (May)	No. of counties affected	No. of farms unlet, unstocked, or only partly stocked	Acreage of farms unstocked, or only partly stocked
1902	14	89	12,181
1903	10	48	5,791
1904	9	42	6,305
1905	10	96	11,203
1906	7	67	6,725
1907	13	174	20,338
1908	16	284	37,507
1909	15	98	18,548
1910	13	44	8,120
1911	16	53	9,521
1912	17	52	10,045
1913	12	49	9,397
1914	12	46	10,153

[a] Information on this subject was not collected prior to 1902.

The consequence is clear enough. The returns from agrarian radicalism were both diminishing and increasingly ambiguous; embarrassingly, for example, many of the leaders of the ranch war of 1906–10 had turned out to have ranching connections themselves. The gap between agrarian radical rhetoric, so beloved of the Irish party, and reality became stretched indeed. Counties as far apart as Leix and Mayo provided celebrated examples of this during the home rule crisis. In June 1913 Patrick Joseph Meehan succeeded his father, Patrick A. Meehan, to the Leix parliamentary seat. P. A. Meehan had been a noted advocate of land redistribution. His son adopted the same stance in public. All went well for two months, then, suddenly, controversy erupted. P. J. Meehan, in robust form, was in the process of denouncing a local land-grabber, a typical theme, when he was rudely interrupted by a party of men in a brake, backed up by their own band.[33] 'Mr Meehan, what about Corbally? What about Corbally?' soon became the principal question of Leix politics.

The essence of the controversy was a simple one. Patrick Joseph Meehan presented himself as the friend of radical land redistribution. At Mountmellick on 19 October 1913 he insisted: 'The land of the people was the old watchword of the Irish party and of the Irish people.'[34] But the Corbally case raised doubts about the strength of his commitment to this principle. Arthur McMahon, already the holder of 1,000 acres in Cashel and Loir, had taken a further 400 acres at Corbally.[35] This soon became a matter of bitter dispute in the locality. Embarrassingly, Meehan was Arthur McMahon's solicitor and friend; Meehan's principal local political opponent, J. J. Aird, was predictably outraged: 'It has been stated that Mr McMahon was a Nationalist and Catholic and he ought to go through. If it be so you will get lots of Catholics and Nationalists to take up ranches, but will that supply the wants of the small holders?' Aird's ally, Patrick Dunne, declared: 'Parnell and Davitt founded the Land League on the principle of land for the people.'[36] These exchanges took place before a mammoth five-hour meeting of the Leix divisional executive of the United Irish League. By twenty-six votes to two (Aird and Dunne) this body supported the local MP. Encouraged, Meehan rounded on his critics: Patrick Dunne was accused of being a land shark himself,[37] while his supporters—who claimed to be seeking the Corbally land for evicted tenants—were substantial farmers who wanted it for themselves.[38] In late September the police had assumed that the whole affair would blow over very quickly, saying the agitation was 'scarcely likely to continue for any length of time', and adding: 'The matter is being carefully watched by the police—but in a very unobtrusive way, as Mr McMahon does not desire police protection owing to the public support he is receiving from Mr Meehan MP for this county.'[39]

But the following summer there were still serious repercussions: rural branches of local land and labour organizations were formed at Maryborough[40] and Stradbally.[41] This happened principally because Patrick Meehan resolved to attack J. J. Aird's base as chairman of the

---

[33] *Leinster Leader*, 30 Aug. 1913.   [34] Ibid., 25 Oct. 1914.
[35] Ibid., 4 Oct. 1913; the date of the Leix meeting was 28 Sept.
[36] Ibid.   [37] Ibid., 25 Oct. 1913.
[38] Ibid., 4 Oct. 1913; 25 Oct. 1913; 14 Nov. 1913.
[39] County Inspector's Office, 1 Oct. 1913, 904/91/146.
[40] *Leinster Leader*, 15 Nov. 1913; 22 Nov. 1913.   [41] Ibid. 2 May 1914.

Maryborough land and labour league. Accusations and counter-accusations flew between them: Aird accused Meehan of failing to support the labourers' strike at Ballyfin;[42] Meehan replied by accusing Aird of being a rent-raiser himself.[43] Stradbally was regularly disturbed by the marching and countermarching of the bands of the two factions.

These events in a normally sleepy constituency were spectacular public evidence of one of the Irish party's major difficulties. Attempts to invoke the principles of Parnell and Davitt on agrarian matters were now highly problematic. The Wyndham Land Act of 1903 had resulted in nearly 300,000 sales, 100,000 of them between 1906 and 1908; the Birrell Act of 1909 had been the focus of much criticism,[44] but the fact remains that by 1914 an estimated two-thirds to three-quarters of farmers owned their own holdings. As a result the Irish party was inevitably heavily influenced by this new rural bourgeoisie, even though at the same time it wished to remain the traditional voice of the rural have-nots. This often left members of parliament in a rather difficult position, particularly in the west where the cattle-driving was most concentrated. Aware of the extent to which unionists were exploiting the issue of rural lawlessness, William O'Malley, MP for Connemara, attempted to cool the passions of cattle-drivers in the locality at the beginning of the home rule crisis. But he was immediately accused of having a personal motive by the Letterfrack United Irish League: 'Whereas although Mr William O'Malley MP had been in communication with certain members of the branch, *re* the recent cattle drivers, he never said a word to discourage such tactics until the farms in the Clifden district, notably the one held by his brother-in-law [Mr O'Flaherty of Ballyconneely] were to be driven by the landless men on the fringes.'[45] According to the police, O'Malley was then summoned before the Tully branch of the United Irish League to explain his negative speeches concerning cattle-driving. After 'a great deal of excitement', he withdrew his remarks about this activity.[46]

Such exchanges became increasingly commonplace and undoubtedly weakened the Irish party's standing in public opinion. The embarrassments were frequently rooted in the nature of Irish rural

---

[42] Ibid., 15 Nov. 1913.   [43] Ibid., 2 May 1914.

[44] See Bew, *Conflict and Conciliation*, chs. 5 and 6; W. F. Monypenny, *The Two Irish Nations: An Essay on Home Rule* (London, 1913), 42–3.

[45] *Mayo News*, 17 Jan. 1914.   [46] Public Record Office, CO 904/92/100.

society in the epoch after the passing of the Wyndham Act. Having rejected the O'Brienite thesis of 1903 that rural militancy should cease to be a defining feature of the party's activity, the Irish MPs found themselves on uncertain and treacherous terrain. The continuation of agrarian radicalism after 1903 tended to be internally divisive of their own support base. While there was still much land hunger in the Irish countryside, which the party's agrarian radicals attempted to mobilize, many Catholic nationalists had made substantial gains during the long, slow decline of landlord power. They were reluctant to share these acres with their poorer neighbours. These men also had an influence over the party machine. In parliament the unionists often had a field day exposing the confused and even greedy behaviour of prominent UIL cadres. Embarrassing though all this was to the Redmond leadership, the fact remained that the confusion of the Irish party on the land issue reflected the confusion within the rural population as a whole. The party was, in effect, in control of the great bulk of political activity generated by the land question. There was no indication that it could be outflanked on the issue and the issue itself appeared to be of diminishing significance.

Matters stood quite differently with respect to the language issue. Fears about the role of the Irish language under home rule came to play an increasingly important part in unionist discourse. At the committee stage of the Home Rule Bill in October 1912, the unionists moved an amendment with the aim of preventing an Irish parliament making the holding of Irish a qualification for holding public appointments.[47] They claimed that this was a necessary safeguard; the nationalists, led by their two most public language enthusiasts, Tom O'Donnell and J. P. Boland, denied it. Birrell's speech in rejection of the unionist position was typically queasy: the language enthusiasts did say some foolish things, he suggested, but the Irish language was a dwindling force in Irish society and nothing could change that. The unionist speeches were rather more pointed. The Orange MP William Moore—of all people—declared that he was proud to have a smattering of Irish. Ronald MacNeill had tried unsuccessfully to learn it. James Craig admired those who took it up in their spare-time. But, said Craig, the language was inevitably dying and its main use would be as 'a political lever'.[48] Bonar Law argued that there was fear of discrimination in public appointments, but for him there was an even

---

[47] *Northern Whig*, 13 Oct. 1912.   [48] Ibid.

deeper problem: the Redmondites had claimed to be 'great imperialists', but their support of the language movement seemed to imply a rather different logic. 'Everyone knew that the real vitality of the movement in support of the Irish language depended on the hope of those who were pushing it that it might be come another factor in the separate nationality of Ireland as distinguished from the rest of the UK.'[49] Dr Hyde, the President of the Gaelic League, had opined in San Francisco in 1906: 'We aim for nothing less than the establishing of a new nation upon the map of Europe.'[50] Hence, for Bonar Law, the acceptance of the amendment was a 'test of sincerity'. Redmond may have been disturbed by these arguments, but he could not afford to offend the Gaelic League. At Aughrim in September 1911 he had declared: 'For my part I have always been in favour of the Gaelic League ... the ideals of the Gaelic League are our ideals.'[51] The amendment was defeated by a government majority of 106. A few days later Redmond did permit the government to accept an amendment excluding both Trinity College, Dublin, and the Queen's University, Belfast, from the remit of the home rule parliament.[52] Here he judged correctly that he had the space to manœuvre and thus to make a substantial gesture of tolerance; but where the Irish language was directly at issue, Redmond felt he had no such space. He left it to John Dillon to control the excesses of the Gaelic radicals. Dillon had, in the 1903–10 period, utilized agrarian radicalism against Redmond's leadership. Redmond's rural conservatism was widely mocked: typically Michael O'Riordan, Arthur Lynch's fictional Irish MP, noted in exasperation, 'sure he's nothing but a little Tory squireen'.[53] It must have given Redmond a certain satisfaction to see Dillon at the wrong end of similar rebukes: denounced because of his coolness on the language issue as the 'Ballaghadereen tolerance prover' or the 'Mayo factionist', who pointedly educated his own children outside the country; or even more rudely as the great opponent of bigotry who refused to do anything about the discrimination against Catholics by the Northern Railway—even though he was a substantial shareholder in that company.[54]

The background here requires some comment. John Dillon had embraced the Gaelic League enthusiastically in 1897, but following a

---

[49] Ibid.   [50] Ibid., 7 Oct. 1912.   [51] Ibid.
[52] Ibid., 22 Oct. 1912.
[53] Lynch, *O'Rourke the Great: A Novel* (London, 1921), 63.
[54] *Leader*, 15 Mar. 1913.

number of disputes, including one involving his Ballaghadereen employees, his attitude cooled considerably.[55] The key conflict came in February 1909, when at a United Irish League convention, Dillon, eloquently supported by Stephen Gwynn, opposed the notion that Irish should be a compulsory subject for matriculation at the National University of Ireland. Tom O'Donnell and J. P. Boland, both keen supporters of compulsory Irish in the university, were astonished by Dillon's open opposition. Boland recalled later:

The vote was taken by a show of hands. It was estimated to be about three to one in favour of my resolution, and it settled the question conclusively in the country in view of the representative character of the National Convention. My own belief is that had any other Irish MP than John Dillon led the opposition, the voting would have been practically unanimous for compulsory Irish. On the other hand, had Dillon used the big shots in his locker, appealed to his thirty years' record, used all the arts of a demagogue to win his point at all costs, he might have carried the meeting with him.[56]

This victory gave the Gaelic League a new impetus. By June 1909 it had the support of some nineteen county councils for its position on compulsory Irish; this was of particular significance because the county councils had the power to give university scholarships. As Vincent Comerford notes: 'County councillors, who were manipulators of a nationalist politics that was comparatively inert much of the time, ran scared before the energy and enthusiasm of the Gaelic League. When the compulsory Irish question was posed as one of being for or against Ireland there was only one answer they could give.'[57] By the end of 1910 the authorities of the National University capitulated and made Irish compulsory for matriculation from 1913 onwards.

Between 1908 and 1910 the battle over Irish in the National University had been won by the Gaelic League. But this still left open the question of the role of Irish in the school system. Professor Osborn Bergin told the *Weekly Freeman's Journal* (12 September 1912) that 'If Irish is to live ... the schools must be gaelicised in the present

---

[55] Shane O'Neill, 'The Politics of Culture in Ireland 1890–1910' (D.Phil. thesis, University of Oxford, 1982), fo. 241.

[56] J. P. Boland, *An Irishman's Day* (London, 1940), 133–4. Ironically, as J. A. Gaughan points out, Tom O'Donnell, who in 1912 denounced the unionist view of the Gaelic League as a Fenian conspiracy, in 1914 took exactly the same view of it himself! Thomas O'Donnell, *A Political Odyssey* (Dublin, 1983), 97.

[57] R. V. Comerford, 'Nation, Nationalism and the Irish Language', in T. E. Hachey and L. McCaffrey (eds.), *Perspectives on Irish Nationalism* (Lexington, 1989), 34.

generation.' Nevertheless, throughout 1912 John Dillon opposed the notion of compulsory Irish in schools: his view was in turn vigorously challenged. Tensions were raised by a draft educational scheme finally published in the *Weekly Freeman's Journal* on 28 September 1912, but widely bruited beforehand. Birrell had responded generously to a request made by the county councils to provide from imperial funds a sum of £10,000 for the purpose of founding a system of scholarships from primary to intermediate schools. So far so good, but Birrell was not prepared to swallow the 'vital principle', as Irish nationalist enthusiasts saw it, of essential Irish. On 3 August 1912 the *Weekly Freeman's Journal* had already carried the angry response of Professor Agnes O'Farrelly (National University of Ireland), speaking to an *aerdheacht* at Kilskeery, County Tyrone: 'Anyone would have thought at this hour of the day, that Irish would in any such scheme be nationally an essential subject. We are unreasonable enough to demand that, above all else, the brilliant pupils leaving our primary schools and starting on a course of education at the national expense shall reflect in the highest degree the instincts of the nation.' Even more insidiously, Professor O'Farrelly felt that Birrell's scheme was an attempt to claw back ground already won by the Gaelic League. The holders of the school scholarships were to be offered—without further examination—county council scholarships to be held at university level, provided that they should be tenable at all three Irish universities. As O'Farrelly made clear, this provoked the fear that candidates would choose to go to Trinity or Belfast and that the National University would have to drop compulsory Irish and, as she vividly expressed it, 'in self defence, unsay its act of national faith'. Twenty-four county councils refused to accept Birrell's grant on this basis: they firmly rejected 'a bid of £10,000 made by the English Chief Secretary of Ireland for the purchase of a principle vital to Irish nationalism'. At a meeting of an executive committee of the Irish County Council's General Council, chaired by P. J. O'Neill, it was decided that Birrell was asking far too much: his conditions were, a commissioned report declared, highly objectionable.[58] O'Neill was a substantial figure who shared national platforms with Redmond and Dillon;[59] clearly, however, he did not feel it necessary to listen too closely to the views of the party leadership on the language issue. Meath County Council lapsed into an ambiguous silence, but one

[58] *Weekly Freeman's Journal* 2 Nov. 1912.
[59] Ibid., 15 Feb. 1913.

county council, Kildare, argued explicitly that it would be unwise and foolish to refuse acceptance of a grant. The official organ of the Gaelic League commented acidly: 'Is there no memory of the Geraldines of Cill Cara?'[60] and what have the 'Gaels of Athy, Naas, Brownstown and Celbridge to say of the action of their County Council?'[61]

Kildare County Council was not allowed to rest on its laurels: the Kildare branch of the Gaelic League was a prominent and vigorous body.[62] A deputation from the Gaelic League (led by Eoin MacNeill) attempted to persuade the council to alter its position: by fourteen votes to eleven, the council retained its original line. The public debate which followed MacNeill's presentation made it quite clear that the issues at stake were widely understood. In particular, the council members fully comprehended the position of John Dillon. MacNeill insisted 'there was no special hardship in making Irish compulsory, and if they adopted a scheme in which Irish was not compulsory they would drive the study of Irish out of the schools altogether'. The objections of the pragmatic majority on the council were equally clearly stated. In the first place, they doubted that it was possible to give the bulk of the children the teaching which would have been required. Michael Fitzsimmons said that only 5 per cent of the teachers in the primary schools were competent to teach Irish. Other councillors were afraid of allegations of sectarianism. The *Weekly Northern Whig* (3 May 1913) had reported that Antrim County Council would allow its scholarships to be held at any university in Ireland. In response, Kildare Councillor John Conlon noted: 'The Nationalists of Louth had been tolerant and were tolerant to every section of the community (*hear, hear*), but he was afraid that they or their representatives in Parliament would not be able to make that boast if the attitude assumed by the supporters of the resolution were adopted. The county council of Antrim had made their scholarships tenable at any Irish university and the County Council of Kildare should not adopt a narrow attitude.' The chairman of the council, Matthew J. Minch, a director of the *Freeman's Journal*, whose own sons attended Trinity College, agreed: was that council to levy a tax on their non-Catholic countrymen and then say 'we will compel you to send your child to a school you don't approve of'? Minch added: 'As a loyal Irishman he was a thorough supporter of the Gaelic League in its objects but on

---

[60] *Leinster Leader*, 1 Mar. 1913.   [61] Ibid., 8 Mar. 1913.
[62] O'Neill, 'The Politics of Culture in Ireland', fo. 314.

this question the Gaelic League was wrong.' Finally one councillor, John Healy, felt that the Gaelic League was standing in the way of the advancement of poor men's sons and 'was surprised that the Gaelic League should be the body to keep the poor man's son without education'.[63]

The Kildare councillors demonstrated a keen awareness of the views of the Irish party leadership on the issue, particularly those of John Dillon. They clearly knew that Dillon supported the Birrell scheme; in fact, there was a hidden dimension here. Dillon had exercised a strong influence over Birrell's thinking[64] on the subject before it was made public, as Birrell had shown him a draft of the scholarship scheme before sending it to the Treasury and responded sympathetically to the Irish leader's ideas: 'Your scheme is a bold one ... but it is a good one.'[65] It is little wonder then that Dillon felt obliged to defend the proposals in public. Angrily, he argued that the supporters of essential Irish were guilty of 'gross oppression ... by depriving Protestant boys of scholarships unless their parents compel them to learn Irish.'[66]

Though the *Freeman's Journal* remained loyal to the Birrell scheme, Dillon's efforts were not well received in sections of the mainstream nationalist press: 'Mr Dillon's advocacy of the cause of the Protestant boy is a superfluous effort to pose as the protector of the interests of an element in Irish life, which does not need it now, no more than in the past.'[67] Such a bland dismissal of the problem infuriated unionist opinion of all shades. The *Irish Times* liked to call John Dillon the most intolerant politician in Ireland, but if even he was to be swept aside as a weak-kneed cosmopolitan liberal by other forces, what then was the future of the Protestant community? In fact, as the *Leader* pointed out, the *Irish Times* and Dillon were effectively united on this issue, and the *Times* gave sympathetic space to Dillon's views.

At Westminster, the unionists urged that schoolteachers be given the same position as civil servants (holding their posts directly under the Crown) in the event of home rule. The *Irish Times* argued that

---

[63] *Weekly Freeman's Journal*, 31 May 1913.

[64] Birrell to Dillon, 19 Dec. 1911, Trinity College, Dublin, Dillon Papers, 6798/182.

[65] Birrell to Dillon, 17 Sept. 1911 ibid. 6798/180.

[66] *Leinster Leader* 1 Mar. 1913. For the hostile or indifferent attitude of Protestant parents to the Irish language—a fact which was well known—see Peter Murray, 'Irish Cultural Nationalism in the United Kingdom State: Politics and the Gaelic League', *Irish Political Studies*, 8 (1993), 62.

[67] *Leinster Leader*, 8 Mar. 1913.

there was 'convincing evidence'[68] that the first move of an Irish parliament would be to introduce compulsory Irish in schools. It is clear that John Dillon no longer held undisputed sway over public opinion, at least on matters of cultural symbolism, though interestingly the majority of County Galway's teachers publicly indicated their support for him on this issue.[69] There is even some evidence that those radical nationalists—who made so much of these matters of cultural symbolism—were capable of inflicting some reverses on the party at the polls on a minor, but not entirely insignificant, scale. For example, in municipal elections held in Dublin, Sligo, Longford, and Wexford in January 1913, several of the candidates put forward by United Irish League branches were beaten by a motley crew of Larkinites, Sinn Feiners, Foresters, and others. Jasper Tully noted: 'This looks a bad preparation for home rule when in important centres East and West and South, official UIL candidates would be rejected at the polls.'[70] He added: 'It can never be forgotten that it was against the old Irish Parliament that the Rebellion of '98 was waged, and an Irish Parliament now, if even only a shadow and a name, gives a loophole for many opportunities in the perilous times that are undoubtedly ahead.'[71] Once again this was precisely the deepest fear of Irish unionism. But Redmond was still entitled to insist that as far as the broad direction of the political destiny of Irish nationalism was concerned, he was still firmly in control. The discontents connected with the language issue apart—discontents which after all had important implications for the rights of a Protestant minority in Ireland—it was still a reasonable claim.

[68] Quoted in the 'In the Gaelic World' column, *Weekly Freeman's Journal*, 12 Dec. 1912.   [69] *Leader*, 1, 8, 15 Mar. 1913.
[70] *Roscommon Herald*, 15 Jan. 1913.   [71] Ibid.

5.

The Road to Civil War?

A difference of opinion has arisen in the Executive committee as to the objects to which the funds . . . should be applied. Some of the Committee urge that constitutional methods of resisting Home Rule have proved useless and that force alone can decide the issue and that, therefore, all funds should be applied to the equipment of the UVF.

The other members of the Committee point out . . . that the funds of the Council . . . should be devoted to the extensive and vigorous prosecution of a campaign by speeches, canvasses and distribution of literature to arouse opposition in England and Scotland.

> Memorandum for submission to Sir Edward Carson,
> 10 June 1914
> Ulster Women's Unionist Council, Public Record Office
> Northern Ireland, D 1507/A/6

The face that is a blend of north and south; the powerful jaw was Ulster, the eye was receptive and communicative like a Southerner.

> Martin Ross Carson in an Ulster village, *Northern Whig*,
> 7 Oct. 1912

The Dublin Castle administration appear to have relied on two principal sources of intelligence on the unionist movement against home rule. One key source was an RIC sergeant, Joseph Edwards, who seems to have penetrated the Ulster Unionist Council. Edwards argued in the summer of 1913 that there was clear evidence that a significant section of the Belfast unionist leadership wished to avoid an explosive conflict with the government. At the private standing committee on 16 May 1913 of the Ulster Unionist Council: ' "the question of compromise" was next brought up by a large amount of correspondence on the subject being read. The majority of those present were in favour of dialogue, but a large minority were in favour of fighting the matter out. The principal speakers in favour of peace were Lord Londonderry, who was in the chair, and Sir James Henderson, the Lord Mayor of Belfast; Sir James Strong and a few others spoke very warmly against anything being done which would savour of compromise.'[1] Carson kept his own counsel and did not side with either faction in this debate, insisting vaguely that he was in the hands of the committee of his Ulster friends. The subject of arming was then broached by Colonel Wallace: 'some warm interchange occurred between Dr William Gibson and Mr Sclater and Captain Hall of the Unionist Clubs and Colonel Wallace and Sharman Crawford and A. P. Dalzell of the Loyal Orange Order as to whether the Council should arm Unionists as Clubmen or Orangemen'. Carson again appears to have kept his views to himself. But, according to Edwards, while there was much grass-roots pressure in favour of the distribution of arms, 'the opinions of those present at this meeting were by a large majority against the purchase of arms'.

On the whole, Carson emerges from the police files as a relative moderate; certainly he was opposed to sectarian violence. 'Among other things dealt with by Sir Edward was the present position of Roman Catholic workers in places where the workers were mixed, and he strongly advised every precaution to be taken in order to secure that such workers would not be interfered with, and it was suggested by some present that this was the right course to adopt and that a great amount of harm had been done to the cause in the past by the neglect of this.'[2] There is evidence that Edwards's reports, which stressed a lack of unionist unanimity on policy issues, were well received by some in the Castle. On 10 June in parliament, Birrell rather tactlessly taunted Carson by coy references to his prime informer's work. But when the district inspectors and county inspectors in Ulster were asked to provide a wider overview, they stressed rather a growing mood of loyalist intransigence. The police could find some fissures, but these were of strictly limited importance: 'Some of those who were not so enthusiastic seem to think that if there were a General Election before the passing of the Home Rule Bill they would, if a Liberal government were returned, be bound to submit and give it a trial, taking no revolutionary action until it was found that the action of the Irish

[1] Report of Sgt. J. Edwards, 20 May, Public Record Office, CO 904/27/302–7.
[2] Report by the same informer, Public Record Office, CO 904/27/298.

government was intolerable.'[3] But, for a government which was determined to resist another election at almost any cost, this was to be of limited comfort. 'Even these say that in the present crisis they are justified in resorting to force if the Bill be passed by the present Parliament which, they hold, has no mandate from the electors to do so.'[4]

It is important to realize that the limits to unionist flexibility were clearly set. At the meeting with businessmen in Belfast when he had urged protection for Catholics, Carson had urged employers to recruit male workers into the UVF. While he had complained about the lack of support for the Carson Fund, the Police Commissioner for Belfast had no doubt that 'some of the most prominent businessmen in the city are associated with the Unionist movement and fulfilling its programme by every means in their power. Probably when called on, those who are less enthusiastic at present will be forced by circumstances to take a more energetic part in the movement.'[5] The County Down inspector confirmed this analysis: 'In County Down, prominent merchants like the Andrews of Comber and Hursts of Drumaness, who were Liberals in their views, as well as many others who held back at first, are now seen to be on Unionist platforms and encouraging others to join the Volunteers.'[6] The county inspector for Antrim voiced the opinion that 'any businessman who held back would be a marked man and his business would be ruined.' His Tyrone counterpart felt that the local businessmen 'will throw in their lot with their protestant fellow countrymen.' Nevertheless, Sir James Brown Dougherty, the under-secretary in Dublin Castle, consistently urged Birrell to discount alarmist police reports of this type. On 13 March 1913 he told his chief Secretary: 'DIs and CIs are lending themselves as willing instruments in a game of bluff.'[7] On rather scrappy evidence—a critique by a Belfast Orange leader of a lack of loyalist activism in Ballymoney—Dougherty concluded: 'It seems reasonable then to assume that the Presbyterian community in Ulster is not prepared to follow hot headed Orange leaders.' He added: 'In reading these reports it is perhaps necessary to remember that these officers are more closely associated with Unionist politicians and with the better classes in Ulster than they are with the masses.' This claim is implicitly reiterated in his effort to

---

[3] Report of the Commissioners of Police, Belfast 1913, Public Record Office, CO 904/27/3. [4] Ibid.
[5] Report on the condition of Ulster, 26 Aug. 1913, ibid. [6] Ibid.
[7] Ibid. See also Leon O'Broin, *The Chief Secretary in Ireland* (London, 1969), 83–5.

discredit the message of the police reports in September 1913. The son of a distinguished surgeon, Dougherty, a former professor at Magee College and a prominent figure at Presbyterian Assembly debates, was personally close to the small minority of Presbyterian home rulers (for example the Revd J. B. Armour), and this undoubtedly influenced his views. This group revelled in its access to government, but almost as an inevitable corollary tended towards a certain self-deception on the subject of popular sentiments. There is considerable evidence that Birrell was fully aware of this and treated Dougherty's opinions with a certain amount of caution: indeed, the government became increasingly circumspect in its attitude towards the Ulster unionist movement.

On 7 July 1913 the unionists won an outstanding admission from the prime minister: 'The soldiers of the King will not be employed against peaceful Ulster protestant opposition to home rule.' It was an important, even critical, development. Carson referred to the subject at a large Orange gathering at Craigavon on 12 July 1913:

Well, the other evening, my colleague and your old friend, Mr James Campbell (*cheers*) made a very remarkable speech, and the most remarkable part of it was that he challenged the Prime Minister to say whether he agreed with Mr Birrell, who stated that it was not the intention of the Government to employ the forces of the Crown against the people of Ulster. Of course, we treat everything Mr Birrell says as a huge joke—and I am not all sure that is not the way he desires to be treated—(*laughter*)—but that was a serious question to ask the Prime Minister but the Prime Minister assented to that proposition. So you see we are getting on. We know now that the forces of the Crown are not to be used against us. I think they have made a wise decision. (*laughter . . .*) The government know perfectly well that they could not tomorrow rely on the army to shoot down the people of Ulster . . . I tell you this, that a day never passes that I do not get—to put it at a really low average—half a dozen letters from British officers asking to be enrolled.[8]

In William O'Brien's view, moderate northern Protestants, infuriated by the lack of government consultation but afraid of large-scale confrontation, now perceived that Carson's strategy had, in effect, been vindicated. Any doubts that they might have had about the wisdom of 'Carsonism' were now rendered irrelevant. 'The Prime Minister and Mr Birrell had allowed themselves to be pushed to the declaration that under no circumstances would the armed forces of

---

[8] *Weekly Northern Whig*, 19 July 1913; *Hansard* lx, 159.

Great Britain be employed to enforce the law made by a Dublin parliament', he told a Cork audience. Such a declaration was a major triumph for the unionist parliamentary party; in this view, O'Brien was quite correct, James Chambers, KC, MP, exulted at Carney Hill: 'He believed no drop of loyalist blood would ever be shed in connection with the fight, they would be able to stave off Home Rule by constitutional means.'[9]

Carson seems to have been greatly encouraged by the apparent crack in the government's resolve. His language became increasingly intemperate. To understand this, it has to be accepted that the home rule crisis was fought primarily through the medium of verbal violence. Any slight hint of public willingness to compromise on Carson's part was seized on by critics as a sign of weakness, and as showing that, in the end, as the liberal *Ulster Guardian* editor W. H. Davey said, his 'bid is higher than the cards he holds'.[10] It must have seemed wiser, therefore, to maintain the rhetorical momentum. At Carney Hill, standing beside Chambers, Carson declared:

Many people ask what will be the use of our drilled men when the time comes. . . . Well, we are not out for oppression, but we are not going to submit to a Parliament composed of the Ancient Order of Hibernians . . . People say to me 'If you resist won't you be doing illegal acts?' I say 'Yes', and the more of them the better. (*great cheers*) You can not carry out opposition to a policy of this kind without illegal acts.

At Banbridge in September, Carson told a UVF demonstration: 'The next time I come to inspect . . . I hope I will see every man with a rifle on his shoulder.'[11] He told another UVF demonstration in the same month:

Drilling is illegal. Only recently I was reading the Act of Parliament forbidding it. The Volunteers are illegal, and the Government knows they are illegal, and the Government does not interfere with them. And the reason is this, the Government knows that the moment they interfere with you you will not brook their interference; the knowledge will be brought home to them that every man is not only in earnest but that you are prepared to make any sacrifice to maintain your liberties. The moment that is understood the Government will know their game is up. Therefore don't be afraid of illegalities. Illegalities are not crimes when they are taken to assert what is the elementary right of every citizen—the protection of his freedom.[12]

---

[9] *Weekly Freeman's Journal*, 23 Aug. 1913.
[10] Ibid., 26 Aug. 1913, 'Protestantism Divided, Will Ulster Fight?'.
[11] Ibid., 27 Sept. 1913. [12] Quoted in *Irish Communist*, no. 58, p. 26.

Towards the end of September, the structure of the Ulster provisional government—to come into effect when the Home Rule Bill was placed in the statute book or 'some other day when appropriate'[13]— was revealed. Despite this rather curious phrasing, this was not an unimpressive exercise. There was a ninety-strong 'military council', supplemented by various smaller departmental committees: a Volunteer Advisory Board; a Personnel Board; a Finance Board; a Railway Board; a Transport Board; a Supply Board, a Medical Board; a Finance and Business Committee; a Legal Committee; an Education Committee; a Publication and Literary Committee; and a Customs, Excise, and Post Office Committee. There were a few notable absentees: why was Robert Lynn, editor of the liberal unionist *Northern Whig*, not on the Publication Committee when the Henderson family, so closely associated with the *Belfast Newsletter*, was so well represented?[14] Nevertheless, the very occasional slightly surprising omission was offset by the remarkably large number of eminent and highly respectable persons—seventeen of them were titled—to give a very public indication of their willingness to serve on the council of a body which Sir Edward Carson had assured them was 'illegal'. The UVF has been described by a distinguished scholar as Europe's 'first fascist army', though in truth much of its style (open drilling, for example) seems to be borrowed more obviously from the local example of Irish Fenianism. Yet several of those on the military council were hardly the fascist type:[15] Sir Robert Kennedy, Viscount Bangor, Lord Dunleath, and Earl Kilmorey were all men of varying, but not insubstantial reputations for broad-mindedness.[16] The marquis of Londonderry shared this approach,[17] while other members of the military council, such as Milne Barbour[18] and Ricardo[19] were later to distinguish themselves by their sense of fair play towards the minority. Lovatt Fraser's picture of another senior military council member, the duke of

[13] *Weekly Northern Whig*, 27 Sept. 1913.

[14] Recently discovered Carson–Lynn correspondence indicates Lynn's unease about the Provisional Government concept. See J. E. Gamble, *Books Relating to Ireland*. (Belfast, 1993), catalogue 94, p. 27, item 270.

[15] Bew, P., Darwin, K., and Gillespie, G., *Passion and Prejudice* (Belfast, 1991), 40–5. For the 'fascist army' theme, see the second note to ch. 1 of Alvin Jackson, *Carson* (Dublin, 1993). [16] Ibid., 20.

[17] Jennifer Pauley's (University of Ulster) work on the Londonderry family is revealing here.

[18] Paul Bew, Peter Gibbon, and Henry Patterson, *The State in Northern Ireland 1921–72: Political Forces and Social Classes* (Manchester and New York, 1979), 77.

[19] Public Record Office CO 906/24–30.

Abercorn, at this moment is suggestive: 'The Duke is sincere enough, but I should say he is d——d uncomfortable at heart in the position in which he finds himself . . . Nevertheless, he can't move back now.'[20] If this was true of Abercorn, who had allowed Baronscourt to be turned into an armed military camp visited by supportive officers on the active service list, it is very likely that it was true of a great many others. But there were those, albeit a minority, who had a decided taste for confrontation.

Inevitably therefore the provisional government was a very dangerous concept. James Craig laudably promised the northern nationalist minority 'equality of treatment' under the provisional government, and that the 'British government would be the model',[21] but who could believe this after the workplace expulsions of 1912? There was a brutal logic of polarization and intimidation at work; at times Carson failed to suppress this tone in his own rhetoric. In a reply to nationalist taunts, he declared at Craigavon: 'They ought to remember, if you commence boycotting, that, just as we are in a minority down in the South and West, there is a minority here—a minority that we desire to live with on terms of amity and friendship.'[22] It is hard to deny the element of threat in such language; this really was the nub of the problem for the provisional government concept. What was its relationship going to be with its own 'disloyal' minority? As Protestant home ruler and Fellow of Trinity College, Dublin, Joseph Johnston, intelligently pointed out:

> The Provisional Government can be given full scope so long as it makes no attempt to govern and remains a mere voluntary association collecting subscriptions, which it prefers to call taxes, from those who are foolish enough to pay them. The trouble will arise when it begins to deal with the half million or so of inhabitants of the province who, though they have signed no covenant to that effect, may safely be depended upon to refuse to pay its taxes or obey its laws? What is it going to do in regard to them? Is it going to ignore them? . . . Is it going to disregard all its own contentions about the rights of minorities and attempt to compel obedience on the part of those who will not recognise its authority?
>
> If it attempts to do so, will they not have as good a moral right to resist as Ulster Unionists say they have to resist the decrees and refuse to pay the taxes of an Irish Parliament, since the impositions of the latter would be at least legal, while those of the former would not.[23]

---

[20] B. Clifford and J. Marsland (eds.), *Lovat Fraser's Tour of Ireland* (Belfast, 1992), 14. Lovat Fraser to Geoffrey Robinson, 8 Oct. 1913.
[21] *Northern Whig*, 17 June 1914.   [22] *Weekly Northern Whig*, 19 July 1913.
[23] *Civil War in Ulster* (Dublin, 1914), 57.

But these problems—all too precisely located—were problems of the future. In the shortrun, the establishment of the framework of a provisional government increased the pressure on the British government, also, in the autumn of 1913, the numbers involved in drilling rose dramatically and with the same effect. As tensions built up, so did the doubts within the UK political élite, and so did the search for an escape route. In a highly publicized letter to *The Times* on 11 September 1913, Lord Loreburn, the former Lord Chancellor and chairman of the 1911 Home Rule Cabinet Committee, suggested a 'conference or direct communication between the leaders in an attempt to reach a common agreement, since parties stood to lose by fighting over the Irish quarrel to the bitter end'. One recent scholar, Patricia Jalland, has correctly insisted: 'For a letter which aroused a storm of controversy it was exceptionally mild and vague . . . Nowhere was any form of Ulster exclusion ever mentioned, since Loreburn disliked the idea, though historians have mistakenly tended to assume that this is what his letter proposed.'[24] Jalland's account of Loreburn's traditional views and of his letter is absolutely correct, but in September 1913 many observers assumed that the letter was a definite sign of softening in the liberal establishment on the Ulster question. It is implicit in Carson's public comment: 'He [Loreburn] is one of those who is accountable for the framing and passing of the Bill, but he now sees the signs that you and I have known all along and that is the warning to the Government.'[25] It is implicit also in Birrell's comment to Dillon on 14 September:

Is not Loreburn too outrageous? Here is a man who for all these years has not only been a pronounced and convinced home ruler but an obstinate and almost pigheaded one, making light of real and outstanding difficulties, pouring intellectual and moral scorn on all those timid and half-hearted Liberals who felt doubts and qualms and *now*, after a lifetime of stress and travail on the eve of the blow being struck, he turns tail and would have us let the stop drop to the very bottom and go back to the days of Isaac Butt and an Inquiry into the best way of governing Ireland![26]

Birrell, who loved a morsel of gossip, angrily attributed Loreburn's sudden loss of resolve to recent conversations with his nearest neighbour in Deal, Ulster Tory Lord George Hamilton. He admitted

---

[24] *Liberals and Ireland* (Brighton, 1980), 127.
[25] *Weekly Northern Whig*, 11 Oct. 1913.
[26] 14 Sept. 1913, Trinity College, Dublin, Dillon Papers, 6799/206.

in the same text: 'I am not altogether happy in my heart about one or two high-placed friends of ours, but I daresay my forebodings are ill-founded. We are all right at the top.'

There followed a week of significant happenings in exalted circles. While Sir Edward Grey was the Minister-in-Attendance on his Majesty the King at Balmoral Castle, the guests included Lord Lansdowne, Unionist leader in the House of Lords. Then Bonar Law, who had visited Lord Lansdowne a day earlier, spent the weekend as a member of King George's house party. Sir John Simon, a much-touted possible successor to Birrell as Irish Chief Secretary, was also known to have visited Balmoral. 'All the movements of eminent politicians have given rise to speculation concerning possible efforts to promote an understanding on the Irish problem.'[27]

Carson wrote to Bonar Law on 23 September 1913: 'As regards the position here I am of the opinion that on the whole things are shaping towards a desire to settle on the terms of leaving "Ulster" out.'[28] At the beginning of October, Winston Churchill confirmed the point in a speech at Dundee. Churchill argued that Carson had often tried to 'restrict and therefore, to consolidate' his case: the claim for 'special consideration' for Ulster was 'very different' from an attempt to block home rule *tout court*. The *Irish Times*, on 9 October 1913, was emphatic: 'Mr Churchill's offer is plain enough. He proposes the exclusion of north east Ulster from the Irish parliament in the hope that she would soon grow weary of her isolation.' Churchill insisted that the government had a mandate for his Irish policies—to the fury of unionists—but, as the *Weekly Northern Whig* shrewdly noted on 11 October, 'There are signs in Mr Churchill's speech that he realises the impossibility of forcing Ulster into a Roman Catholic parliament.'

On 12 October Redmond replied to Churchill from Limerick: 'Mr Churchill in his speech in Scotland alluded to a possible exclusion of a part of Ulster (*cries of "Never!"*) on condition that both parties in England agree to pass the Bill and make it work. Now I have to say here that the suggestion is a totally impracticable and unworkable one. (*cheers*)'[29] Churchill had implied that he had nationalist support for his offer—it was plain now that he had not. Redmond was followed by Joe Devlin, who was most fervently received, and who insisted that 'Ulstermen and Munstermen are bound together by the common bond

[27] *Ballymoney Free Press*, 18 Sept. 1913.
[28] Montgomery Hyde, *Carson* (London, 1953), 339.
[29] *Freeman's Journal*, 13 Oct. 1913.

of nationality ... we demand ... a united Ireland ... under a free constitution'. Redmond was closely observed at this moment by Lovat Fraser, an experienced journalist working for *The Times*. Fraser, who had for many years been editor of the *Times* of India, was unknown in Ireland and travelled with his wife, both adhering 'strictly to the character of tourists'. Fraser reported directly to Geoffrey Robinson on 12/13 October 1913:

I watched Redmond very closely at dinner and at breakfast this morning, as well as at the meeting, and if he is not d——d anxious about the situation I am no judge of men. His speech may read like a poean of triumph, but there was no triumphant note in his voice and demeanour, only intense anxiety. Still his declaration of defiance was absolutely resolute. I should say he has not the slightest intention of receding from his emphatic statement today; and, if he had, then Devlin has not, and he must toe the line as Devlin directs.[30]

Churchill, at any rate, refused to be deflected; on 18 October he told a Manchester audience: 'We shall, I think, progress much better towards a settlement if we Liberals cultivate a habit of thinking about the genuine needs and legitimate apprehension of Ulster Protestants, and if Conservatives all over the country turn their minds increasingly to the problem of satisfying the rights and claims of the overwhelming mass of Nationalist Ireland.'[31] The Ulster unionist Ronald McNeill, who was MP for Canterbury, responded a few days later: 'The people of Ulster would not dream of offering physical resistance for the sake of preventing home rule being given to the rest of Ireland.'[32] As part of this mood in favour of greater dialogue, Carson and Asquith met for two informal discussions, the first on 16 December 1913 and the second on 2 February 1914. Having received Redmond's very public message from Limerick, Asquith was nevertheless still reluctant to grasp the nettle of Ulster exclusion and attempted to keep the talks focused on 'home rule within home rule'. This proposal was too close to the nationalist ideal to be acceptable to Carson; indeed, the very offer of such an impossible package might have aroused Carson's fears as to Asquith's motives. It is clear that Asquith was following a policy of delay, but why? It seems that Asquith simply wanted to keep the Opposition guessing as to his ultimate policy, while perhaps also demonstrating to the nationalist leadership that he was prepared to

---

[30] Clifford and Marsland, *Lovat Fraser*, 18.
[31] *Irish Times*, 28 Oct. 1913.
[32] *Weekly Freeman's Journal*, 25 Oct. 1913.

pursue their strategic objective in so far as it was possible. But there were others in the cabinet who perhaps had darker reasons for supporting a policy of delay. A fortnight before his second meeting with Asquith, Carson received a communication that was both interesting and worrying: on 14 January Constance S. Williams, an informant within the household of a junior minister, wrote:

I am a private Secretary to the wife of one of the Under Secretaries. Members of the government meet at this house secretly and informally at all hours and discuss matters with considerable freedom. Less than a week ago, Mr Asquith, Mr McKenna and Mr Pease were here about the same time. The plan is to procrastinate until the patience of the hooligan element in Belfast is exhausted and they begin to riot. This is the moment when troops (they have decided which regiments are to be sent) will step in and crush the riot and incidentally a few of the loyalists. Mr Asquith still hankers after a compromise and is not much in favour of this policy and is being overruled.

They have agents in Belfast—some pretending to be friendly to your people—who send regular reports and are to say when it is the right moment to strike or not. Mr Lloyd George is the only one who does not think things are serious. He said casually over the tea table: 'Put the Crimes Act in place and the whole thing will fizzle out within a week.'[33]

It is difficult objectively to evaluate this warning: but it was certainly taken seriously by Carson, who intensified his propaganda against mob outbreaks. But this was not, of course, the only aspect of the problem. If some members of the government still hankered after decisive military action of some sort, despite Asquith's apparent disavowal in July 1913, then how was the UVF placed? On 20 January 1914, Carson appears to have been warned by the Antrim UVF (Arthur O'Neill, MP, was commanding officer) that 'if the government acted against the UVF in its present unarmed condition then the Volunteers would be broken: it was insinuated that the supine political masters of the UVF would be to blame for its destruction.'[34] It may be significant that O'Neill was married to Lady Annabel Hungerford Crewe-Milnes,

[33] Public Record Office, Northern Ireland, D 1507/A/5/3. See also Elizabeth Muenger, *The British Military Dilemma in Ireland* (Dublin, 1991).

[34] Jackson, *Carson*, ch. 5. For clear evidence of Carson's earlier reservations, see his Sept. 1913 correspondence with Lady Londonderry, Public Record Office Northern Ireland, D 2846/1/105, quoted in Vivien Kelly, 'Irish Feminists: Britons First, Suffragists Second, and Irish Women Perhaps a Bad Third: An Examination of the Difficulties Facing Suffragists in Ireland at the Time of the Home Rule Crisis' (M.Sc. thesis, Queen's University, Belfast, 1992), fo. 39.

elder daughter of Asquith's cabinet colleague, the earl of Crewe; it is clear that he too was exceptionally well informed about the mood within government circles. On 20 or 21 January, Carson reluctantly gave his support to a most risky course of action—large-scale gun-running. As A. T. Q. Stewart observes: 'Here was a distinguished King's Counsel, a former Solicitor-General, contemplating an act of breath-taking illegality which led to international complications.'[35] Nor could he assume that he would carry all his parliamentary colleagues with him; Godfrey Fetherstonhaugh, MP for North Fermanagh—'I see feeling growing very tense and excited, and as I love Ireland I dread what may follow'—declared at Derrygonnelly that he would 'go far for a settlement that would give us a chance to unite on equal terms with our fellow countrymen'. Fetherstonhaugh stressed that for this to happen the government had to introduce genuine safeguards for the minority; their current proposals in this respect were worthless. Without doubt, 'dread of civil war', in his own phrase, had led Fetherstonhaugh to moderate his unionism. Reading the sympathetic nationalist coverage of Fetherstonhaugh's language in the *Weekly Freeman* on 10 January 1914 can only have infuriated Carson. Would Asquith, still anxious to avoid an open conflagration, take a more nationalist line, encouraged by the emergence of the doubt within the unionist parliamentary party? Carson need not have worried; the prime minister was more worried by the drift towards confrontation.

On 2 February, the eve of the new parliamentary session, Asquith held a critical private meeting with John Redmond.[36] It was a deeply disturbing occasion for Redmond. Asquith made it plain that 'establishment' opinion was shifting in favour of the 'exclusion' of north-east Ulster. In particular, the king had 'become thoroughly convinced of the reality of the civil war threat' and was prepared to consider seriously the dismissal of his ministers and the calling of a general election. Asquith suggested a way out: local administrative control in Ulster and a right of appeal on the part of the majority of its members to the imperial parliament against intolerant action by the Irish parliament. This was a principle which the O'Brienite minority of Irish MPs was prepared to accept; Redmond, however, was not,

---

[35] A. T. Q. Stewart, *Sir Edward Carson* (Dublin, 1981), 83.

[36] For this exchange between Redmond and Asquith, it is now necessary to turn to the brilliant and full account in Nicholas Mansergh, *The Unresolved Question: The Anglo-Irish Settlement and its Undoing*, (New Haven, Conn., 1991), 67–70.

adhering still to a readiness to consider only those proposals which were consistent with an 'Irish Parliament, an Irish Executive and the integrity of Ireland'.

Asquith opened the debate on 9 February by hinting, albeit in exceptionally vague terms, that the government was considering a new 'initiative' with the objective of avoiding civil war. Bonar Law was momentarily disconcerted and felt unable to respond seriously. Carson chose the moment to sound a statesmanlike note. He proposed to discuss an exclusion proposal with his Ulster support base. He also made a striking plea to his 'nationalist fellow countrymen', to try to win over Ulster by sympathetic understanding rather than by force.

Stephen Gwynn regarded this speech of Carson's as a *tour de force*. Gwynn, who was close to John Redmond, insisted that it had had a profound effect on the Irish leader: after all, as junior barristers Redmond and Carson had worked the West Munster circuit together.[37] The speech had contained no reference to the UVF or any possible collision of forces. It drew instead on Carson's own personal brand of liberal unionism; a philosophy which Gwynn acknowledged to be without the taint of sectarianism or the spirit of ascendancy. In response, Redmond felt compelled to make further efforts in the cause of peace.

Carson quickly received an interesting letter from the prime minister's wife. 'You made a noble speech tonight, really brilliant and touching. Even if Henry goes right under in this very difficult and anxious business, I shall never change my opinion about you nor indeed will he. Personality is after all greater than political faith, and when they go together as they go with you, they command a very large world. All the men on our side who count were moved to the core by your speech but I am not writing for them just for myself.'[38] Margot Asquith rather specialized in non-partisan gush but, nevertheless, this letter must have lifted Carson's spirits. Less surprisingly Bishop D'Arcy also wrote, a few days later: 'Your speech in the House has stirred our hearts here and how thankful and grateful we are for it and for the effect which it has obviously produced. A few days ago the outlook was very black. There is a break in the clouds now.'[39] *The Times* embraced Carson's rhetoric: 'No true Irishman . . . nor any

---

[37] Despite his father Malachi's wishes, Trollope's Phineas Finn had avoided the Munster circuit of the Irish Bar; Carson and Redmond did not.

[38] 11 Feb. 1914, Public Record Office Northern Ireland, D/1507/A/5/7.

[39] 12 Feb. 1914, Public Record Office Northern Ireland, D/1507/A/5/8.

Englishman wanted a permanently divided Ireland; the solution was clear, leave Ulster out . . . and trust to the healing influences of time.'[40]

By mid-February mainstream home rulers felt they had cause to worry. On 17 February 1914 the *Westminster Gazette*—'hitherto a staunch and sterling supporter of the Irish claim'—significantly suggested 'compromise'. The heart of nationalist Ireland was troubled. The *Tuam Herald* declared, with more hope than certainty: 'there must be no separation of any single city or county for any time or for all time.'[41] In March 1914 Asquith was finally driven to make a proposal which, he said, was designed to avert civil war and bring about peace. He proposed an amendment which would allow the electorate of each Ulster county, together with Belfast the Derry City, to vote on whether it wished to opt out of home rule for a period of six years and to be treated practically as an English county.[42] At the end of six years, an excluded county was to come in automatically, unless the imperial parliament voted it out. Asquith was clearly depending upon the ambiguities in the scheme to gain the support of both the unionists and nationalists. The provision for inclusion after six years was intended to please the Nationalists, whereas the Unionists were supposed to focus on the possibility of a reprieve provided by the intervening elections. But had Asquith done enough? In mid-February the *Witness* summed up mainstream unionist opinion:

We are sure Ulster Unionists would be prepared to make any sacrifice for peace, but to sacrifice the peace and safety of the future for a period of suspense, which would not be peace, but a preparation for more trouble, is what no Ulster unionist would do, could do or should do, if he was true to his principles and professions and to the Covenant by which he bound himself.[43]

The unionists criticized Asquith's proposals with some vigour.[44] In particular, they disliked the idea that Derry City would be in the Irish parliament but the county of Derry outside it.[45] Above all, they disliked the notion of living 'under a sentence of death', as Carson was to put it in a famous phrase.[46] Redmond had clearly been moved to compromise, but the question remained: had he gone quite far enough? Would he have achieved more by being more generous on the question of a time limit to exclusion? His close aide and colleague, Stephen Gwynn,

---

[40] *The Times* (quoted in *Weekly Freeman's Journal*, 9 May 1914).
[41] *Tuam Herald*, 21 Feb. 1914.   [42] Ibid., 14 Mar. 1914.
[43] *Witness*, 13 Feb. 1914.   [44] Ibid.   [45] Ibid.
[46] Ibid.

certainly felt that this was so and that an opportunity for reconciliation had been missed. 'If a clear proposal of local option by counties without time limit had been put before Parliament and the electorate I do not think our position in Ireland would have been worse than it was made by the proposal of temporary exclusion, and it would have been greatly strengthened in Parliament and in the United Kingdom.'[47]

A difficulty obviously remains about Redmond's motivation during the home rule crisis. His eventual acceptance of some form of exclusion for Protestant Ulster reveals that he was not unalterably wedded to the principle of Irish unity. One of his admirers, J. A. Rentoul, was convinced that Redmond accepted the principle of county option.[48] Why then did Redmond not concede this explicitly earlier in the crisis and thus attempt to gain the initiative by splitting his unionist opponents? As the Ulster unionist MP David Trimble has recently put it: 'If [he] had made a clear offer of four counties in 1913, would there have been a UVF? Would it have fought alone for Fermanagh and Tyrone?'[49] The answer, of course, lies partly in the appeal of the idea of Irish unity to some of his followers. Jasper Tully described the concession of temporary exclusion thus: 'It is an outrage against the ideal of Ireland, a nation for which our patriots poured out their red blood in the days of old. It would not be listened to by the men of '98 or '67, why is it tolerated for a moment now?'[50]

But many more worried about minority rights in the north. As David Sheehy expressed it: 'If the Catholics were deserted, the Orange ruffians would make an end of them.'[51] It is for this reason above all that Redmond believed that he could not afford the domestic political cost of an earlier explicit acceptance of partition. It was an understandable, perhaps unavoidable, decision, but it was no longer one which all Redmond's colleagues could accept with conviction. In 1911 John Redmond had written a glowing introduction to Stephen Gwynn's *The Case for Home Rule*. This text had taken the classic nationalist line: 'Can it seriously be contended that a section of the population in one corner of Ireland have the right to resist the declared will of our Imperial Parliament to which they express their allegiance? Is it loyalty to rebel in sheer excess of loyalty? But a threat of armed resistance in

---

[47] Stephen Gwynn, *John Redmond's Last Years* (London, 1926), 103
[48] J. A. Rentoul, *Stray Thoughts and Memories* (London, 1921), 237.
[49] David Trimble, *The Foundation of Northern Ireland* (Lurgan, 1991), 30.
[50] *Roscommon Herald*, 27 July 1914.
[51] *Western News*, 17 Jan. 1914.

Ulster is no new thing and it cannot be taken seriously.'[52] But by 1914 Gwynn was convinced of the need for explicit compromise. In later years, he felt that Redmond had missed the key moment, but he explained it thus: 'He [Redmond] probably underrated the influence he possessed. It is always easy to persuade Irishmen that if you are going to do a thing you should do it "decently". What is more, a real effect could have been produced on much moderate opinion in Ulster by saying to Ulster: "Stay out if you like, and come in when you like. When you come in, you will be more than welcome." '[53]

The Ulster unionists rejected the new proposal. Their Tory allies, however, had to tread more carefully: to many in England, Asquith seemed to have offered a fair compromise. He had certainly placated Churchill and Lloyd George, who had wanted some special concession on Ulster. Churchill in particular began to direct his fire against unreasonable unionists. Bonar Law found it necessary to respond in apparently flexible terms by making an alternative offer: the prime minister should submit his proposals to a referendum of the whole United Kingdom, rather than just the Ulster counties. Such a notion was entirely unacceptable to the nationalist leadership; Bonar Law had apparently offered to respond positively to Asquith's proposals, but had in fact forced Asquith into a corner. Asquith's offer of a compromise was therefore in itself a failure, but the terms of political debate had been decisively altered—and the alteration was in the favour of the Ulster unionists. As the *Witness* noted: 'He [Asquith] and the Nationalists were telling us for weeks that there would be no exclusion of Ulster or any part thereof, that it was unthinkable and impracticable, and that it was madness of the Unionists to ask for or contemplate it.' With a certain grim satisfaction, the editorial noted that matters had now changed: 'At the eleventh hour and on the verge of the twelfth he has now told us that exclusion is not only thinkable but practicable, that any Ulster county that wants exclusion can have it for six years.'[54] The conclusion of all this was clear: 'The principle of exclusion has been brought into the region of practical politics and it is for the extension of that principle, and without a time limit, that Ulster Unionists should contend.'[55]

There is some evidence that the nationalist leadership failed to realize how much ground they had lost. Redmond insisted that if the

[52] *The Case for Home Rule* (Dublin, 1911), 4.
[53] Gwynn, *Redmond's Last Years*, 103.   [54] *Witness*, 13 Mar. 1914.
[55] Ibid.

concession was not accepted, he would expect Asquith to return to a policy of 'full steam ahead', yet he had demonstrated, however reluctantly, that Irish unity was not an inviolable principle. Fraught as the issue was, the nationalist leaders were inclined to suppress—for their own benefit as much as anyone else's—the full scale of the concession. Recalling these events five years later, John Dillon insisted in a letter to a close constitutionalist ally, John Horgan of Cork, that the Irish party leadership had accepted only a temporary exclusion. Horgan replied that he accepted Dillon's point, but added significantly: 'personally I consider that once the principle of exclusion was conceded it would have been impossible to limit it in time.'[56] It is worth noting that Redmond retained support in nationalist Ireland for this approach: one leading nationalist newspaper rallied behind him:

> The principle of exclusion is in direct antagonism to the views of nationalist Ireland, and to the pronouncements made by Mr John Redmond and the Irish party. While holding out for the maintenance of the nation intact under the Irish Parliament, Mr Redmond has repeatedly declared that there is no length to which he would not go, short of the sacrifice of the principle of the Bill itself, in order to win the consent of Ulster, and the starting of the nation with its new career and with the good will and support of all sections of Irish life. By waiving the principle of exclusion, Mr Redmond and the Irish party have, in our opinion, more than redeemed their pledges to win a settlement by consent if that were possible.[57]

Symptomatically, though, Redmond felt it wise to cancel a Derry mobilization of Ulster nationalists planned for mid-March: most of nationalist Ireland still preferred the notion of allowing unionists to leave *after* a period of inclusion. As Patrick White, MP, told Meath United Irish League: 'If after a time any evidence was shown by the rest of their fellow countrymen that they were intolerant or unfair, I for one, would say that they had the right to get out after a number of years.'[58] Even John Devoy, speaking for American separatists, was prepared to accept this idea,[59] and Horace Plunkett tried unsuccessfully to get Carson to take it up. Most striking of all, however, is the absence of a serious debate reflecting the strategic realities.

---

[56] Horgan to Dillon, 16 Nov. 1919, Trinity College, Dublin, Dillon Papers, 6753/312.   [57] *Leinster Leader*, 14 Mar. 1914.
[58] Ibid., 13 July 1914. For the Derry decision, see J. J. Campbell, *Fifty Years of Ulster* (Belfast, 1941), 58–9.   [59] *Mayo News*, 18 Apr. 1914.

The failure of Asquith's initiative infuriated the cabinet, in particular Winston Churchill. On 14 March Churchill made an explosive speech at Bradford. He described the Ulster provisional government as a 'treasonable conspiracy'. He called for conciliation, but ended his speech with the ominous words: 'Let us go forward and put these grave matters to the proof.'[60] The *Witness* noted on 20 March 1914:

Mr Winston Churchill's bellicose harangue in Bradford on Saturday afternoon indicated a serious and sudden drop in the political barometer of peace . . . It is not long since the meteoric genius was a flamboyant Unionist; now he is a rampant home ruler with the noisy zeal of a turncoat.

But yesterday he was the advocate in Dundee of local parliaments including one for Ulster; today he is all for mobilising the forces of the Crown to shoot Ulster Unionists if they do not at once proclaim his latest shibboleth for the parcelling out of Ireland.

In frustration, Asquith gave his consent to a plan proposed by Churchill and Colonel Seely, the Secretary of States for War, to overawe the Ulster Volunteers by swift and decisive military action. Elizabeth Muenger argues that 'a real fear produced the urge to have it out if Ulster reacted adversely to the troop movements'.[61]

Churchill, it seems had found Carson's provocation—'the government dare not interfere'—too much to bear. The Ulster unionists had been offered a reasonable compromise. They had refused it. Now it was time to bring them to an awareness of the limits of their power. The scheme backfired: at the Curragh Camp, County Kildare, Sir Arthur Paget, the GOC in Ireland, explained his orders so incoherently to his senior staff that fifty-seven cavalry officers, led by their brigadier, Hubert Gough, declared they would resign if ordered north. The government did its best to explain its actions. A White Paper containing eight documents was published on 25 March; on 22 April a further White Paper containing fifty-five documents was published. After the second and more revealing publication, the *Quarterly Review* commented: 'No one could any longer dispute that naval and military preparations, on a larger scale than any carried out by this country since the Crimean War, had been concerted against Ulster by Mr Churchill and Colonel Seely with the general knowledge of the Prime

---

[60] Muenger, *British Military Dilemma*, 198. See also Stewart, *Carson*, 87.
[61] Muenger, *British Military Dilemma*, 202.

Minister.'[62] Seely resigned, but insisted that 'it was never a plot on his part. He simply meant to see that government property was safeguarded.'[63]

On 26 April, the UK public was suddenly made aware that there had been a highly effective unionist counterstroke: the Larne gun-running. 'No amount of organising skill could have carried out such a stroke unless the sympathy and determination of the whole country had been behind it.'[64] Shortly before, Birrell had boasted to a hapless loyalist Portrush fisherman: 'I may tell you that I know everything that is passing in Ulster.'[65] He now looked patently absurd. To the delight of the more ardent Liberal home rulers, Asquith pledged his government to vindicate the full authority of the law. It was an empty enough pledge but, revealingly, the unionist opposition did not act in such a way as would force him to attempt to give his words any real substance. This was not because they feared that Asquith could have vindicated his pledge; rather it was due to a general unease which Carson's tactics had generated. Most British Unionist MPs were characterized by what the *Quarterly Review* called a 'natural reverence for authority'; they felt themselves placed on the defensive by the gun running incident and wished simply to say as little as possible about it. English unionists were much happier with themes of peaceful resistance. On 18 April A. V. Dicey had been moved to address a Belfast audience directly through the columns of the *Northern Whig* on precisely this point: 'I know nothing of Belfast except through the newspapers.' He had, after all, been the advocate, to take the title of his first book, of *England's Case against Home Rule*, but he did not know the strengths and weaknesses of the English character. 'It would never tolerate the violence of a mob. It would never support the side which struck the first blow.' He added ominously: 'the future of the union, which is comparatively nothing, and the welfare of the whole United Kingdom, which to a true Unionist is everything, may be ruined by a sudden exercise, however provoked, by the protestants of Ulster.' Both the government and opposition, therefore, colluded in a defensive reaction to repress the Larne events in so far as it was possible. Carson

---

[62] 'The Home Rule Crisis', *Quarterly Review*, 221/440 (July 1914), 279. For Gough's precise position, see F. W. Beckett (ed.), *The Army and the Curragh Incident* (London, 1986), 371–2.   [63] *Weekly Freeman's Journal*, 18 Apr. 1914.

[64] *Quarterly Review* 221/440 (July 1914), 281. See David Hume, *For Ulster and Her Freedom: The Story of the April 1914 Gun Running* (Larne, 1989).

[65] *Ballymoney Free Press*, 6 Nov. 1913.

himself claimed to be exultant, telling a Bolton audience: 'For years we were jeered at . . . But all this is changed . . . It is no longer jeering. It is all flattery now.'[66] Nationalists could only hope that the effect on *bien pensant* sentiment in Britain would be traumatic. 'The gun-running at Larne', declared the *Weekly Freeman's Journal*, 'has doubled the effect of the Curragh incident upon progressive opinion. It has added a few more drops of steel to that tonic.' Augustine Birrell, Irish Chief Secretary, later summarized the implications rather frankly:

There will always be a difference of opinion as to whether the leaders of the Ulster rebellion against the supremacy of the law should have been prosecuted. As to the offence, the law officers had no doubt. Whatever or how—the rebels were to be tried or how many of them should be put in the dock were more difficult questions to answer. The consequences of not doing anything were obvious to everybody, but politics often consists of balancing one set of grand evils against another set; after consideration the Cabinet, with my concurrence, decided to leave it alone, although by doing nothing they almost negatived their right to be called a government at all.[67]

The parliamentary debate which followed was therefore surprisingly discursive: its most notable feature was Balfour's indication that he was prepared to sacrifice southern unionists in the cause of peace.

The *Northern Whig* defended the Larne operation as a defensive response to Churchill's manœuvres when, in a revealing image, it declared that an entire community had been 'threatened with repetition of the St Bartholomew Day's massacre'.[68] In fact, of course, it had been planned by Colonel Fred Crawford and others some months before. J. L. Garvin probably gives us the clue as to the real originating moment: the signing of the Covenant. By such a public demonstration, the unionists deliberately left themselves without any room for dignified retreat. Contingency plans for the direst doomsday scenarios had to be drawn up by the local leadership.[69] In his classic unionist text, *Ulster's Stand for Union*,[70] Ronald McNeill uneasily acknowledged that the methods of unionism might be said to constitute a 'bad example'. They were only justifiable he says, as the 'lesser of two evils', adding drily: 'But there was something humorous in the pretence put forward in 1923 and afterwards that the violence to

---

[66] *Weekly Freeman's Journal*, 2 May 1913.
[67] *Things Past Redress* (London, 1937), 201.
[68] *Northern Whig*, 27 April 1914.
[69] Public Record Office Northern Ireland, D 1295/2/7.
[70] London, 1992, p. 149.

which the adherents of Sinn Fein had recourse was merely copying Ulster. As if Irish nationalism in its extreme form required precedent for insurrection from Ulster.'

Nor should it be assumed that the guns were in any immediate sense utilizable. As James Craig wisely continued to insist—proving that the *World* journal had been right in its 'celebrity at home' profile to describe him as 'neither a visionary nor a fanatic': 'The effects of a civil war in Ireland would prove calamitous for generations to come and memories of the event would be associated with cruelties that would not readily be forgotten.'[71] A key letter to Sir Edward Carson from Lord Dunleath, who had been involved in the gun-running himself, carefully revealed the gap between belligerent rhetoric and political reality. There were important constraints still in operation.

The general idea in the minds of the men who promoted and organised this movement was to give as strong an expression as possible of their resolve to resist the policy of home rule. Speeches had apparently failed ... we commenced by drilling our Orangemen and our Unionist clubs; [we] gradually trained and equipped them into a fairly efficient force of volunteer cavalry. Finally, we succeeded in providing them with a good supply of arms ...

... Many of us are undoubtedly willing if necessary to risk our lives in defence of what we believe to be our rights and liberties, but I venture to think that our encounter with the armed forces of the Crown would inflict a serious injury upon our cause ... Moreover, I do not believe our men are prepared to go into action against part of His Majesty's Forces.

I quite understand that Unionist politicians would like very much to assert in their speeches that the Volunteers would undoubtedly come out and fight at the first attempt to administer the Home Rule Act, but I venture to express a strong hope that this assertion will not be made or encouraged by the leaders of the Unionist party.

If Ulster is not to be excluded by an Amending Act, I submit with all deference to your superior wisdom ... that our policy should be, in the first instance, one of passive resistance, (especially against the payment of taxes to a Home Rule Parliament. If the enforcement of taxes is left to the Home Rule government, the Volunteers would always be available to resist; our men would like nothing better than to go out against the Nationalists.)[72]

In an important gloss to this passage, Charles Townshend has made the point that in 'a full scale military clash the UVF weaponry would

[71] *Northern Whig*, 17 June 1914.
[72] Lord Dunleath to Sir Edward Carson, 9 Mar. 1915, Public Record Office Northern Ireland, D 1507/A/6.

have created a logistical nightmare'.[73] Expanding on the implications of this observation, Alvin Jackson has noted that Larne merely turned an 'unarmed force' into a 'badly armed force'.[74] There was, as Jackson shrewdly notes, a further complication: 'The UVF had only the capability to fight a "dirty" war, which would certainly have sacrificed political opinion in England to the point where Asquith could have imposed a settlement with impunity.' He summarizes the implications with admirable precision: 'If Larne made the Unionist leadership a more formidable adversary in the eyes of the Liberal government, then it also made a negotiated settlement all the more desirable—and for *everyone* concerned, pre-eminently the Unionists.'[75]

It is, therefore, far from obvious that Larne was the decisive *coup* that it has so often been presented to be. Certainly, those unionists and Conservatives who had depended on the supposed 'plot against Ulster' to inflict terminal damage on the Asquith government were bitterly disappointed. After Larne, Churchill could dismiss their criticism as an 'attack by the criminal classes on the police'.[76] Nevertheless, in localities such as Fermanagh and Tyrone where the two sides lived cheek by jowl in a state of political rivalry, one was now armed and the other was not. Inevitably, nationalist Ireland felt compelled to redress the balance.

The National Volunteers, a smallish organization dominated by nationalist independents and Sinn Feiners, had managed to build up a membership of 7,000 or so by the end to March 1914. Many areas of the country had been left untroubled, however ('Will the tramp of Volunteers soon be heard by the people of Newport?'[77]) But, after Larne, nationalists savagely contemplated 'double standards' in the matter of law and order. Even the *Leinster Leader*, which had supported Redmond's stand on exclusion, observed: 'Why even at the present moment there are batches of decent farmers in the West of Ireland awaiting trial for no greater offence than clearing out a ranch of its cattle in pursuit of an agitation to have the terms and spirit of the Land Purchase Act complied with in order to enable them to return to the possession of the land from which they or their fathers have ruthlessly been evicted.'[78] There is some evidence of middle-class reluctance.

---

[73] *Political Violence in Ireland* (Oxford, 1983), 255.

[74] 'Unionist Myths 1912–85', *Past and Present*, 136 (Aug. 1992), 183.

[75] Ibid. 182–3.

[76] David Dutton, *His Majesty's Loyal Opposition: The Unionist Party in Opposition* (Liverpool, 1992), 237.   [77] *Mayo News*, 14 Feb. 1914.

[78] *Leinster Leader*, 2 May 1914.

John Gleeson, a key figure in the Athy volunteer leadership, noted in mid-May: 'In Athy he regretted that many of the so-called "respectable" classes had not yet joined the movement (*hear, hear*). That class was, however, always on the ditch (*cheers*); and they watched always to see if a movement would be successful before they came in.'[79]

But the world was rapidly changing. For a brief moment Redmondite loyalists like J. P. Farrell tried to hold the line against the advance of the Volunteers. At the beginning of May, Farrell still withheld his support in his Longford constituency, saying that 'for the present I think the time is not opportune.'[80] One of his local critics, Joe Callaghan, declared angrily: 'Longford is a laughing stock for the rest of Ireland.'[81] In truth, it was a hopeless struggle. In reaction to the unionist counterstroke, the membership of this body doubled and perhaps even trebled by the end of May. One of its most notable separatist leaders, Michael O'Rahilly, claimed in mid-May: 'Precautions had been taken to see that no one party or section would get hold of the Volunteer movement.'[82] John Redmond was rather less than happy with this arrangement. On 10 June he issued a manifesto suggesting that the existing provisional central committee of twenty-five members of the Volunteers should be strengthened by the addition of another twenty-five, nominated by the nationalist party, failing which he indicated that the party would take measures to secure control in the different counties and ignore the central body. The provisional committee collapsed after a short struggle. With the whole sentiment of the Irish party behind it, the movement spread like wildfire, and was soon claiming a membership of 100,000. Militarily speaking the Irish Volunteers were perhaps less impressive than the Ulster Volunteers, but politically they were of great importance. For unionists the existence of such a force rendered irrelevant 'the whole system of safeguards' (reserved rights, the power of veto, and the power of overriding legislation) which the Liberals had used to defend the Home Rule Bill.

What becomes of the Home Rule itself in this diabolical process? Home Rule is only possible to a united, homogenous, peaceful people. But Home Rule which is brought about by two-thirds of a community bludgeoning the other third under its jurisdiction is, by no figure of speech, entitled to be called Home Rule. Half the radical platforms of England will be robbed of their

[79] Ibid., 23 May 1914.
[81] Ibid.
[80] *Longford Leader*, 9 May 1914.
[82] *Leinster Leader*, 16 May 1914.

finest rhetorical points. If Sir Edward Carson was a rebel, Mr John Redmond has now gone one better. If it is treason to combine for the purpose of defending your civil and religious liberty it is worse treason to combine on a military basis to coerce a province under your yoke of Home Rule.[83]

This charge may have been unfair, but it was one that gave Redmond genuine grounds for concern.

In this heightened sense of nationalist expectancy Redmond increasingly felt that he could offer no further concessions beyond those he had already offered at the beginning of March. So, despite hints that the government might have wished to offer more to the opposition, on 23 June the Government of Ireland (Amendment) Bill was introduced in the Lords. This proposal did allow for temporary exclusion for six years on a county option basis; but it is worth noting the actual arrangements for the governance of the excluded counties. They were controlled by a makeshift administration under the Lord Lieutenant in Dublin—in other words, so the Ulster unionist felt, under the indirect control of the new Irish parliament. As the *Quarterly Review* noted acidly: 'In fact it is not too much to say that the principle of the so-called exclusion is that the excluded counties are to be represented in a Parliament at Westminster which will not govern them and to be governed by a Parliament in Dublin in which they will not be represented.'[84]

The country seemed to be sliding towards civil war. In July, the Lords returned the bill after amending it to provide permanent exclusion for all nine counties. The Lords also felt that a position of 'Secretary of State' should replace that of Lord Lieutenant—though it is clear that the government remained committed to the idea that one or perhaps two senior figures should handle both relations with Dublin and the excluded area at the London end. Asquith indicated that he could accept little of the argument advanced by the Lords. The Buckingham Palace Conference on 21–4 July failed to find a way out, despite the genuine warmth of the Redmond–Carson relationship. Going into the conference, Carson received advice from Lord Milner: 'I hope you stick out for six counties as a minimum. It really is too monstrous that they should make a row about leaving some of their people under the imperial parliament, when we are asked to leave an

---

[83] *Witness*, 19 June 1914.
[84] 'The Home Rule Crisis', *Quarterly Review*, 221/440 (July 1914), 290. For similar fears, see the House of Lords debate on 2 July 1914, *Hansard*, xvi. 911–18.

even larger number of ours in the rest of Ireland under a brand new government in Dublin.'[85] Carson hardly needed such advice but he kept to it anyway. As Stephen Gwynn records: 'Even if adjustment had been possible on the question of the time limit, neither would give up the debatable counties, Tyrone and Fermanagh, in which nationalists had a clear though small majority of the population, but in which the Ulster Volunteer organisation was very strong.'[86]

Which way was the government to turn now? It did not need John Devoy to tell it that the nationalist Volunteers proved 'that Ireland cannot be trifled with.'[87] But the *Witness* reporter inevitably felt that the UVF were a very much more formidable force. 'As I looked into the faces of the Volunteers I saw the firm set features and the flashing eyes of men such as I never saw in the Phoenix Park. Every man had a Mauser rifle on his shoulder, and screwed on the Mauser rifle was a flashing pointed bayonet.'

Turning to the academic Sir Henry Craik, Tory MP for Glasgow and Aberdeen universities, who was on a visit to the province, the *Witness* reporter commented 'these are the men that Mr Winston Churchill wants to shoot down as not fit to live'. Sir Henry's reply was brief and to the point: 'The idea is monstrous—the Empire will probably soon need these men to protect the East coast of England from the invasion of the Kaiser.'[88] Craik was correct: the First World War transformed the context of Irish political manœuvring; but not before one last local drama.

Inevitably, the gun-running at Larne provoked a nationalist response in July. The Irish Volunteers elegantly designed their Howth gun-running as an open challenge to the authority of the government. Even with military assistance, the police were unable to prevent the distribution of the arms. Tragically, however, soldiers shot dead three members of a hostile crowd at Bachelor's Walk. This disaster had

[85] Public Record Office Northern Ireland, D 1507/A/6/40.

[86] Gwynn, *Redmond's Last Years*, 122. On the afternoon of 24 July Asquith persuaded Dillon and Redmond to drop the time limit idea (see B. B. Gilbert, *David Lloyd George, the Organiser of Victory* (London, 1992), 105), but lost the benefit because of events at Howth on 26 July.

[87] *Mayo News*, 20 June 1914.

[88] *Witness*, 12 June 1914. For a recent discussion of the outbreak of war in relation to the Irish issue—concentrating on Asquith, Churchill, and Prince Lichnowsky, (the German Ambassador in London)—see Brendan Clifford, 'How to Start a World War Without Obviously Trying (1914)', *Problems of Communism and Capitalism*, 36 (Feb. 1992), 8–12.

important consequences. Naturally, Redmond, in a dignified parliamentary intervention, drew attention to the apparent partiality in the administration of the law. Ulster unionists were able to import arms and march in large armed groups—why not Irish nationalists? Interestingly, neither Bonar Law nor Carson made the slightest attempt to deny that Redmond had a strong case. Bonar Law declared: 'I do not blame in any shape or form the Nationalist volunteers for what they did yesterday.'[89] They simply argued that, confronted with the depth of Ulster resistance, the Liberal government had had two choices: either to retreat in its legislative proposals or to enforce the law with vigour. It had failed to do either. The government reacted by scapegoating—with, some felt, an indecent degree of haste—the unfortunate assistant commissioner W. Harrel, son of Sir David Harrel, one of Dublin Castle's most reflective, moderate, and respected senior officials.[90] Inevitably this left a bad taste in the mouth; Harrel believed that he had obtained the consent of Birrell's most senior subordinate, the Under-Secretary Sir James Brown Dougherty, for his attempt to stop the gun-running. Twenty years later when Dougherty died, his *Irish Times* obituarist argued that his behaviour on that critical day had been indecisive at best:

Harrell, having heard of the landing of arms, sent a large body of constables to Howth. At the same time, he told Dougherty of the facts. [Harrell then] 'failed to get into communication' with the constabulary . . . [and] decided it was his duty to send troops . . . It has never been denied that the Under Secretary at first concurred in sending out the police with the object of seizing the arms. Some time after Mr Harrell left the telephone, Sir James Dougherty seems to have changed his mind, and accordingly he drew up a minute to Mr Harrell directing that forcible disarmament of the Volunteers should not be attempted, but that their names should be taken and the destination of the arms traced. This was drawn up at five o'clock—after the affray was over—and did not reach Harrell, after a further delay, until 5.45. At first Birrell hid these facts of timing from the House of Commons.[91]

In fact, this version is open to challenge. It was denied at the time that Dougherty had made such a verbal order (see, for example, the

---

[89] *Hansard*, 5th ser., 1040, 27 July 1914.

[90] K. Tynan, *The Years of the Shadow* (London, 1919), 59–63. The war allowed Harrel to reconstruct a naval career outside Ireland. Cf. L. Ginnell, DORA *at Westminster*, (Dublin, n.d.), 15.

[91] *Irish Times*, 5 Jan. 1934. For Dougherty's side of the question, see J. R. B. McMinn, *Against the Tide* (Belfast, 1985), 151. J. B. Armour to J. B. M. and W. S. Armour, 1 Oct. 1914.

Weekly Freeman's Journal on 1 August 1914) and his written clarification was said to have been written at three o'clock, the eventual confrontation taking place an hour later. Harrell, it was claimed, was unavailable because he was consulting with associates in Kildare Street, 'the headquarters of militant Unionism in Ireland'. Whichever of these versions is correct, many believed that Harrell had, at the very least, been placed in a rather difficult position. The government's moral authority suffered a blow; Birrell had shown a queasy willingness to sacrifice the son of a friend. Only the war allowed young Harrell to reconstruct his career, and then only in the navy a long way from Ireland. Dublin Castle had revealed a fatal incapacity; some felt even a moral numbness.

The Howth gun-running also created a new hero for radical nationalists—the egotistic, apparently brave Anglo-Irish literary figure of Darrell Figgis who, along with Hobson and MacDonagh, had 'talked Harrell to a standstill'[92] at the celebrated confrontation on the Malahide Road. Privately, the Irish party leaders feared Figgis. William Doris, MP for Mayo West, whose constituent Figgis was, wrote to John Dillon: 'I know that during some land troubles in Achill about a year ago he [Figgis] was asking the people to smash and shoot all before them—just what I was telling them to avoid at the time.'[93] But such reservations could hardly be voiced in public. The *Western People*, a mainstream constitutionalist journal, referred glowingly to 'the role played by Figgis in the Achill land war'.[94] Figgis himself penned an article for *TP's Weekly* on the Redmondite theme of a reconciliation between Ireland and the empire: 'It is early days to speak of Ireland and the Empire', he declared ominously.

---

[92] Townshend, *Political Violence in Ireland*, 275. For a 'fictional' account of this and other episodes, see Eimar O'Duffy's eye-witness novel *Wasted Island* (London, rev. edn. 1929).
[93] Doris to Dillon, 3 Oct. 1914, Trinity College, Dublin, Dillon Papers, 6753/355.
[94] *Western People*, 6 Sept. 1914.

6.

The Project of 'Redmondism':
Articulation and Collapse

In fact the national movement itself was almost hijacked by his
Majesty's Imperial Government . . . [which] persuaded John
Redmond, the leader of the Irish parliamentary party, to become
a recruiting sergeant for the imperial forces.

> Fr. Brendan Bradshaw, *Irish Times*, 20 Apr. 1992

Was there any perceptible change in public opinion in Ireland
towards the parliamentary party and the British government
during those short twenty months, or did a lightning change
result after the Rising? A cursory glance at the facts corroborates
the view that Redmond and his party had no serious challenge in
Ireland (except for Carson and the Orangemen) before 1916.

> F. X. Martin, '1916—Myth, Fact and Mystery', *Studia*
> *Hibernica*, 7 (1967)

The outbreak of war immediately changed the rules of the game for
the leaderships of the two principal Irish factions. The Irish unionist
leadership was now inhibited; they felt that they had lost their freedom
of action. They also felt that the government—taking unionist support
against Germany for granted—would make new efforts to placate
Redmond, thus increasing the nationalist leadership's bargaining
power. As John O. Stubbs has recently concluded: 'The Unionists as a
result of the war had lost their greatest weapon, the threat of civil war
in Ulster. They were imprisoned by their patriotism. Conversely, the
nationalists had gained considerable political leverage.'[1] On 30 July,
Bonar Law had persuaded Asquith that the issue of home rule—and
any amending bill—should be postponed until after the impending
war. Redmond, however, insisted on the Home Rule Bill being placed

---

[1] 'The Unionists and Ireland 1914–18', *Historical Journal*, 33/4 (Dec. 1990), 871.

upon the statute book. Despite angry unionist objections, Asquith accepted Redmond's arguments on this point. The prime minister attempted to mollify the unionists by suspending the operation of the bill until the end of the war and undertaking to bring in an amending bill before the implementation of home rule. There is little doubt that Redmond had at this moment extracted the maximum from a complex and difficult situation. The hidden danger lay in the government's need to make a 'compensating' action in favour of the unionists.

Redmond's speech on the 15 September 1914 gives us a vital clue to his future strategy. Perhaps, because the unionists had already left the House of Commons in disgust, its genuinely conciliatory content—especially on the theme of coercion of unionist counties—did not have the effect it deserved. Redmond clearly also hoped that common sacrifice in the war effort would transform nationalist–unionist relations in Ireland. It was to be a major theme of the last phase of his leadership.

The amending bill is still on the stocks—that is to say an Amending Bill. . . . I believe this delay, this moratorium may lead—and I pray and hope that it will—to an amending Bill very different from that about which we have been quarrelling in the past. There are two things that I care most about in the world of politics. The first is that this system of autonomy which is to be extended to Ireland shall be extended to the whole country and not a single sod of Irish soil and not a single citizen of the Irish nation shall be excluded from its operation. Let me say—and this may perhaps surprise some Honourable Members, but it has been my view all through—that the second thing that I most earnestly desire is that no coercion shall be applied to any county in Ireland to force them against their will to come into an Irish government. At the moment, as everybody knows, these two things unfortunately are incompatible. Will they be incompatible after an interval of some months, as these months will be occupied by the Irish people?[2]

Nevertheless radical nationalists have always argued that Redmond threw away a great political opportunity in the months of August and September 1914. It is claimed that he should have exploited Britain's international vulnerability for Irish purposes. As the son of one of the leading separatists, Aodogan O'Rahilly, has recently noted:

It does not seem to have occurred to Redmond that this was his chance to hold the British up to ransom. The least he should have insisted on, if the Irish promised not to make any trouble, was a written assurance from Carson and

[2] *Hansard*, 5th ser., 907.

Bonar Law that in return for his commitment, they would accept the Irish Home Rule Bill which had been passed by Westminster.[3]

Such a course would have implied a willingness on Redmond's part to allow the triumph of German arms in France. John Redmond implemented instead another strategy: despite contrary advice from a group of his close supporters including Colonel Maurice Moore, chief of the Volunteers, and his brother Willie he moved towards open advocacy of Irish enlistment in the British armed forces. When the Home Rule Bill was formally given the royal assent on 18 September, Redmond immediately emphasized his support for the British cause in the war. Elizabeth, countess of Fingall, declared: 'The Irish leader, being a gentleman, put his cards on the table and did not try to bargain with England in her hour of need.'[4] At a review of Irish volunteers at Woodenbridge on 20 September, with a 'full heart' and 'amongst friends',[5] Redmond at home in Ireland made his message absolutely explicit. He urged them to fulfil their twofold duty: to defend the shores of Ireland and to 'account for yourselves as men, not only in Ireland itself, but wherever the firing line extends, in defence of right and freedom and religion in this war'. Colonel Moore reportedly believed that this 'political harangue' was a mistake; Redmond himself had wanted to delay such a speech. But, as Stephen Gwynn acknowledges, such a formal declaration could not have been long delayed in any event.

Although Redmond's words were received without challenge, it is worth noting that one of his allies, Thomas Scanlan, MP for Sligo, was already facing difficulties. Scanlan, an active constituency MP, had particularly close relations with the British Liberals, and he was understandably anxious to support Redmond's stand. Immediately after the royal assent, he returned to his Sligo constituency and seemed to defend the policy of the Irish party leader with enthusiasm. James Connolly, one of the most eloquent critics of 'Redmondism', had visited the town a few days before.[6] Against Connolly's message, and not without some exaggeration, Scanlan told the crowd in Sligo town: 'We have got home rule not for a part of Ireland but for the whole of Ireland. The statute which was yesterday enacted on the

---

[3] *Winding the Clock: O'Rahilly and the 1916 Rising* (Dublin, 1991), 141.
[4] *Seventy Years Young: Memories of Elizabeth, Countess of Fingall, told to Pamela Hinkson* (Dublin, 1991), 360.
[5] Stephen Gwynn, *John Redmond's Last Years* (London, 1926), 355–60.
[6] Greaves, *Connolly*, p. 378.

statute book makes Ireland free but the same statute binds Ireland indissolubly to the British Empire.'[7]

At this point, Scanlan's speech—which obviously slurred over the danger of partition—ran into trouble. His positive reference to links with the British empire provoked an outburst of indignation. A voice from the crowd cried out: 'You are a damned liar Scanlan',[8] and disorder ensued. Scanlan attempted to continue: 'without the recognition of our rights', but another voice shouted 'to hell with the Empire',[9] and there was further disorder. Scanlan again attempted to continue: 'Without the recognition of our rights Ireland had been discontented but now Ireland takes alongside Canada, New Zealand, South Africa and Australia her rightful place in the British Empire.'[10] At the request of the mayor, Mr Joseph O'Beirne, the platform party proceeded to sing 'A Nation Once Again' from the upper window of their hotel. As this was in progress, several members of the crowd in the street below engaged in a spirited bout of fisticuffs and the proceedings terminated abruptly. There was a significant sequel: immediately the Sligo United Trades Council debated the incident because it was clear that prominent figures in the Sligo labour movement had been involved in the anti-party disturbance. The exchanges between the pro- and anti-Redmond factions were explicit. Pro-Redmondite F. F. Gallagher told J. McGowan: 'You want the Germans to come out on top but we don't.'[11] But the condemnation of the President of the Trades Council, John Lynch, by that body was withdrawn a week later.[12] This second meeting was chaired by a leading Larkinite, P. T. Daly, secretary of the ITUC and a man with strong Irish Republican Brotherhood and Sinn Fein connections.[13] In short, the radical nationalist subculture of Sligo labour had made its point and stood its ground. Within a few weeks, Jasper Tully, also a sarcastic and long-standing critic of Redmondism, was alleging that a later attempt by Scanlan to recruit for the British army in Sligo had provoked a 'hot scene'.[14]

---

[7] *Sligo Independent*, 26 Sept. 1914. For his connections with Liberalism see Scanlan to Dillon, 23 Feb. 1912, Trinity College, Dublin, Dillon Papers, 6760/158.
[8] *Sligo Independent*, 26 Sept. 1914.   [9] Ibid.   [10] Ibid.
[11] Ibid.
[12] Ibid., 3 Oct. 1914. For Sligo generally, see M. Farry, *Sligo 1914–21: A Chronicle of Conflict* (Trim, 1992), ch. 3; and D. Carroll, *They Have Fooled you Again* (Dublin, 1993), 37–9.
[13] Adrian Pimley, 'The Working Class Movement and the Irish Revolution, 1896–1923', ch. 9 in D. G. Boyce (ed.), *The Revolution in Ireland 1879–1923* (London, 1988), 200.   [14] *Roscommon Herald*, 26 Oct. 1914.

Redmond's position on the war immediately initiated a split in the volunteers. Overwhelmingly the rank and file supported the Irish party leader: out of 170,000 volunteers, only 12,000 supported Eoin MacNeill's breakaway group of 'Irish Volunteers'. Redmond's 'National Volunteers' were obviously much the larger group. But as Stephen Gwynn, a strong supporter of Redmond, admitted, the split in Dublin was a rather different affair: 2,000 out of 6,700 volunteers supported MacNeill. Indeed, Redmond had lost two of the strongest battalions in the city.[15] This was the group which, Gwynn acknowledged, along with James Connolly's Irish Citizen Army, was to 'change the course of Irish history' by planning a rising with German assistance.[16] In part, this development reflected the material conditions of life in the Irish capital. Almost alone of the large cities of the British Isles, Dublin experienced not prosperity but depression during the war, with rising prices for foodstuffs and fuel and high unemployment.[17] The basis for serious disaffection clearly existed. Those sections of the Dublin working class and the middle-class intelligentsia who provided the constituency for the Easter Rising were decidedly outside the traditional constituency of the Irish parliamentary party. Yet it would be a mistake to lay exclusive emphasis on Dublin.

The private correspondence of the Irish party confirms the existence of difficulties in some significant rural instances. On 8 October 1914 J. P. Farrell, MP for North Longford, wrote to Dillon; in particular he noted the defection of South Longford's Irish Party MP, ex-Fenian John Phillips:

I am sorry to have to tell you we are getting a good deal of trouble here as to Redmond's action *re* recruiting. Phillips has gone pro-German mad and is fiercely denouncing Redmond in all directions. Frank McGuinness, who was secretary for years and a staunch supporter of the Party in all weathers up to this, has gone dead against us and is using all his influence there against the Party and the policy of its leader and is quite Sinn Fein.[18]

---

[15] Gwynn, *Redmond's Last Years*, 180.

[16] D. Greaves, *1916 as History* (Dublin, 1991); *Sunday Press*, 31 Mar. 1991.

[17] D. G. Boyce, *Nineteenth-Century Ireland: The Search for Stability* (Dublin, 1990), 247. See also Peter Murray, 'Citizenship, Colonialism and Self-Determination: Dublin within the United Kingdom 1880–1918' (Ph.D. thesis, Trinity College, Dublin, 1987), chs. 5 and 6, and the stimulating article by Tom Dooley, 'Southern Ireland, Historians and the First World War', *Irish Studies Review*, 4 (autumn 1993), 5–9. On wartime taxation, though, see Redmond's key statement, *Weekly Northern Whig*, 1 Apr. 1916.

[18] Trinity College, Dublin, Dillon Papers, 6753/701.

Tom O'Donnell sent similar news from Tralee, while Sir Walter Nugent passed on to Dillon a significant letter from Father O'Reilly, curate of Tang, County Westmeath. The news was not good: 'Our branch has taken neither side', but the 'general tendency' of the Volunteers 'is against Mr Redmond. The priests of Ballymore, Ballinacargy, Miltown and Tubberchase tell me that things among the rank and file are likewise in their district.'[19] The priest suggested a compromise, but one implicitly weighted against Redmond: those who joined the volunteers had to give a commitment to defending Ireland. This rule was to be so stringent that no volunteer was to be accepted for any future Irish corps unless he could present a written discharge from the superior of his company or battalion. While billed as a 'compromise', nothing could have been further from Redmond's 'tone' on this issue.

Redmond devoted much of October to the measured exposition of his case. He felt he had been forced into a hasty exposition by local pressure at Woodenbridge; in later speeches he outlined what he considered to be a rather more rounded explanation of his views. J. J. Lee has explained the underlying basis of Redmond's strategy: 'No one genuinely committed to Irish unity could have acted differently from Redmond in the autumn of 1914'.[20] This is clearly true; but it is possible to go even further—even assuming the existence of some form of partition, Redmond had no choice but to act as he did, in order to retain at least some influence on the shape of such a settlement. In response to his critics, Redmond gave two classic statements of his position. They are as pointed and as serious as anything he ever said in his public career, and go to the heart of the whole case for parliamentary nationalism. The first speech was given at Wexford at the beginning of October 1914:

People talk of the wrongs done to Ireland by England in the past. God knows standing on this holy spot it is not likely any of us can ever forget, though God grant we all may forgive, the wrongs done to our fathers a hundred or two hundred years ago. *But do let us be a sensible and truthful people.* Do let us remember that we today of our generation are a free people. (*cheers*) We have emancipated the farmer; we have housed the agricultural labourer; we have won religious liberty; we have won free education; . . . we have laid broad and

[19] Ibid. 6758/760, 3 Oct. 1914. For O'Donnell, see his biography by J. A. Gaughan, *A Political Odyssey* (Dublin, 1983), 96. For Father O'Reilly, see B. MacGiolla Choille, *Intelligence Notes 1913–16* (Dublin, 1966), 119.

[20] *Ireland 1912–85: Politics and Society* (Cambridge, 1990), 21.

deep the foundations of national prosperity and finally we have won an Irish Parliament and an Executive responsible to it. (*cheers*) I say to Ireland that all these things, every one of them, is at stake in the war.[21]

This relatively relaxed attitude towards Ireland's historic grievances against England—or at any rate their contemporary relevance—became a marked feature of Redmondism. A United Irish League organizer, M. J. Conway, fused it with concern for Belgium's fate at German hands: 'if their lot was cast in with Belgium they would know what despotism was. They would see their cathedrals ... a pile of smoking ruins, their Cardinal Primate a prisoner, hunted like a felon ... a thousand times worse than the accursed Cromwell himself.'[22] Of course, it was a new experience for Irish audiences to learn from their leaders that their own sufferings were now firmly in the past or that other peoples were being treated more savagely by history. Then at Kilkenny a week later Redmond offered a rare glimpse of his vision of the future:

On this question of industries, town industries, I have never been one of those who desire to see Ireland turned into what is called an industrial country—that is, into a country studded over with Belfasts or Manchesters or Liverpools or great cities of that kind. Our people are far happier, far better off, both socially and morally, in my opinion (*hear, hear*), in a country which is in the main an agricultural country, than they are in these great seething masses of population like those to be found in the Black Country in England. (*hear, hear*) I therefore have never been ambitious of seeing great industries spreading over our country. But what I do want to see, and what we must see in the future, is, in every city like Kilkenny a certain number of small industries which will provide employment for the surplus population (*hear, hear*).[23]

This was the commonsense wisdom of the Irish parliamentary party. Daniel Boyle, the Manchester AOH alderman who was MP for Mayo North, fully supported Redmond's vision: 'I have shared that view for a long time.' Boyle told the North Mayo executive of the United Irish League at Ballina: 'I hope to see a comparatively prosperous, happy, pastoral people, retaining their native purity and singularity of habit and manners and their pure morals.' There were many things more important than the mere accumulation of wealth. These included 'the old traditions of bygone days, our charming family and Catholic life,

[21] *Weekly Freeman's Journal*, 10 Oct. 1914.
[22] *Tipperary People*, 15 July 1915.
[23] *Weekly Freeman's Journal*, 24 Oct. 1914.

the brave chivalry of our men, the purity of our women, the things that we are proud of before the world.'[24] These agreeable arrangements would, however, be enjoyed by a population of some twenty million, according to South Mayo MP John Fitzgibbon.[25] The social vision of 'Redmondism' was strikingly similar to the social vision of 'de Valeraism' as expounded in inter-war Ireland. It is clear that unrealistic assumptions about Irish population growth and economic development in the twentieth century were shared by both the parliamentary and the separatist tradition.

Nevertheless, it is worth noting in this context that late Redmondism—partly as a result of Joe Devlin's prompting—was offering a rather different view of Westminster's recent and also future role in Irish affairs. The United Irish League leadership, which had initially been rather suspicious of 'new liberalism', became an increasingly relaxed advocate of the application of such welfare reforms (especially in the field of pensions and insurance) to Ireland. It is true that, at the onset of the home rule crisis, mainstream nationalist opinion insisted on the importance of fiscal independence: Ireland should learn to shoulder her own responsibilities instead of being demoralized by 'British doles'. It was openly acknowledged that by 1910–11 Irishmen received over 1 million more in benefits, mainly for old-age pensions and land purchase, than they paid in taxes. But the unionists who wanted this arrangement to continue were denounced, not for the last time, as 'spongers'.[26] Many nationalists felt that old-age pensions paid a debt owed to history: the imperial exchequer should assume responsibility for all Irish pensions granted before home rule, but beyond this temporary charge Ireland should be responsible for her own revenue expenditure, and pursue a broadly independent economic policy. But under pressure from Joe Devlin dependence was further increased when the Irish party accepted the application of National Insurance to Ireland. Irreversibly, as the crisis unfolded, both unionist and dissident Liberal pressure forced Asquith to reduce the amount of fiscal autonomy on offer: publicly reluctant, the Redmondites—with only a tiny number still attending the financial debate—conceded their ground in order to preserve the principle of a Dublin parliament. 'Self government without the control of taxation and

---

[24] *Western People*, 1 Nov. 1914.   [25] Ibid., 14 Nov. 1914.

[26] Tom Kettle, *Home Rule Finance* (Dublin, 1911), 22, 70. Patricia Jalland, 'Irish Home Rule Finance: A Neglected Dimension of the Irish Question 1910–1914', *Irish Historical Studies*, 23/91 (May 1983), 233–53.

expenditure is at best an unhopeful experiment',[27] noted Stephen Gwynn.

Gwynn presented Redmond as having no realistic alternative. In theory, he conceded, their opponents were right: the O'Brienites argued cogently that Ireland was already over-taxed and needed to free up resources for development. But Redmond simply could not have achieved major reductions in the unproductive expenditure of the Irish government. Gwynn presents this as inevitable in any policy of conciliation of vested interests, and this is perfectly true, though it is worth remembering that the RIC was an 80 per cent Catholic body.[28] In other words, the political space to cut expenditure did not exist. On the other hand, Irish taxes might be paying for welfare schemes more appropriate to a highly industrialized country—or so the argument went. Nevertheless, it was receiving these social benefits at a bargain price. The logic then was to accept a continuing subvention of £2 million—after all this was hardly an ungenerous offer from London. The painful choice between nationalist principle and immediate economic advantage was resolved in favour of economic advantage— although bitter nationalist critics could always insist Ireland was owed some £300 million in over-taxation since the 1850s.

The result was a certain ambiguity in nationalist tone. Tom Kettle, one of the most ardent exponents of economic nationalism in theory— he coined the phrase 'spongers' to describe the unionists—now accepted 'a subsidy, and what we prefer to call conscience money and restitution for past over-taxation. It would enable them to face the future as a going concern.'[29] At the end of 1911 Tim Healy, who tended to be authoritative about such clerical views, claimed that the Irish bishops were opposed to the Insurance Act. But not all bishops took this view. The Most Revd Dr Clancy observed: 'we have been in the habit hitherto of indulging in abuse of the English government in this country . . . But at last, a change has come over the spirit of the scene, and the English government apparently is ashamed of its treatment of Ireland in the past, has earnestly set itself to the task of making amends for its misdeeds . . . We may take it, therefore, that the National Insurance Act, which is the most recent expression of the policy of the present government, contains many benefits which will

---

[27] *Redmond's Last Years*, 74–5.
[28] *Weekly Freeman's Journal*, 23 Aug. 1913.
[29] Ibid., 6 Jan. 1912. See also Kettle's lecture, 'The Economics of Unionism', given to the National Liberal Club, *Weekly Freeman's Journal*, 20 Jan. 1912.

prove of the utmost importance to our people.'[30] John Dillon was of a similar sanguine view:

Let me say one word as to the Insurance Act. The Insurance Act undoubtedly will require a good deal of amendment in order to fit it to Irish conditions (*hear, hear*) but what I want to recommend to the attention of the people of Ireland is this, that by applying the Insurance Act to Ireland we obtained a sum of £500,000 a year which would undoubtedly have been lost to Ireland if we had not taken the Act, and when we get Home Rule we have the money and we can alter the Act just as we like. (*cheers*) What I look forward to is this, and I look forward to it with confidence, that with the aid of the Insurance Act and the money that is coming to us under it, and the Old Age Pensions Act, we shall be able under a Home Rule Government to completely sweep away the whole poor law system of Ireland and reduce, and substantially reduce, the rates of the country. (*cheers*)[31]

Devlin, of course, was the most ardent exponent of social reform. The Irish party did in fact act to eliminate the medical benefits for Ireland from the new legislation. This led even an ardent nationalist like James Connolly, in a moment of despair, to suggest that the union was likely to bring more social progress than home rule.[32] But Devlin soon changed his mind, and the government, under pressure, appointed a committee to look at the issue.[33] Devlin was also quite prepared to draw out the 'politics' of the 'new economics'. At the National Convention of the United Irish League in Donegal on 17 August 1915, Devlin argued:

It is all very well to say that Ireland has no interest in the war. Thirty years ago, or still more, fifty or seventy years ago, that might have been true. But the relations between Ireland and the Empire have undergone a transformation since then . . .

I am not forgetting the Report of the Financial Commission, nor any fact connected with the past, when I say that it is the truth that the fortunes of Ireland are inextricably and willingly bound up with the fortunes of Britain in this present war . . .

England today is not our enemy. For twenty years we have been winning back our own, and day by day the effect of the legislative measures which have been passed for this country is doing much to build up the fabric of Irish prosperity. The winning of Irish land, the housing of our agricultural workers,

---

[30] *Weekly Freeman's Journal*, 18 May 1912.   [31] Ibid., 21 Sept. 1912.

[32] Brendan Clifford, *James Connolly: The Polish Aspect*, (Belfast, 1985), 97.

[33] See Ruth Barrington, *Health, Medicine and Politics in Ireland 1900–70* (Dublin, 1987), 39–63.

the improvement in the educational system, the beneficial influences of old age pensions and many other of the reforms that have been won for Ireland have created new and happier conditions.[34]

Even more significantly, the next day, Joe Devlin, as president of the Ancient Order of Hibernians, drew attention to the growth of that body at a meeting in Parnell Square, Dublin. Membership had increased by some 29,000 in the last four years, making a total of 234,500, including some 159,000 in the insurance section. Devlin's enthusiastic embrace of UK social reform went further than that of the Redmondite leadership as a whole; but it remains the case that it was compatible with Redmond's broad and increasingly impassioned disavowal of separatism. In this Redmond insisted that he was merely expounding the mainstream Irish political tradition. As he noted in a formal presentation of his underlying political philosophy in the *Weekly Freeman's Journal*:

What is the theory of Home Rule? What is the basic theory of the whole constitutional movement for the last century in Ireland? The theory all through the century, put forward by Daniel O'Connell, put forward even by the '48 men when they quarrelled with Daniel O'Connell, put forward by Isaac Butt, put forward by Parnell (*applause*), put forward by us since Parnell's death with the unanimous consent of Nationalist Ireland—the theory of that constitutional movement has been that we in this country claim to become an autonomous nation within the circle of the Empire (*hear, hear*), and we always stated— O'Connell stated it, Parnell stated it, Butt stated it, I stated it—every responsible leader of the constitutional movement for the last quarter of a century has over and over again to England, that if that were done, if Ireland were brought into the Empire as an autonomous unit, as an autonomous nation within the Empire, that Ireland was quite willing while taking any advantage that might flow from her connection with the Empire to manfully and honestly bear her share of the burdens that that Empire cast upon all the nations comprised within its organisation. (*applause*)[35]

Redmond was not alone in the expression of these sentiments: sentiments which quietly dropped the Fenians from the national tradition. The party organ wished to support him with reasoned arguments. Redmond was placed in the great tradition of O'Connell and Parnell. The same issue of the *Weekly Freeman's Journal* commented in a supportive editorial:

That demand [for an Irish Parliament] throughout the century that had elapsed since O'Connell first formulated it had been accompanied and

[34] *Weekly Freeman's Journal*, 21 Aug. 1915.   [35] Ibid., 24 Oct. 1914.

sanctioned by an offer on the part of Ireland that, while taking all the advantages that might flow from her connection with the British Empire, a self-governing and calculated Ireland might be willing 'manfully and honestly' to bear her share in the burdens freely borne by the other free nations of the Empire. The leaders of the Irish people had consistently repudiated the charge of separatism made by reactionaries. O'Connell was one of the best friends the British democracy ever had. The men of '48 when they seceded from O'Connell did not unfurl the standard of separation. Their demand was a Federal Parliament which would have been less national than that actually won. Parnell made no change in the programme. He said at Wolverhampton in the Gladstonian days before home rule what Mr Redmond is saying now. Nay more, as Mr Redmond recalled on Sunday, the platform upon which the society of United Irishmen was founded was not a separatist programme.

Finally, at the end of the year, Redmond outlined his case at Limerick. He noted that it was important to prove that home rule was not based on 'a lie or a fraud'. In other words, there could be no abandonment of constitutionalist principles. It was essential also to vindicate the rights of small nations in the European conflict. Then there was the Ulster question. 'I say, as sensible men and fair women, put yourselves in the position of Englishmen . . . if it were proved to you that nationalist Irishmen had broken faith and that Ireland had refused to do her duty and that the only men who had done their duty were the Ulster volunteers, what would you do? You know very well what an ordinary man would do under the circumstances. He would say I will stand by the men who stood by me.'[36] Redmond denounced nationalist groaning of Ulster volunteers as 'the wrong spirit'. John Dillon took a more cynical line, implying that the nationalist recruits in the British army might eventually be used against the Ulster unionists. Redmond was capable of flirting with this notion, but it is clear that he was not happy with it. Dillon and Redmond were, however, in authentic agreement when it came to a defence of the basic integrity of the constitutional nationalist tradition. Dillon was even prepared to exploit the senile vagaries of the Fenian hero, O'Donovan Rossa, at the Tipperary convention of the United Irish League: 'If England had given repeal in the days of O'Connell they would have had an army of half a million Irishmen equal to the best in Europe, men of the type of Sgt.O'Leary . . . A voice—what about O'Donovan Rossa? Mr Dillon— what about him? For the last two years O'Donovan Rossa has been a

[36] Ibid., 25 Dec. 1915.

supporter of the Irish party and stood on the same platform with Mr Redmond.'[37]

It should be stressed however, that Irish party rhetoric did not lose all its nationalist bite. It is true that the separatist element was now denounced in strong terms. John Cullinane, the Tipperary MP who had a long personal history of militant agrarian radicalism, went so far as to declare: 'If the Irish people were foolish enough to allow division to come amongst them, then the English people would be perfectly justified in refusing to have the home rule act put into operation.'[38] But in the same speech he maintained a consistent attack on Carsonism and all its works, 'mean, pitiful and malign' as they were. In particular, accusations of Ulster unionist bigotry were frequently discussed at length.

The *Weekly Freeman's Journal* spoke of 'a better feeling . . . between north and south'[39] shortly after the outbreak of war; but in early 1915 it was back to the usual language: 'there remains here in Ireland a very noisy and bigoted gang . . . raised in the foetid atmosphere of the Orange lodges.'[40] The paper featured strongly a story that a Derry man had been ejected by a recruiting sergeant in Belfast because he was a Catholic. The most notable apparent example of anti-Catholic bigotry came—as even Cullinane stressed—in the summer of 1915; the Belfast corporation was accused of wanting to evict 160 nationalist families in the Hamill Street area of west Belfast. The families were to be offered other houses, but it was widely claimed that the underlying purpose of the whole manœuvre was to weaken Joe Devlin's political base. As many of the men in these families were at the front, the eviction by the corporation was criticized not only by Irish party MPs, but by the senior British military officer in Belfast. This necessity to keep up the attack on 'mean, pitiful, malign' Carsonism obviously reduced the coherence of the broad Redmondite appeal. It opened up the possibility of a collapse back into inter-ethnic rivalry which would undermine the moral basis of Redmond's rhetoric.

It is worth noting, however, that Redmond's line had considerable support in the Irish provincial press. His tone—in particular his attitude to historic grievances—was widely reproduced. In Munster, the *Kerry Advocate*, closely linked to local MP Tom O'Donnell, picked up on the criticisms of Redmond by Irish American separatists: 'We

---

[37] *Tipperary People*, 30 July 1915.
[39] *Weekly Freeman's Journal*, 22 Aug. 1914.

[38] Ibid., 6 Aug. 1915.
[40] Ibid., 22 Feb. 1915.

must look on the situation as reasonable people. Ireland, no doubt, has been wronged in the past, but that should not allow us to make fools of ourselves.'[41] The *Limerick Leader* reported on the routing of the Sinn Fein 'Clique' who had 'ruled' the local volunteers by 'questionable' means.[42] In Connaught, the *Western News* urged Mr Redmond's critics to realize that they were in a 'hopeless minority'.[43] The *Tuam Herald* added in solidarity: 'In the present situation of Imperial affairs for this country to withold any aid which it could give would be treachery to the cause the Irish people have at heart—that of independence within the Empire and under it—and would be calculated to do that cause irreparable injury.'[44] In Leinster, the *Westmeath Examiner* declared: 'The alternative is to remain sullen and aloof from the rest of the free nations of the Empire which have shown such friendship to our country and rendered her invaluable aid in her struggle for freedom.'[45] Adding for good measure a week later: 'In this respect the foes of Irish liberty in the North of Ireland are giving an example of trust and confidence and of statesmanship which those cranks have sought to prevent the Nationalists of Ireland from exhibiting. Ireland is at war with the forces of despotism.'[46]

The same editorial addressed one of the great fears of the Irish masses: the issue of conscription. 'The action of Mr Redmond and the Party is calculated to save the people from Compulsory Service. Should the war be prolonged, as seems probable, and should the Volunteer system break down, which seems unlikely, there is not the slightest doubt that conscription would be established.'[47] This type of comment had the unfortunate side-effect of increasing popular fears of conscription—fears which tended to undermine the Irish party's appeal. In a historically well-informed analysis the *Wicklow People* also sympathetically stated Redmond's rationale; 'On hundreds of platforms in that country he had promised in the name of his country that when Ireland's rights were admitted by the English democracy Ireland would become the strongest arm in the defence of the Empire. The test had come sooner than he had expected, but he told the Prime Minister that it would be honourably met. He would feel himself dishonoured if he did not say to his fellow-countrymen as he said to them from that place, that it was their duty and should be their honour to take their

[41] *Kerry Advocate*, 15 Aug. 1914. See also Gaughan, *A Political Odyssey* 95–108.
[42] *Limerick Leader*, 25 Sept. 1914.   [43] *Western News*, 17 Oct. 1914.
[44] *Tuam Herald*, 3 Oct. 1914.   [45] *Westmeath Examiner*, 10 Oct. 1914.
[46] Ibid., 17 Oct. 1914.   [47] Ibid., 12 Oct. 1914.

place in the firing line in this war.'[48] But it should be noted that there was vigorous opposition as well. On 8 August the *Leinster Leader* opined: 'At present we are receiving a kind of patronising indulgence from British political parties, which must not blind us to the realities of its meaning. The Irish Volunteers today occupy the position they held in 1782 when, backed up by their swords, the old constitution was wrung from a unwilling government, and today if it proves necessary the difficulties which confront England present Ireland with that opportunity which she is at liberty to seize to enforce the recognition of our claims.'[49] The *Tipperary Star* observed equally sourly: 'Ireland has not been consulted about this recruiting business and the response from rural parts is likely to be nil', adding: ' "Business as usual", say the Britons; "politics as usual", say the Irish.'[50] There is no clearer example of the 'business as usual' approach than the *Mayo News*. It reacted to the outbreak of world war by stressing parochial agrarian concerns: 'We have no doubt that the present war will bring home to the minds of all Englishmen the evils and dangers of a land system which allows land to go out of cultivation and be given over to grass.' It added, for good measure: 'We have no doubt we will yet reach a stage in the land movement where every man who wishes to till land will have it and that wherever land is required for tillage no man will be allowed to retain it for pasture.'[51] Other accounts stress the parochial nature of much peasant consciousness, particularly in the west. Katherine Tynan has described the predominant attitude which she encountered a few months into the war: 'They knew very little about the war at Claremorris. A few days after I arrived I heard the statements: "There are submarines in the Irish Sea and eggs are down to one and four." So did Claremorris correlate the things of war.'[52]

But the *Mayo News*, edited by P. J. Doris, brother of local loyal Redmondite MP William Doris, soon raised itself to consideration of the wider political issues. The editorial commented only on a proposal that Redmond and Dillon should address recruiting meetings. 'Surely

---

[48] *Wicklow People*, 19 Sept. 1914. [49] *Leinster Leader*, 8 Aug. 1914.
[50] *Tipperary Star*, 3 Oct. 1914. [51] *Mayo News*, 8, 15 August 1914.
[52] *The Years of the Shadow* (London, 1919), 176. Katherine Tynan believed that even the Easter Rising had such a limited initial impact: 'Mayo is given to minding her own business. Having given birth to the Land League and accomplished that revolution, Mayo had ever been content to rest on her laurels. A "strong" farmer came away from his tillage to tell us, "and now we shall get no money for land purchase", he said sorrowfully. "Was ever anything so uncalled for?" The little war in Dublin left Mayo as unmoved as the great war—in our part of it.' (Ibid. 192)

the South and West of Ireland, whatever their sympathies may be, and they are decidedly with outraged Belgium, can spare very little of their manhood for the march from Paris to Belgium. . . . We think in the South and West, Mr Asquith, Mr Redmond and Mr Dillon must be content with strong resolutions. They might draft them and send them over for adoption by our public Boards. They know well this has been the well recognised system in the past to overcome awkward situations and it might now be of some effect on the German Emperor.'[53] But, as the same editorialist later darkly noted: 'Raising resolutions and shouldering rifles are very different performances.'[54]

The critics were there from the start, but the least that might be said for the Redmondites is that they were able to stage-manage remarkable scenes of United Kingdom or imperial patriotism. Dr Foley of Kildare was soon to declare himself 'proud to belong to the great British Empire'.[55] Thousands attended a Galway meeting as local MPs Stephen Gwynn, William O'Malley, and W. J. Duffy supported Redmond's call for an Irish brigade. William O'Malley proudly told the crowd that his son had taken a commission in the army as soon as the Home Rule Bill was put on the statute book. W. J. Duffy, an ardent agrarian radical, described Sinn Fein as 'skulking behind backs instead of doing their duty'.[56] One moment, in particular, gives the flavour of this event:

Soldier Addresses Meeting

Mr Gwynn introduced a Connaught Ranger named Tully who had been in the Battle of Mons. The young soldier commented on the bravery of the Irish troops, and asked every man in the vast crowd to join him on his next visit to the front. Three cheers were then given for the Connaught Rangers, after which the crowd repeated 'God Save the King' with Mr Gwynn. The proceedings closed with the playing of the 'Marseillaise' by the band, and the shouldering of Mr Gwynn through the streets by a cheering crowd.[57]

The northern unionists at first reacted sourly to these displays. They claimed that there was evidence that Redmond's calls were not being heeded in nationalist Ireland: Redmondite imperialism, they argued, was a very superficial phenomenon. They picked up on any signs of disenchantment with Redmond. 'We do not believe in the Imperialism of Mr Redmond or his followers; we do not believe in their love of

---

[53] *Mayo News*, 19 Sept. 1914.
[55] *Weekly Freeman's Journal*, 21 Nov. 1914.
[57] Ibid.

[54] Ibid., 14 Nov. 1914.
[56] Ibid., 10 Oct. 1914.

Empire—the profession is a falsehood and the fulfilment will be a failure. Mr Redmond has made his appeal with all the assistance of Mr Asquith. It has been before the country for a week. What has been the response? In the words of the Dublin *Independent* "it has been very disappointing".'[58] On 20 March 1915, the *Weekly Northern Whig* editorialized: 'Irish Protestants are barely one third of the population, but they have supplied three fourths of the new recruits who have joined in Ireland since the beginning of August.' Parliamentary nationalists can hardly have been surprised. They bitterly denounced this begrudging attitude: 'Nothing is more depressing than the disposition of our unionist fellow countrymen . . . to fail to see any good in the Nazareth of Irish Nationalism.'[59]

By 24 October 31,000 men had joined the British forces from all over Ireland. Of these, some 15,000 came from Belfast and the surrounding districts, 4,000 from the unionist northern counties, and 5,500 from Dublin. Interestingly as far as Dublin was concerned, Catholics and Protestants joined up in roughly similar proportions;[60] 2,000 came from Cork city. The weak areas for recruitment were obvious enough: the nationalist north-west of Ulster and the agricultural districts of the south and west of Ireland. These figures omitted the large Catholic and nationalist minority in Ulster and consequently exaggerated the Unionist and Protestant commitment, impressive though it was. There is little doubt that Irish agriculturalists, as opposed to urban labourers, were less likely to join up. The town of Wexford had an excellent recruiting record, but this was not so of the surrounding rural areas.[61] John Dillon made the same point about Limerick.[62] Many agricultural areas, having traditionally experienced heavy emigration, now found that there was a shortage of labour at the

---

[58] *Witness*, 2 Oct. 1914.   [59] *Tuam Herald*, 28 Nov. 1914.

[60] Laura Dooney, 'Trinity College and the War', in David Fitzpatrick (ed.), *Ireland and the First World War* (Gigginstown, Mullingar, 1988), 38–9; N. Marlowe, 'The Mood of Ireland', *The British Review*, 11/1 (1915).

[61] See also the excellent article by Pauline Codd, 'Recruiting and Responses to the War in Wexford', in D. Fitzpatrick (ed.), *Ireland and the First World War* (Gigginstown, Mullingar, 1988), 15–26, esp. the interview with John Codd, cited on p. 16: 'Not many fellas from the country joined up. It was mainly the poor people from the towns, who had nothing much to lose anyway. I remember one or two lads from around here joining up all right. I think most of them went for the excitement of it all. It was better than staying here.' Ballina is another case in point, as Stephen Gwynn pointed out in *The Charm of Ireland* (London, 1934), 281: 700 out of 4,500 inhabitants joined the British army. Rural Mayo was in the mind of Darrell Figgis when he noted that 'not one of the volunteers in Mayo'—regardless of the side taken on the split—had actually been 'drawn into the recruiting lists', *Mayo News*, 31 Oct. 1914.   [62] *Tipperary People*, 6 Aug. 1915.

very moment when there was an increased demand for their produce. Others had a keen eye for the market. As the *Roscommon Herald* put it: 'For Ireland this war should mean big fortunes for the farmers who have bought out their lands.'[63] Nicholas Marlowe summed up: 'Many a peasant finds it impossible to spare the son who is still at home',[64] a calculation which he did not consider to be a 'directly political one'. Nevertheless, Marlowe acknowledged that a 'direct patriotic feeling was lacking in parts of Ireland'.[65] Marlow felt that Arthur Griffith of Sinn Fein expressed a certain mood accurately when he wrote: 'England having destroyed our constitution, suppressed our Parliament, loaded her debt on to our shoulders, turned our tillage fields into cattle ranches, trebled our taxation and halted our population, and within a century—wants what is left of us to fight for her supremacy in the rest of the world.'[66] The significance of this formulation lies in the fact that it was close enough to the traditional rhetoric of many parliamentary nationalists: in 1915 Redmondism attempted to change this rhetoric, but the effort was being made rather late in the day.

The public comments of Stephen Gwynn reveal some of the difficulties faced by the pro-recruitment forces. He noted in Galway in early 1915: 'The landlord class had played its part like men. No class in Europe had given more of their sons to this war than that class.' Given the traditions of the Anglo-Irish gentry, this was perhaps only to be expected. But he noted that there was virtually no recruitment in other sectors: 'the whole middle-class of clerks and shop assistants seemed, however, to have completely dropped out of touch with the profession of arms.'[67] Gwynn calculated that only 1 per cent of the drapers' assistants in Galway had joined; these comments clearly reveal the existence of substantial blockages to recruitment even before War Office strategy became clear.

In his subsequent analysis of this period Stephen Gwynn was to lay great stress on the fact that John Redmond was never able to overcome the suspicion—or perhaps, more accurately, simple lack of understanding—of the British military establishment. This could clearly be seen in the War Office's handling of the status to be accorded to the 10th and 16th Irish divisions. Redmond desired that these predominantly Catholic and nationalist regiments be accorded special recognition: he wanted them to be grouped into an Irish brigade. His strategy

---

[63] *Roscommon Herald*, 8 Aug. 1914.
[64] Marlowe, 'The Mood of Ireland', 6.   [65] Ibid.
[66] Ibid.   [67] *Weekly Freeman's Journal* 23 Jan. 1915.

was to create an emotional focus for Irish identification with the war effort. He easily won Asquith over to this idea, but failed to attract support from General Kitchener. Elizabeth, countess of Fingall, who knew Kitchener socially and whose husband shared recruiting platforms with Kettle and Gwynn, later recalled: 'Kitchener never liked or trusted the Irish and I always believe that but for him, Ireland would have been wholeheartedly in the war and there would have been no rebellion.'[68] A flag prepared for the Irish Brigade at Geraldine Mayo's School of Art was returned: 'questions were asked in the House about that incredibly stupid and hurtful gesture.' Augustine Birrell agreed: 'Lord Kitchener was not a real Irishman only an accidental one. . . . Had he possessed even a tincture of sympathy with the Irish national sentiment, the Irish attitude towards the war would have been materially affected.'[69] But in Kitchener's defence it has to be noted that he was also cordially loathed by Carson. 'Surely you are not going to hold out for Tyrone and Fermanagh?' Kitchener asked Carson in August 1914, adding with some arrogance: 'If I'd been on the platform with you and Redmond, I should have knocked your heads together.' Carson wrote in exasperation to Lady Londonderry on 22 August 1914: 'The War Office are great funkers in relation to Ireland. I believe they would let everything go to H[ell], rather than offend Redmond.'[70] A week later, Carson met Kitchener again and offered unconditionally to put the Ulster Volunteers at his disposal, assuring him that 35,000 of them were willing, if accepted, to enlist and go abroad. Carson wrote to Spender on 30 August: 'I am going to do my best to get our force to join the new army.' He added sourly: 'I have to do this without any conditions on Home Rule.'[71] Under this pressure the War Office finally conceded. Previous doubts were waived and no objection was made to the formation of an exclusively Ulster unionist division, so described. At some level, the placing of the Home Rule Bill on the statute book implied such a concession by the government, keen anyway to get the highly rated Ulster soldiers. Nevertheless, however reluctantly Kitchener had conceded to the Ulster unionists,

---

[68] *Seventy Years Young*, 348. For the Anglo-Irish attitude in general see P. Buckland, *The Anglo-Irish and the New Ireland* (New York, 1972), vol. i, ch. 3.

[69] *Things Past Redress* (London, 1937), 218. On this whole issue, see the judicious summary in Terence Denman, *Ireland's Unknown Soldiers* (Dublin, 1992), 178–9.

[70] For Kitchener and Carson at this point see Montgomery Hyde, *Carson* (London, 1953), 378; A. T. Q. Stewart, *Sir Edward Carson* (Dublin, 1981), 94.

[71] Public Record Office Northern Ireland, D 1295/2/5.

the fact remains that he had conceded to them—and that he would continue to deny the same conditions of service to Irish nationalists. Gwynn also pointed out that Redmond experienced one other crucial failure in his dealings with the War Office. 'Running all through this critical year 1915 is the history of one long failure—his attempt to secure the creation of a Home Defence Force for Ireland. Given that, he should be confident of possessing the foundation for the structure of an Irish army, an army which would be regarded as Ireland's own.'[72] Yet the War Office remained consistently opposed, though it should be noted that belated efforts were made to put a nationalist gloss on recruiting propaganda:

God Save Ireland!
When you sing these words you think you really mean them.
But since the war began, what have you done to help make them a reality?
If you are an Irishman between 19 and 40, physically fit and not already serving your country as a sailor or a soldier, or in the munition factory, there is but one way for you to help save Ireland from the Germans . . .
You must join an Irish Regiment and learn to sing God Save Ireland with a rifle in your hands.[73]

Some of the difficulty arose simply from the fact that the War Office had different priorities from those of Redmond. It wanted at all costs to win the war. Its mind turned towards conscription; Redmond knew that conscription would destroy his base in Ireland. War Office officials were disappointed by the existence of separatist pro-German sentiment in Ireland; Redmond retorted that the policy of the Government intensified such sentiment. Despite such irritation, it is worth noting that in the end, during the war itself, over 140,000 Irish volunteered, including 65,000 Catholic Irish.[74]

Redmond's life was made even more difficult by the change in the nature of the British cabinet. Due to growing criticism of the government's conduct of the war following Churchill's disastrous Dardanelles adventures, Asquith was forced by Bonar Law to widen the basis of the government. Sir Edward Carson, with a display of

---

[72] *Redmond's Last Years*, 202.   [73] *Nenagh Guardian*, 19 June 1915.
[74] For a good discussion of their role, see Terence Denman, 'The Catholic Irish Soldier in the First World War: The Racial Environment', *Irish Historical Studies*, 27/108 (Nov. 1991), 352–65. See also Patrick Callan, 'Recruiting for the British Army in Ireland during the First World War', *Irish Sword*, 17/66 (summer 1982), 42–56.

considerable and probably genuine reluctance, was included in the new coalition cabinet in May 1915. Tom Garvin has recently written: 'The humiliation of the emergent Catholics was completed by the favouring of Carson over Redmond in 1914, the former getting a cabinet post while the latter was ignored.'[75] In fact, as a balancing move, Redmond was also asked to join the cabinet. Symptomatically, when the emissaries from Dublin Castle came to Redmond's country house saying they 'wanted Mr Redmond' the door was slammed on them by Redmond's Wexford cook, who feared they had come to arrest the Irish leader![76] Redmond made this incident into a favourite after-dinner story, but it is a potent enough indicator of Anglo-Irish understanding that Redmond refused the offer. He told Stephen Gwynn later that 'under no conditions did he think he could have accepted'.[77] But this rather overstates the case. In an interview with J. A. Spender published in the *Weekly Freeman's Journal* on 18 May 1912 Redmond himself had declared: 'After home rule was granted . . . There will be no reason why Irish members elected to Westminster should not join British cabinets.' Perhaps this is why Redmond added to Gwynn: 'If I had been Asquith and had wished to make it as difficult as possible to refuse, I should have offered a seat on the Cabinet without portfolio and without a salary.' Needless to say, Asquith had not the grasp of Irish sensibility required to make such a precise offer. As Gwynn concluded: 'Redmond saw fully how disastrous would be the effect on Irish opinion if he were not in the Government and Sir Edward Carson was.' John Dillon for once understated the case when he referred in June to a 'painful knock'.[78] As the *Freeman* wretchedly acknowledged at the same time: 'The government can no longer be described as a home rule government, as it could have been two months ago.'[79] D. P. Moran of the *Leader*, one of the party's most percipient if sectarian nationalist critics, always felt that Redmond's refusal of a cabinet post had been a mistake, leaving him responsibility without prestige.

Despite these increasingly unpropitious political circumstances,

---

[75] 'The Rising and Irish Democracy', in Mairin Ni Dhonnchadha and Theo Dorgan (eds.), *Revising the Rising* (Derry, 1991), 24–5. See also John Turner, *British Politics and the Great War* (New Haven, (Conn.,) and London, 1992), 56–61. Lillian (later Lady) Spender confided to her diary (28 May 1915): 'How dramatic that the arch rebel should be asked to govern us by the very men who wanted to arrest him as a criminal only a year ago.' (Public Record Office Northern Ireland, D 1633/2/20)

[76] *Weekly Freeman's Journal*, 10 July 1915.   [77] *Redmond's Last Years*, 192.

[78] *Weekly Freeman's Journal*, 16 June 1915.   [79] Ibid.

Redmond ploughed on. There is no question of the integrity of the Irish party's commitment to its policy of support for the war. The families of the party leadership gave their sons freely and paid an awful price: Joe Devlin, perhaps, stands out as one who did not join up but he was personally persuaded by John Redmond that his political services in Ireland were too valuable to lose; Devlin himself gave the impression that he had wanted to go; the stay-at-home Kerry MP Tom O'Donnell was perhaps the only Redmondite recruiting platform orator who was open to the charge of operating a personal double standard. One critic of the party, J. Dwyer, protested at the Tuam Board of Guardians: 'Why does not Redmond or Kettle send their sons to join the British Army?'[80] Such an attack was quite unwarranted: Redmond's son joined up, and both Tom Kettle and Redmond's brother, Willie, were to die at the front. Sometimes indeed these Irish party members were robust yet naïve. Recalling his own lengthy commitment to agrarian class conflict in Ireland, John Fitzgibbon told the South Mayo United Irish League that his son who had joined up would 'not incur greater risks than his father ran'[81] as a soldier in the land war. It is painful to record that this optimism was not justified. When the war broke out Fitzgibbon's son Michael, immediately after the royal assent to the Home Rule Bill, sought and obtained a commission in the army, and went out to Gallipoli with the rank of captain. But within a few days of landing he had died in action. John Fitzgibbon's sorrow was intensified when another son, the Revd John Fitzgibbon, SJ, who had joined the army as a chaplain and obtained the rank of colonel, was killed while rendering spiritual aid to a fallen comrade.[82] Even in the context of the traditional bitterness of Irish politics, such deep personal sacrifice was bound to have some effect. The unionists, too, suffered: Arthur O'Neill, MP for mid-Antrim, became the first MP to die at the front. Former Presbyterian moderator, John McDermott, a bitter critic of Fitzgibbon's agrarian radicalism, lost his son—the first UVF officer to die at the Somme. Serjeant Sullivan, one of the keenest Redmondite supporters of the war effort, noted that amidst continued mutual suspicion: 'Cork acknowledged the courage of Portadown and Belfast admitted that Kerry men could fight.'[83] Even the *Whig* managed to draw attention to

---

[80] *Western People*, 26 Sept. 1914.   [81] Ibid., 14 Nov. 1914.
[82] *Roscommon Messenger*, 13 Sept. 1914.
[83] *Old Ireland* (London, 1927), 175.

the 'unionjacks' carried by nationalists at a Strabane St Patrick's Day procession that turned into a pro-recruitment rally.[84]

Within the élites there was a change of tone. Although it was not unconditional or unguarded, Basil Brooke promised a friend, Hugh MacManaway, that he would never again resort to anti-Catholic rhetoric.[85] At the end of September 1915, John Redmond had a long and productive interview with Lord Kitchener at the War Office. After this meeting Redmond decided to make a visit to the front. Before setting out on his journey, Redmond symbolically entered the vice-regal lodge in Dublin for the first time to discuss ways of promoting the war effort. He was impressed by the 'extreme friendliness of attitude'[86] displayed by the senior Ulster unionist political represent-atives who were there.

On his return, Redmond addressed a recruiting meeting for the Royal Irish Rifles in London. In an emotional passage he declared:

In the part of the trenches I went to I found a battalion of the Ulsters from Belfast side by side with the Dubliners, and spoke to them all. I found that so far from having friction between them, they were like comrades and brothers. I pray God that may go on. (*cheers*) I pray that whenever an Irish battalion goes into action there may be an Ulster division alongside them. (*more cheers*) I would point out that is the way of ending the unhappiness, the discord and confusion in Ireland.[87]

Unionist reaction to Redmond's speech requires some study. The *Irish Times* commented sympathetically: 'In Ireland though the war has worked miracles the taint of religion and bigotry still persist in public life. At the front that microbe perished long ago in an atmosphere of duty and patriotism. Ulstermen and Munstermen are at last comrades and brothers.'[88] Provided that Irishmen really *did* join up, then the southern unionist *Times* was happy to identify with Redmond's theme of reconciliation. In the northern unionist camp, however, there was still some suspicion. Was not Redmond simply playing nationalist games? The *Weekly Northern Whig* editorialized: 'The other day Mr Redmond was claiming the tenth division as his own, but as a matter of

---

[84] 20 Mar. 1915

[85] Hugh MacManaway, dean of Enniskillen, to General Hugh Montgomery, 17 Aug. 1935, Public Record Office Northern Ireland, D 2661/C. This promise, rather famously, was not kept; Brooke explicitly explained this by referring to the Easter Rising. On all this, see B. Barton, *Brookeborough: The Making of a Prime Minister* (Belfast, 1988), 24.   [86] *Redmond's Last Years*, 199.   [87] *Irish Times*, 24 Nov. 1915.

[88] Ibid. Cf., for similar testimony, Tom Johnstone, *Orange, Green and Khaki* (Dublin, 1992), 255.

fact there are more Ulster Unionists than Irish nationalists in that division, which contains no fewer than five battalions from the north.'[89]

A particularly sour note was struck in a letter from Colonel Spender to Carson: 'I am moved to write about Redmond's latest and not least wicked speech. I will only deal with that point in which he refers to the Dublin and Ulster divisions fighting side by side. If anything would be more likely to stir up trouble amongst them than a speech like that, I should not like to know it. I hear the Fifteenth Brigade at the front has done very much good work like the good soldiers that they are and getting along very well with those southern Irishmen—none too many—who had the courage to fight.'[90] Redmond was to be disappointed when Carson displayed unwillingness to come to Newry to share a recruiting platform with prominent nationalists. On the Ulster unionist side, there were fears that their greater recruitment rate would leave them exposed to nationalist aggression after the war.[91] Sectarian outbreaks continued in the north: in March 1916 in a particularly nasty incident, there was shooting at an AOH hall in Portadown.[92] On the nationalist side there was an equal fear: that their troops were being used as cannon fodder. Nevertheless, Carson soon gave a sign of his recognition of Redmond's qualities. Early in March 1916 Carson took part in an interview for the *New York Sun*. His remarks were obviously intended to appeal to American public opinion. The British government was clearly anxious to ensure that the flow of American sympathy for the war effort was not diminished by any negative publicity arising from the 'Irish question'.[93] Carson, in particular, was aware that his personal image in America was a poor one. Nevertheless, his tone towards Redmond and the Irish party is of some interest:

At present while the nation struggles against Germany a truce must be observed by all the parties in Irish affairs. We must settle our domestic differences after the war and see how far the war may affect them . . . I am well aware that John Redmond is having his own difficulties with the extreme anti-English factions in Ireland, and do not wish in the slightest measure to add to

[89] *Weekly Northern Whig*, 22 May 1915.

[90] Public Record Office Northern Ireland, D 1507/19/14.

[91] Nicholas Mansergh, *The Unresolved Question: The Anglo-Irish Settlement and its Undoing* (New Haven, Conn., and London), 91.

[92] Birrell to Carson, 26 Mar. 1916, Public Record Office Northern Ireland, D 1507/1/15/16.

[93] For an excellent analysis, see F. M. Carroll, *American Opinion and the Irish Question 1910–1923* (Dublin and New York, 1978), 14–54.

his trouble by emphasising the deplorable facts which have facilitated against recruiting in Ireland for the war. For them he is no wise responsible . . .

Is it not true that Irishmen are great enough, noble enough, have pride and commonsense enough, to let men realise it is wisest and most honourable for them to fight out their domestic battles amongst themselves, upon a lofty plane, without comforting the international assassin of the high seas and of Belgium, of the Balkans and North France? I would a thousand times rather shake the hands of, and declare my friendship for the most bitter and most extreme among my fellow Irishmen, no matter how pronounced their enmity for my belief and my ideals may have been, than to contaminate my fingers with one touch upon the hand of any of those who wrought such damning outrage against every tenet of my work . . .[94]

In this context, the most 'bitter' and 'extreme' of his fellow Irishmen is a reference to the left wing of the parliamentary party rather than to Sinn Fein. Carson's words do not commit him to any change of position on the Irish question; but they do acknowledge Redmond's good faith. This was a point which registered particularly with Andrew Bonar Law. At Balmoral, Bonar Law had insisted upon the potential strategic damage to Britain arising from a home rule parliament. Redmond's behaviour since the outbreak of war had made this an implausible argument. This element at least of the pre-war anti-home rule case was irrelevant. Shortly before the rising, Bonar Law and Redmond had a private discussion of the political situation. This so impressed Redmond that he immediately had notes of the meeting typed up. They are filed in his papers, alongside Bonar Law's later letter of sympathy following the death of Willie:

He then said to me, 'Anyhow, Mr Redmond, our Irish quarrel can never be revived in the same way as it existed before the War.' I said that this was always my view. He then said he had to say, for fear I would misunderstand him, that he did not see daylight on the Irish question at present; but that he felt, at the same time, instinctively that a way out would be found and that the position which existed before the war could never revive. He said he appreciated most fully the action of the Irish party and of Ireland in the war. He only hoped, he said, that the reports about the Sinn Feiners were exaggerated.[95]

[94] Interview given to *New York Sun*, 6 Mar. 1916, quoted in *County Cork Eagle*, 12 Mar. 1916.
[95] D. Gwynn, *The Life of John Redmond* (London, 1932), 467; National Library of Ireland, MSS 15201. In this case the text of the interview, unlike the Asquith interview of Feb. 1914 (see Mansergh, *Unresolved Question*, 67–9), has not been altered by the biographer. See also Bonar Law's letters (15 June 1917) following the death of Willie Redmond.

Tragically for Redmond the reports were not exaggerated. The preparations for the Easter Rising were continuing apace. The Redmondite reaction to the event itself is worth recording. The members of the Irish party tended to emphasize the social aspects of the revolt. It was a revolt, declared P. J. Meehan, MP for Queen's County, of the 'people with nothing against the people with something'.[96] John Pius Boland, MP for Kerry South, made the same point in a rather more laconic way when he recalled the fate of one of his family's business concerns: 'A propos of the Ringsend Mills, it is of some interest to record that they came into some notoriety at a later period of Irish history, for at the time of the Sinn Fein Rising in Easter Week 1916 they were seized by Sinn Feiners as a point of vantage and they were severely bombarded. If I mistake not de Valera was in command there.'[97] John Redmond, however, thought only of the implications for the Irishmen who served at the front. 'Is it not an additional horror that on the day when we hear that men of the Dublin Fusiliers have been killed by Irishmen in the streets of Dublin, we received the news of how men of the 16th Division—our own Irish Brigade and of the same Dublin Fusiliers—had dashed forward and by their unconquerable bravery retaken the trenches that the Germans had won at Hulluch?'[98] Redmond's words here reveal a mind preoccupied with a broader international context—to the neglect of his own political base in Ireland. His traditionally benign attitude towards imperialism had not prepared him for its dark side: the massive carnage of international conflict. Nevertheless, it cannot be presumed that up to this point Redmond had failed to take majority sentiment in Ireland with him.

A debate has recently opened up on this issue: J. J. Lee has argued at some length that Irish public opinion during the Easter Rising may have been less critical of the rebels than has normally been thought.[99] B. A. McKenzie, the Canadian journalist, insisted at the time on a 'vast amount of sympathy' for the rebels in the 'poorer districts' of Dublin. ' "Shure we cheer them", said one woman, "Why shouldn't we? Aren't they our own flesh and blood?" '[100] But so far the evidence presented has been largely impressionistic; there has been no serious attempt to track the evolution of public opinion from 1914 to 1916. This is all the

[96] Meehan, *The Members of Parliament for Laois and Offaly 1801–1918* (Portalolse, Leinster, 1972), 74.   [97] *Some Memories* (Dublin, 1928), 32.
[98] *County Cork Eagle*, 6 May 1916.   [99] *Ireland 1912–85*, 29–36.
[100] Quoted by P. Beresford Ellis in the *Irish Democrat*, Feb. 1991.

more surprising as the substantial number of by-elections in the period mean that evidence clearly exists. The Irish party's electoral perform-ances in the period between the outbreak of the First World War and the rising require some analysis: there were five contested seats, each possessing considerable political interest; in addition, two seats— Wicklow West in August 1914 and Galway East in December of that year—fell vacant and were uncontested and Sir James Brown Dougherty took Londonderry city as a Liberal pro-home ruler with Irish party support in December 1914 without a contest, thanks to the wartime political truce. But what do the five contested seats reveal about the evolution of nationalist opinion? Let us take the three rural seats first.

Following the death of the sitting candidate, Haviland Burke, MP for King's County (Tullamore), the UIL selection convention in November 1914 was split three ways: Adams 42, Birmingham 37, and Graham 27. The Tullamore convention had been small enough in size; at the East Galway gathering held at the same time some 261 conventioneers voted.[101] By the time of the parliamentary election, the supporters of the second- and third-place candidates at the convention had belatedly united, leading to the defeat of the officially selected candidate: Edward John Graham eclipsed P. F. Adams by 1,667 votes to 1,588 on 8 December 1914. The defeat of the convention's candidate led to a degree of criticism of the 'convention system': why had it failed to produce an acceptable candidate for the constituency? Redmond and Dillon defended the system, insisting that they had no particular interest in the convention's choice, all the candidates having declared themselves to be fervent supporters of the Irish parliamentary party line. As John Dillon pointed out, in the actual election Adams had secured a larger proportion of the nationalist vote than he had of the delegates to the convention.[102] The defeat of the official candidate therefore, was not a reflection on the party's procedures or ability to sense the public mood; rather it was the product of a freakish combination of the supporters of the second- and third-placed candidates behind the third-placed man (Graham). It was also alleged that the disaffected unionists in Tullamore had seized their chance to inflict a blow, however nominal, on the UIL machinery, thus helping to give Graham his narrow victory. The official UIL view of the

[101] *Tuam Herald*, 28 Nov.1914.
[102] *Weekly Freeman's Journal*, 9 Jan. 1915.

Tullamore defeat thus effectively treated the event—for perfectly understandable reasons—as being of no political importance. But it is not possible to go quite so far. P. F. Adams was an enthusiastic agrarian radical; indeed, he was unable to hear in person the returning officer's announcement of his narrow defeat because he was in court facing charges arising out of the Geashill cattle-drive.[103] At the very least, his defeat indicated that, for many nationalist electors, cattle-driving was no easy route to instant popularity. Equally, the party's broad stance appeared to be somewhat confused: Adams, as the official candidate, was warmly supported by other Irish party MPs who were well known to be hostile to, or at least lukewarm about, cattle-driving. As both candidates stressed their loyalty to Redmond, the Tullamore defeat was hardly a harbinger of doom for the Irish party, but it did reveal a debilitating lack of clarity on the key area of agrarian radicalism. Given the importance of this question in the growth of the Irish party this was in itself rather discouraging.

The next crucial rural contest followed on the death of Dr John Esmonde (family seat Drummagh Castle, on the banks of the Shannon) in Tipperary North. Esmonde's last major speech at Toomevara had insisted: 'We are a constituent part of the British Empire, for we are now a nation.'[104] He died in April, having contracted a cold in Tipperary, where he had been serving as a captain in the Royal Army Medical Corps.[105] At this point a convention of the Tipperary UIL should have been held to elect a successor. But, as Redmond publicly acknowledged, this was impossible 'because the branches of the organisation have been allowed to die out'.[106] Instead, Robert P. Gill, an experienced product of a well-known nationalist Tipperary family, put himself into the field.[107] A few days later a Tipperary man resident in London, Patrick Hoctor, joined the fray, Finally, a fortnight later, Dr Esmonde's son, Lieutenant John Lymbrick Esmonde, was the last to declare. Gill's uncle, Peter, had had well-known connections with Fenianism in the early 1870s; Hoctor's manifesto stressed the 'Fenian spirit'; nevertheless, all candidates emphasized their loyalty to Redmond as leader. Gill had

[103] *Westmeath Examiner*, 12 Dec. 1914.
[104] *Nenagh Guardian*, 3 Mar. 1915.
[105] Ibid., 24 Apr. 1915.
[106] *Weekly Freeman's Journal*, 10 July 1915.
[107] *Nenagh Guardian*, 24 Apr. 1915. For the Gill family, see E. Larkin, *The Roman Catholic Church and the Home Rule Movement in Ireland 1870–74* (Dublin, 1990), 248–9.

shared John Esmonde's last platform. The contest was fought out in the 'utmost good humour' and 'friendship'.[108] John Esmonde won by 1,691 votes, against Hoctor with 1,293 votes and Gill with 1,192.

The third rural seat to be fought was Louth North, following the death of Augustine Roche. This time there actually was a UIL convention, which selected Patrick Joseph Whitty, the son of Dr Whitty, former High Sheriff of Waterford City. Perhaps more to the point, Whitty was the nephew of Richard Hazleton,[109] who had contested the seat in 1910 but had been unseated on petition. Whitty was a completely unknown figure up to this point. However, the candidate chosen by the convention was soon challenged by Bernard Hamill, who declared he would never have entered the field if the convention had nominated a local man. The force of this observation was somewhat diminished by the fact that he was not himself from the locality.[110] But, unlike the contests in King's County and Tipperary, the Louth election did take on an explicit political hue: while the earlier contests had focused on personality issues, Louth acquired a broader significance. The *Drogheda Independent* saw Hamill's supporters as 'dreamers' and 'ultra nationalists'.[111] Hamill had started out by saying that he hoped to join the Irish party's ranks at Westminster, but Joe Devlin was soon implying that he was not a sincere believer in the parliamentary process: 'If Mr Hamill does not believe in constitutional-ism, if he is a revolutionary . . . let him say so . . . let him leave the recruiting associations of Dundalk for the hillsiders in the city of Dublin.'[112] Whitty was also subjected to criticism from the Dublin *Independent* because he was not a serving soldier. It was replied in his defence that his brother had lost his life at the Suvla Bay landing while his only other brother was serving in the 6th battalion of the Dublin Fusiliers. Whitty won by 2,299 votes to Hamill's 1810; thanks partly to a very good vote in the Carlingford area of the constituency. Thomas Lundon, MP, prematurely, but understandably, declared: 'We have buried forever Sinn Fein in North Louth.'[113]

The three contested rural seats all tell a story. All of them were won by loyal Redmondites; only in the last case was there a Sinn Fein challenge in any sense. But none of the contests went smoothly: the UIL machine was clearly not in good working order. In theory, the conventions were models of democratic practice: a mix of locally

---

[108] *Nenagh Guardian*, 19 June 1915,   [109] *Drogheda Argus*, 5 Feb 1916.
[110] Ibid., 29 Feb. 1916.   [111] *Drogheda Independent*, 4 Mar. 1916.
[112] Ibid.   [113] Ibid.

elected officials, clergy, and activists in the national organizations. But throughout 1915 Irish MPs were increasingly frank about the weakness of the UIL structures. J. J. Clancy openly said that North County Dublin was not properly organized;[114] P. J. O'Shaughnessy acknowledged the same of Westmeath,[115] and W. J. Duffy found the lapsing of Galway branches 'impossible to account for'.[116] During the year most of the UIL county machinery was overhauled. By the end of August Waterford, Tipperary, Donegal, Derry, Sligo, Longford, and Limerick had enjoyed this experience;[117] they were soon to be joined by Kerry.[118]

It was repeatedly declared that, indeed, there had been a degree of local laxity, but now the party machinery was once again in excellent working order. The very need for this whole publicly proclaimed process had, however, indicated a degree of rustiness. Moreover, there were profound reasons for local apathy: the land question in particular had lost its capacity to generate excitement. 'There had been', as James McCarthy concisely put it at the South Drogheda UIL, 'a departure from the ethics of the Land League.'[119] Every effort was made to keep up morale. Joe Taggart, vice-president of Cavan UIL reminded V. P. Kennedy, MP, that 'farmers who had bought out should continue to help others'.[120] But the majority who had bought out were less than concerned about the minority who had not. Indeed, sections of the strong farming community were positively hostile towards the latecomers. As John Fitzgibbon explained:

The spirit of jealousy showed itself in the division of the grass lands: men, instead of being thankful for what they had, were annoyed at seeing their neighbours get so much, and this was particularly so in the case of the strong men of the village. The strong men who saw their neighbours creeping up on them are the very persons who claimed the congested Districts Board was doing no good in this country. (*hear, hear*) This spirit must disappear and a feeling of gratitude take it place . . .[121]

The Irish parliamentary party also faced contests in two urban seats. On 11 June John Dillon Nugent, the leading figure of the Dublin AOH, defeated a Labour candidate, Thomas Farren of the Irish

---

[114] *Weekly Freeman's Journal*, 23 Jan. 1915.
[115] Ibid., 30 Jan. 1915.
[116] Ibid., 20 Feb. 1915.
[117] Ibid., 28 Aug. 1915.
[118] Ibid., 9 Oct. 1915.
[119] *Drogheda Argus*, 12 Feb. 1916.
[120] *Weekly Freeman's Journal*, Mar. 1915.
[121] *Western People*, 14 Nov. 1914.

Neutrality League by 2,445 to 1,816 votes at College Green. At first sight it was a comfortable victory. But in fact it as undoubtedly the worst Irish party performance since the outbreak of the war. Throughout the campaign, the party stigmatized Farren as a radical socialist, and he was indeed well known to be a close associate of the republican Labour leader James Connolly.[122] The O'Brienite *Cork Free Press*, then edited by Frank Gallagher, later to be de Valera's chief propagandist, declared icily that College Green was proof of 'process of putrefaction' at work in the party machine. Only a quarter of the electorate had voted for the Irish party; half the voters had declined to use their franchise at all. 'A reverse in vigorous warfare can easily be repaired; one proceeding from public indifference and contempt, never. It is the fifty per cent who abstained from the polls who will by and by be the ruling and driving force in the College Green division and everywhere else.'[123] James Connolly's election address for Farren admitted that he would rather have ignored the election and that his mind lay elsewhere: 'We deprecate any action turning the eyes of Irishmen towards England in the present International Crisis. Ireland as a Nation has her own destiny to achieve and there is no law of nature which makes it necessary that that destiny must forever be worked out in terms of British Acts of Parliament.'[124] This was clearly the view of a man actually preparing for a rising. But on the other hand Nugent had thrown the weight of the AOH machinery behind the Dublin employers in 1913: 'the selection of Nugent was a studied insult to the Dublin working class and that class would not be worth its salt did it not answer this insult by striking back.'[125] Also 'a fomenter of sectarian strife' in his role as the leading figure of the AOH, Connolly had no doubts: 'John Dillon Nugent is the active figure behind all that is foulest and most loathsome in Irish life.'[126]

Given the absolutely explicit nature of this campaign, Farren's vote was a respectable share of a low poll, a share which carried a worrying implication of relative urban weakness for the Irish party. The party leaders, of course, would have replied that if the radical nationalists

<hr />

[122] D. Greaves, *The Life and Times of James Connolly* (London, 1961), 372.

[123] *Cork Free Press*, 19 June 1915.

[124] James Connolly, 'Manifesto to the Electors of College Green', in J. Connolly, *The Workers' Republic* (Dublin, 1951), 181.

[125] Id., 'College Green: A Labour Candidate', *ibid.* 179.

[126] Id., 'Manifesto to the Electors', in D. Ryan (ed.), *The Workers' Republic: A Selection from the Writings of James Connolly* (n.p., n.d.), 181.

could not take a seat like College Green, how could they ever take a mainstream Irish rural constituency? On 2 October 1915 Alfred Byrne, the Irish party candidate, comfortably defeated Pierce O'Mahony at Dublin Harbour by 2,208 votes to 913. J. J. Farrell also stood, but obtained only 677 votes. O'Mahony, a Parnellite ally and close friend of Redmond in the 1890s, had grown disillusioned with Redmond's toleration of AOH influence at the heart of the UIL machine.[127] Now again a loyal Redmondite, he may have shared Connolly's dislike of Hibernianism—which, of course, was also felt by William O'Brien and the All For Ireland League—but not his radical perspectives. Nevertheless, there was one very important issue at stake in Dublin Harbour. All three candidates had professed equally enthusiastic support for Redmond, but their political styles varied: Both Byrne and Farrell were typical members of Dublin corporation and they stressed humdrum local issues; 'the O'Mahony' campaigned in his uniform and was an indefatigible supporter of the recruitment drive. He told a meeting in the constituency: 'if they elected him they would elect a man who has made up his mind to do his very utmost to win the war'. The two other candidates failed to express any opinion at all of the recruiting issue. The unionist *Irish Times* advised the 500 or so unionists in the constituency to vote for O'Mahony; in this context they noted Bonar Law's comment on the eve of the election that some pre-war controversies seemed to belong to 'a previous life'.[128] In fact O'Mahony was easily defeated, but it should be recalled that out of an electorate of 8,624, 2,000 were believed to be serving with the colours. Dublin Harbour sounded a muffled warning note to John Redmond; a professedly loyal Redmondite won the seat, professedly loyal Redmondites took all the votes, but the candidate closest to his own personal vision was heavily defeated.

The conclusion of any analysis of wartime by-elections in nationalist Ireland is clear enough. The Irish party won all five of the contested seats, as well, of course, as retaining the non-contested ones. The *Weekly Freeman's Journal* was quite correct to criticize the separatists for their failure to put up candidates: 'There were vacancies in the South, in the West, in the East and in the North. They could have tested their views in Tipperary, in Galway, King's County or Derry but they did not budge.'[129] The two seats where separatists stood—

---

[127] Paul Bew, *Conflict and Conciliation* (Oxford, 1987), 186–7.
[128] *Irish Times*, 1 Oct. 1915.   [129] *Weekly Freeman's Journal*, 6 Nov. 1915.

College Green and North Louth—were won by the party. Nevertheless, there is clear evidence of the weakness of the UIL's structures. In
general, the rural results are better than the urban; in Tipperary, given
a choice of three parliamentarians, the electors selected the candidate
closest to Redmond's personal philosophy; in Dublin Harbour, in the
same situation, they did not. But even in rural areas, there was
evidence of a correspondingly low level of involvement in the party's
apparatus. This was due in significant measure to the fading resonance
of the land question. But, when all is said and done, it is clear that
before Easter 1916 Redmond had the support of the majority of Irish
nationalists. It is true to say that there was traditionally in Ireland a
widespread desire for as much independence as possible; but the
success of the new Liberal welfare reforms had added a new economic
argument in favour of a 'home rule' compromise which retained
beneficial links with England. In this sense, the events in Easter week
constitute a technical *coup*; a successful *coup* in the end, but none the
less one lacking a substantive claim to democratic legitimacy. The
unionists, of course, were immediately challenged by critics who
argued that their resort to arms had provided the impetus for the
Easter Rising. Carson replied at once: 'there have always been certain
anti-English elements which have been accountable at one time for
Fenian outbreaks, and at another time for the horrible outrages of the
Phoenix Park . . . the leaders of the Nationalist party have been doing
their best to help us in the present rising and I am sure they would
agree with me that no useful purpose can be served by reviving these
controversies.'[130] Despite Carson's advice, one unionist R. D. S.
Megaw, who still retained the dumdum bullet fired at his house during
the rising, was moved to protest. He recalled a celebrated Ulster
Liberal meeting at Ballymoney addressed by Sir Roger Casement on
24 October 1913: 'It is unseemly to say the least of it, that the dupes
and tools of Sir Roger Casement, who gave him such an effusive
welcome on his first appearance in Irish politics, should for their
wretched political ends attempt to drag the name of Sir Edward
Carson to any association with the later rebellion.'[131] Yet, as Carson's
reply indicates, unionist attitudes towards Redmond were slowly
changing. As late as 28 May 1915, an entry in Lillian Spender's diary
ran: 'I think Redmond is very wrong to hold aloof at such a time and
the whole attitude of the Nationalist party is most unpleasant.'[132] Yet

---

[130] *Weekly Northern Whig*, 6 May 1916.	[131] Ibid., 20 May 1916.
[132] Public Record Office Northern Ireland, D 1633/3/20.

four decades later Sir Wilfred Spender recalled Redmond's name in a more mellow and reflective way: 'The southern Irish MPs included men such as Redmond and Dillon who were supporters of the British Empire.'[133]

The heartbreak of Redmondism lies here. The unionists had good grounds for concern about the home rule project: reasonable grounds when it came to the economy, militant Catholic sectarianism, or even Irish language fanaticism. None of this justifies the mob violence of the summer of 1912. It is simply reductionism on an excessively grand scale to reduce these arguments to the status of mere rationalization of 'supremacism', even though the difference in socio-economic standing of the two communities buttressed unionist assumptions. But the unionists had no reason to doubt Redmond's basically tolerant Parnellian vision of a home rule government. As the *Leader* bitterly put it, in a comment on his rhetoric: 'The end of the land fight was Ireland buying out the alien landlords at exorbitant prices. Is the end of home rule to be that the Unionists are to run the country?'[134] Nor had they any reason to doubt his imperial loyalty.[135] The *Leader's* comment links Redmond's broad, if at times inconsistent, espousal of a 'policy of toleration'[136] in the 1890–1910 period with the Irish Chief's more recent hints in 1912 concerning the non-nationalist elements he wished to embrace in a new home rule dispensation. *Nationalist Fairplay*, one of the more powerful unionist leaflets[137] took up the issue from a different angle. Redmond, it correctly pointed out, had argued in 1898—following the democratization of Irish local government—that Protestants would receive the fullest toleration.[138] In fact, by 1912 only fifteen out of 703 Irish county councillors outside Ulster were unionist. More to the point was the record of these councils in salaried appointments: fourteen of them had not made one single Protestant appointment, it was claimed, while five others had made only one each. 'In face of a record like this is it any wonder that Protestants put no faith in Mr Redmond's professions of toleration?

---

[133] Ibid., D 1295/2/16.　　　　　　　　　　　　[134] *Leader*, 1 Mar. 1913.

[135] D. G. Boyce accurately observes: 'Redmond saw himself as a potential imperial statesman, joining the ranks of the Canadians, Australians, the New Zealanders—and the latest members of the club, the South Africans, in the family of nations that formed the core of the British Empire. Redmond was a kind of imperialist nationalist.' *Ireland 1828–1923: From Ascendancy to Democracy* (Oxford, 1992), 80.

[136] Bew, *Conflict and Conciliation* (Oxford, 1987), *passim*.

[137] Ulster Unionist Council leaflets, series UC 69, Cambridge University Library.

[138] Bew, *Conflict and Conciliation*, 57–69.

Even if he is perfectly sincere, he could not carry out his promises, as he failed to carry out those of 1898.' It was an understandable reaction,[139] but it begged a most important question: can the refusal to explore the common ground between the two main Irish traditions ever help in the struggle to protect minority rights?

[139] For similar fears see *The Unknown Power behind the Irish Nationalist Party* by the editor of *Grievances from Ireland* (London, 1907), 170–1.

Epilogue

Ulster Nationalists can be helped but not satisfied. Nationalist Ireland has the force to do one but not the other, force must be used in proportion to its object. Nationalist Ireland should concentrate on preventing any new legislation that would stereotype Orange ascendancy in Ulster of the Ulster Nationalists. Let it be clearly understood that the part of Ulster that is left outside Home Rule shall remain under modern British rule directly and indirectly in small and large affairs. Orangemen must not be allowed to dominate Ulster Nationalists, according to law, under the cover of refusing to come in under Home Rule. Modern British law and protection is better than out-of-date, seventeenth-century Orange law and principles. No delegation of the authority of the British Parliament and Government to an Ulster Council—administrative or legislative—should be tolerated by Nationalist Ireland. This attitude and policy is so reasonable that the Ulster Unionists would not resist it. The thing is feasible, because it is reasonable and practicable.

R. J. S. Irish Opinion, 21 Nov. 1916

Anniversaries are often problematic, and few in recent times have been as loaded with ambiguities and contradictions as the seventy-fifth anniversary of 1916. The interpretation of this key event in modern Irish history has prompted fractures and disputes among historians, politicians and citizens—but, outside the realms, of embattled historiography, open and general discussion has been curiously muted, not to say inhibited.[1]

These are the words—at the beginning of the preface—of the editors of a recent collection, *Revising the Rising*. In fact, it would be a mistake to exaggerate the amount of critical reflection on the meaning of the Easter Rising, either among the general public or amongst academics. Superficially, at least, there was much evidence of an uncomplicated

---

[1] Mairin Ni Dhonnchadha and Theo Dorgan (eds.), *Revising the Rising* (Derry, 1991), p. ix.

nationalist sentiment, though Conor Cruise O'Brien[2] and unionist MP David Trimble[3] have published tersely critical articles from outside the consensus of nationalist Ireland. The *Irish Independent*'s survey of public opinion (30 March 1991) revealed that 65 per cent of the Irish people 'look back with pride' on the events of 1916, though interestingly only 27 per cent felt the rising made the Irish political situation any better. There has been no shortage of writers willing to defend the rising, but often these writers have avoided the most difficult questions of context. As Brendan Clifford has accurately observed: 'The independent Irish State originated in the Great War on the anti-British side. But Nationalist Ireland never produced directly out of its own culture a single history of that war. That monumental oversight is at the source of the embarrassment which was so widely felt on the seventy-fifth anniversary of the Rising.'[4] In fact *Ireland in the Great War*, Clifford's edition of the writings of C. F. O'Donnell (1849–1934), is an attempt to remedy this deficiency and is much the most intellectually audacious defence of the rising to appear on print. In Clifford's analysis the Redmondites were responsible for a 'Gadarene' rush 'to slaughter': this serves to place Connolly's revolt in an even more heroic light. Connolly's attempt to strike a blow for a German victory in the face of anti-German war-mongering being fostered and led by fellow Irishmen saved the honour of Ireland, and its cultural significance gave substance to Irish separatism in a way that Redmondism could never do. Ireland, building on Connolly's act of war against decadent British imperialism, has now exercised its 'national will and embraced the Germanic leadership of Europe'.[5] But, as Clifford notes, the 'West British influence' of 'recent decades'[6] in Irish society was so strong that few others felt able to embrace this resolute if logical conclusion.[7] Others felt that later Irish membership and British membership of the EC raised a different question. The Inter-Church Group in Faith and Politics roundly declared,

Since 1973 both Ireland and the UK as members of the EC are part of a supranational entity and political community . . . It is, at best, not immediately

---

[2] *Irish Independent*, 30 Mar., 1991.   [3] *New Ulster*, 15 (winter 1991), 2–6.

[4] 'Nemesis: Casement and Connolly', in Clifford (ed.), *Ireland in the Great War, The Irish Insurrection of 1916 Set in its Context of the Great War* (Belfast, 1992), 86. See also 'The Spirit of 1916: A View from Beyond the Back of Mushera', *Irish Political Review*, 6/5 (May 1991), 8–13.

[5] Dick Spicer, 'Ireland in the Great War', *Irish Political Review*, 7/12 (Dec. 1992), 10–11.   [6] Clifford, *Ireland in the Great War*, 84.

[7] Dhonnchadha and Dorgan, *Revising the Rising* is revealing here.

obvious what conclusions the logic of 1916 points to in the face of the democratically secured commitment of the majority of the people to constructing a single community.[8]

This posed a problem for an ardent Europeanist, former premier of Ireland Garret FitzGerald, who, on the other hand, was the son of a 1916 revolutionary. In a series of articles in July 1991 FitzGerald attempted a resolution of sorts.[9] Drawing on Tom Kettle's 1911 work, *Home Rule Finance*, Dr FitzGerald pointed out that the rising took place at precisely the moment when Ireland began to gain substantial economic advantages from the union. If it had been delayed, the spirit of Irish independence would have been sapped by a sense of material well-being. In brief, FitzGerald argued, it was essential to break the links with Britain in the early years of this century if the Irish state 'was to have any chance of creating a fully independent economic infrastructure which would enable us to become members of the European community.'[10]

In a later, expanded version of this argument in the *London Review of Books*, 24 October 1991, Dr FitzGerald acknowledged this was 'a matter of pure hindsight—presenting a case that no one in the first half of the century could conceivably have made'. (It is the strength of Clifford's case that he stays close to the subjective intentions of men like Connolly and Casement.) FitzGerald returned to his main theme: the Royal Commission on Financial Relations of 1896 provided the intellectually reputable basis for the century-long Irish claim of over-taxation; but by the time of the Home Rule crisis of 1912–14 matters had substantially changed.

Political historians recognise the significance of the impact upon Nationalist opinion, of the Report of this Commission. What seems to have been less generally grasped is the manner in which the turn-of-the-century policy of killing Home Rule by kindness raised local spending to a level that for the first time equalled Irish revenue, thus eliminating the century-long Irish subsidy to Britain. As a result, the subsequent introduction by the Liberal Government of old-age pensions in 1908 reversed by a significant margin the traditional out-flows from Ireland to Britain.

Thereafter the traditional argument for separation from Britain—that a

---

[8] Report of the Inter-Church Group in Faith and Politics (Belfast and Dublin, 1991), p. 11, no. 9. Dr FitzGerald admitted being disturbed when A. P. Ryan, the veteran journalist who had known his father, charged him with the abandonment of his father's views.   [9] *Irish Times*, 13–18 July 1991.

[10] Mary Holland, 'Garret's Legacy to the Brooke Talks', *Irish Times*, 17 July 1991.

separate Irish polity would be cheaper to run in the absence of the overhead of Imperial defence, and that this would make possible a lower level of taxation— disappeared. From then on, the question was rather how soon the expansion of social expenditure, involving ever-increasing transfers from Britain to Ireland, would reach a level at which the short-run social cost of independence would be so high that there would be a reluctance to pay this price in order to secure the long-run, and more intangible, benefits of independence. If the issue of independence had been postponed beyond the first third of the century—and more especially if national sentiment had not been aroused by the Rising of 1916—might not Ireland have remained in the United Kingdom with some limited form of Home Rule?

There was a considerable price to pay for the course actually followed. If Ireland had remained within the United Kingdom it would have obtained agricultural protection and benefited from rising public expenditure.[11] Perhaps even, as Arthur Green has claimed, 'by the 1980s it would have had low taxes, negligible public debt, better public services and migration as low as Northern Ireland's'.[12] But the most striking thing about FitzGerald's defence of the rising of 1916 is that it is an essentially *accidental* defence: it makes no sense in terms of the aspirations of the insurrectionists. They had in the main expected that the mix of political sovereignty, nationalist economic policy, radical agrarian policy, and compulsory Irish in the schools would produce a Gaelic nation of twenty to thirty million people. By 1956–7 a quarter of a century of such policies had, in fact, brought about near collapse with, ironically, higher levels of emigration than in the last decades of British rule. Not the least of the problems was the way in which the revolutionary generation clung on to power long after it had run out of ideas. In 1956 the *Irish Times* commented; 'If the trend continues . . . Ireland will die, not in the remote unpredictable future but quite soon.'[13] The fact that no such editorial is conceivable today is a tribute to the transformation in Irish economic policy brought about by Sean Lemass and T. K. Whitaker, a transformation which is indisputably

---

[11] Arthur Green, 'Unionist Horizons', *Irish Review*, 4 (spring 1988), 28. We need not surmise as Alan J. Ward, understandably does in *The Easter Rising: Revolution and Irish Nationalism* (Arlington Heights, Ill., 1980), that 'the evident willingness of the Irish party to accept bills which give them less financial power . . . is suspicious because it suggests they were accepting Home Rule simply in order to gain a foothold on Irish independence' (p. 93). It is more likely that new liberalism was promoting an Irish party retreat from economic nationalism.   [12] Ibid.

[13] Quoted in Paul Bew and Henry Patterson, *Sean Lemass and the Making of Modern Ireland* (Dublin, 1982), ch. 3.

based on a rejection of the mainstream Irish Republican thinking on the economy boasted in the pre-war era.

Interestingly, however, Garrett FitzGerald did fully acknowledge that independent Ireland has had, in effect, to erase 'Redmondism' from its memory. Redmond's strategy of support for the British war effort had been designed to ensure a maximum degree of influence when the final arrangements for the north-eastern excluded area were sorted out: he had also in any case hoped for better relationships with unionist leaders such as Carson and Bonar Law. There is some evidence that he had personally achieved a limited degree of success here: though more with Bonar Law than Carson, and more with both than their lieutenants. It seems fair to say that Redmond had created the possibility of better north–south relations but not of Irish unity. There is a powerful symbol here: Redmond's brother, Willie, and James Craig's brother, Charles, had the sharpest exchanges during the Home Rule crisis. However, after 1914 both men wore the same uniform in a common cause. Even more poignantly 'the same gazette would publish both men's names as enrolled on the same day in the French Legion of Honour. On that day Mr Charles Craig was a prisoner in Germany, wounded in a famous fight, and Willie Redmond was in a grave towards which his Ulster comrades had been the first to carry him.'[14] Redmond's supporters felt that his strategy had been destroyed in 1916 by men and women who did not even understand it. The Ulster unionists, in consequence, were placed in a much stronger bargaining position. They had stood by Britain in the conflict with Germany; Redmond and his supporters had also done so but, by 1917 at the latest, they had lost the initiative to apparently pro-German forces in Ireland. A key British politician like Winston Churchill—who had been very sceptical about Ulster unionism in the 1912–14 period—became a strong and absolutely crucial supporter of Sir James Craig, the new unionist prime minister of Northern Ireland in all the critical phases of the crisis of 1921–2.[15] This is why the great leaders of northern Nationalism (Joe Devlin and Cahir Healy) were so cynical about the spirit of 1916.[16]

[14] Stephen Gwynn, *John Redmond's Last Years*, (London, 1926), 51.

[15] Paul Bew, Peter Gibbon, and Henry Patterson, *The State in Northern Ireland 1921–72: Political Forces and Social Classes* (Manchester and New York, 1979), 51–6.

[16] Alexander Tsipko, one of the most astute Soviet commentators, has recently noted: 'Perhaps the most dangerous element of our radical thinking did not consist so much in the cavalier attitude towards violence and destruction but rather in the conviction that

One final irony. Redmondite home rule was conceived essentially as democratization; a more sensitive, more intimate form of government than Dublin Castle bureaucracy. For Redmond and his colleagues, once this debt owed to history was paid by Westminister then the Irish could for the first time play a full part as equals in wider UK parliamentary and imperial concerns. Ever since Lemass started to unpick the elements of economic nationalism in the 1950s we have been moving back to the world of Redmond. Of course, the intimate Redmondite involvement in Westminster—which would have survived home rule—is impossible to recreate, but a more relaxed, less charged version of Irish political destiny already exists, with Brussels to some degree playing the role Redmond envisaged for London. Redmond would easily recognize a world in which a government in Dublin exists predominantly for political and democratic reasons and in which economic and social policy evolves pragmatically with relatively little input (save perhaps on the North) from nationalist ideology. Even here the current policy of support for the Anglo-Irish Agreement—direct rule with a green tinge—bears a remarkable resemblance to that pursued by Redmond after 1914.

The Major–Reynolds Downing Street declaration of 15 December 1993 permits a gloss on this point. In his subsequent speech to the Irish Association in Dublin Castle the Taoiseach, Albert Reynolds, observed: 'The historic nature and importance of the declaration has, however, I regret to say, not yet been fully appreciated. The Joint Declaration, if accepted as a basis for peace and implemented by all, spells an end to the coercion or attempted coercion of either community whether nationalist or unionist.'[17] Identifying 'the spirit of coercion' as the great evil of modern Irish history, Mr Reynolds insisted that in future 'the democratic right of self-determination by the people of Ireland as a whole must be exercised with, and subject to, the agreement and consent of a majority in Northern Ireland'.[18] It is easy to pick up the Redmondite echoes. John Redmond made clear his opposition to the principle of coercion in his speech in parliament on

the strength of the future edifice depended on the thoroughness of the initial destruction and that nothing of importance can be built without sacrifice. Sometimes one gets the impression that many Soviets hold dear not that which has innate value in itself but rather that which has cost them much suffering.' (Quoted in John Lloyd, 'The Party's Over', *London Review of Books*, 25 July 1991.) Does this comment have an Irish resonance?

[17] *Irish Times*, 11 Jan. 1994.   [18] Ibid.

15 September; earlier in the year his lieutenant, John Dillon, had belatedly but decidedly come to a similar conclusion: 'He [Dillon] now says "How can we coerce Ulster with our own record against coercion?" and that we can not face civil war as a beginning of home rule.'[19]

There will always be two views of the 1916 rising. There will be those who identify with the themes of the revolutionary press on the eve of the rising. The republican socialist *Workers' Republic*—whose moving spirit was James Connolly—expressed the insurgent mood: 'Now or never . . . are you going to oblige John Bull, the butcher of your priests and people, by remaining quiet till he is in a position to finish you off?'[20] The *Spark*, anti-socialist and obsessed with the conversion of England, none the less insisted that the *Workers' Republic* was entirely compatible with what was its own credo: an explicit 'Catholic nationalism'.[21] *Nationality*, edited by Arthur Griffith, insisted on the economic oppression of Ireland on England; Ireland was the 'most heavily taxed country in the history of nations since the fall of the Roman Empire'.[22] Today Desmond Fennell, for example, speaks approvingly of the 'humanist dream and project of the Irish Revolution'.[23] Fennell notes sympathetically Connolly's 'final theoretical adaptation to the national revolution',[24] when he ended a twenty-year estrangement and reconciled with Catholicism. Indeed, on the eve of his execution, Connolly asked his Protestant wife, Lily, to convert to

---

[19] Tim Healy, *Letters and Leaders of My Day* (London, 1928), 538. It has to be admitted that at this point, Joe Devlin did not accept any scheme of 'exclusion', insisting that the 'weight of opinion' if not the 'actual numbers' in the north-east supported Irish unity; *Irish News*, 16 June 1914. See also W. R. K. Sweeney, 'Loyal to the End: Redmond in the Irish News' (MSc thesis, Queen's University of Belfast, 1993), fo. 19; J. J. Lee, *Ireland 1912–85* (Cambridge, 1989), 4–5 is scathing about the Unionist variant of this argument. By June 1916, however, Devlin fully accepted Dillon's thesis: 'Ulster Unionists may be conciliated. Who says they should be coerced? Does anyone light heartedly propose to provoke another rebellion in the North, and if such were provoked, what hope would there be for many a long year of wiping out the fatal legacy it would leave behind?', *Armagh Guardian*, 23 June 1916. I owe this reference to S. Day.

[20] *Worker's Republic*, 19 Feb. 1916.   [21] *Spark*, 16 Apr. 1916.

[22] *Nationality*, 2 Oct. 1915.

[23] For a discussion, see Paul Bew's 'Things Still Fall Apart', *Times Educational Supplement*, 21 Jan. 1994.

[24] Desmond Fennell, *Heresy: The Battle of Ideas in Modern Ireland* (Belfast, 1993), 31. For a different treatment of similar problems, see M. Goldring, *Pleasant the Scholar's Life: Irish Intellectuals and the Construction of the Nation State* (London, 1993), and Roy Foster's impressive *Paddy and Mr Punch* (London, 1993).

Catholicism,[25] thus more than justifying the *Spark*'s faith in him: even Connolly's bitter capitalist enemy in the Dublin lock-out of 1913, William Martin Murphy, felt 'every drop of Catholic blood in [his] veins surge up'[26] following Connolly's execution. Nevertheless, the Redmondite Serjeant Sullivan refused to be impressed by the exalted but in his view the inflated parochial rhetoric of the insurrectionists. Sullivan sourly noted: 'The departure of the bravest leaves the comedian to play the hero.'[27] After all, in early 1916 Ireland had produced some 78,852 recruits as against 5,000 revolutionaries.[28] But at the moment when the official discourse of the Downing Street declaration insists upon, and is organized around, a formal distinction between the 'people of Ireland' and the 'people of Britain' it is worth remembering how diverse the sympathies of the 'people of Ireland' have actually been.

[25] Patrick Maume, 'Lily Connolly's Conversion: New Light on James Connolly's Last Days', *History Ireland* (forthcoming).

[26] Healy, *Letters and Leaders*, 562.

[27] Serjeant Sullivan, *Old Ireland* (London, 1927), 185.

[28] Public Record Office, CO 904/91/5. For the best recent analysis of 1916, see Charles Townshend, 'The Suppression of The Easter Rising', *Bullan* vol. 1, no. 1 Spring 1994.

Index

The direction 'see also' refers to closely connected but not identical persons or organizations